An Altitude
SuperGuide

Walks and Easy Hikes *in the* Canadian Rockies

An Altitude SuperGuide

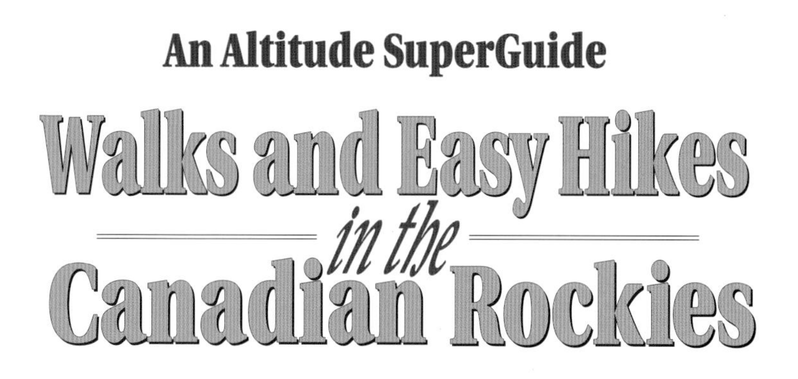

Graeme Pole

Altitude Publishing Canada Ltd.
Canadian Rockies/Vancouver

Publication Information

Altitude Publishing Canada Ltd.
1500 Railway Avenue, PO Box 1410
Canmore, Alberta T0L 0M0

Extreme care has been taken to ensure that all information presented in this book is accurate and up-to-date, and neither the author nor the publisher can be held responsible for any errors.

Canadian Cataloguing in Publication Data
Pole, Graeme, 1956-
Walks and easy hikes in the Canadian Rockies
(SuperGuide)
ISBN 1-55153-700-1
1. Trails--Rocky Mountains, Canadian (B.C. and Alta.)--Guidebooks.* 2. Hiking--Rocky Mountains, Canadian (B.C. and Alta.)--Guidebooks* 3. Rocky Mountains, Canadian (B.C. and Alta.)--Guidebooks.* I. Title. II. Series.
FC219.P64 1996 917.1104'4 C94-910967-3
F1090.P64 1996

Made in Western Canada
Printed and bound in Canada
by Friesen Printers, Altona, Manitoba.

Altitude GreenTree Program
Altitude Publishing will plant in Canada twice as many trees as were used in the manufacturing of this product.

Front cover photo: Peyto Lake
(inset left: Glacier lily, inset right: Golden-mantled ground squirrel)

Frontispiece: Moraine Lake

Back cover photo: Cavell Meadows

Project Development

Concept/Art Direction	Stephen Hutchings
Design	Stephen Hutchings
	Sandra Davis
Editing/Proofreading	Noeline Bridge
Indexing	Noeline Bridge
Maps	Catherine Burgess
Drawings	Stephen Hutchings
Electronic Page Layout	Sandra Davis
Financial Management	Laurie Smith

A Note from the Publisher
The world described in Altitude SuperGuides is a unique and fascinating place. It is a world filled with surprise and discovery, beauty and enjoyment, questions and answers. It is a world of people, cities, landscape, animals and wilderness as seen through the eyes of those who live in, work with, and care for this world. The process of describing this world is also a means of defining ourselves.

It is also a world of relationship, where people derive their meaning from a deep and abiding contact with the land–as well as from each other. And it is this sense of relationship that guides all of us at Altitude to ensure that these places continue to survive and evolve in the decades ahead.

Altitude SuperGuides are books intended to be used, as much as read. Like the world they describe, *Altitude SuperGuides* are evolving, adapting and growing. Please write to us with your comments and observations, and we will do our best to incorporate your ideas into future editions of these books.

Stephen Hutchings
Publisher

Acknowledgements

The author gratefully acknowledges research assistance provided by the following people with Parks Canada: Dave Palmer at the Western Region Library, Calgary; Larry Halverson at Kootenay National Park; Heather Dempsey and Dave Gilbride at Banff National Park; Joanne Cairns, Edwin Knox and Rob Watt at Waterton Lakes National Park; Wes Bradford and Interpretation staff at Jasper National Park; and Harry Abbott at Yoho National Park.

Cia and Ben Gadd kindly opened their Jasper home to a couple of tired truck campers during a spell of poor weather, and didn't kick us out when it became sunny again. They also offered a wealth of information concerning Jasper National Park. Thank you, Cia and Ben.

Dr. Ian Spooner of the University of Calgary reviewed the geological and glaciological passages of the text.

For Marnie, companion on and off the trail

Most of all I would like to thank my wife, Marnie, for her devotion to the fieldwork, tireless editing of the manuscript, and for her help in coordinating the project. The hiking schedule was often dictated by the need to acquire photographs at particular times of day. It was a schedule only a photographer would follow without complaint, and meant rising early, backtracking often, and frequently waiting interminably for the sun to peer through a summer of fickle weather. Even on repeat visits to the same location, Marnie remained patient and enthusiastic. Her organizational skills and penchant for making lists kept me from coming adrift in a raft of scribbled field notes. Thank you Marnie.

Notice of Assumption of Risk

Trail walking and hiking in the Canadian Rockies can involve dangers. These dangers include, but are not limited to the following: black bears and grizzly bears, aggressive wildlife, insect bites, rough trails, slippery bridges, logs and rocks, suspension bridges, inclement weather, lightning, forest fires, falling trees, contaminated drinking water, avalanches, late-lying snow, rockfalls, mudslides and flash-floods.

The author has walked every trail in this book at least once, and has endeavoured to render trail descriptions with accuracy and with safety in mind. However, trail conditions are not static, and the inclusion or exclusion of any information does not mean that you will find conditions as described. In particular, bridges and trail signs may or may not be present as described in the text.

Walks and Easy Hikes contains ample information to assist you in preparing for safe trail travel. However, you are responsible for your well-being on trails in the Rockies. Neither the author nor the publisher can be held responsible for any difficulties, injuries, misfortune or loss of property that arises from using the information presented.

Contents

Introduction

Walks and Easy Hikes in the Canadian Rockies

Banff National Park

Jasper National Park

Yoho National Park

The Walks and Easy Hikes in the Canadian Rockies are organized according to this colour scheme:

Banff National Park

Jasper National Park

Yoho National Park

Kootenay National Park

Waterton Lakes National Park

Information

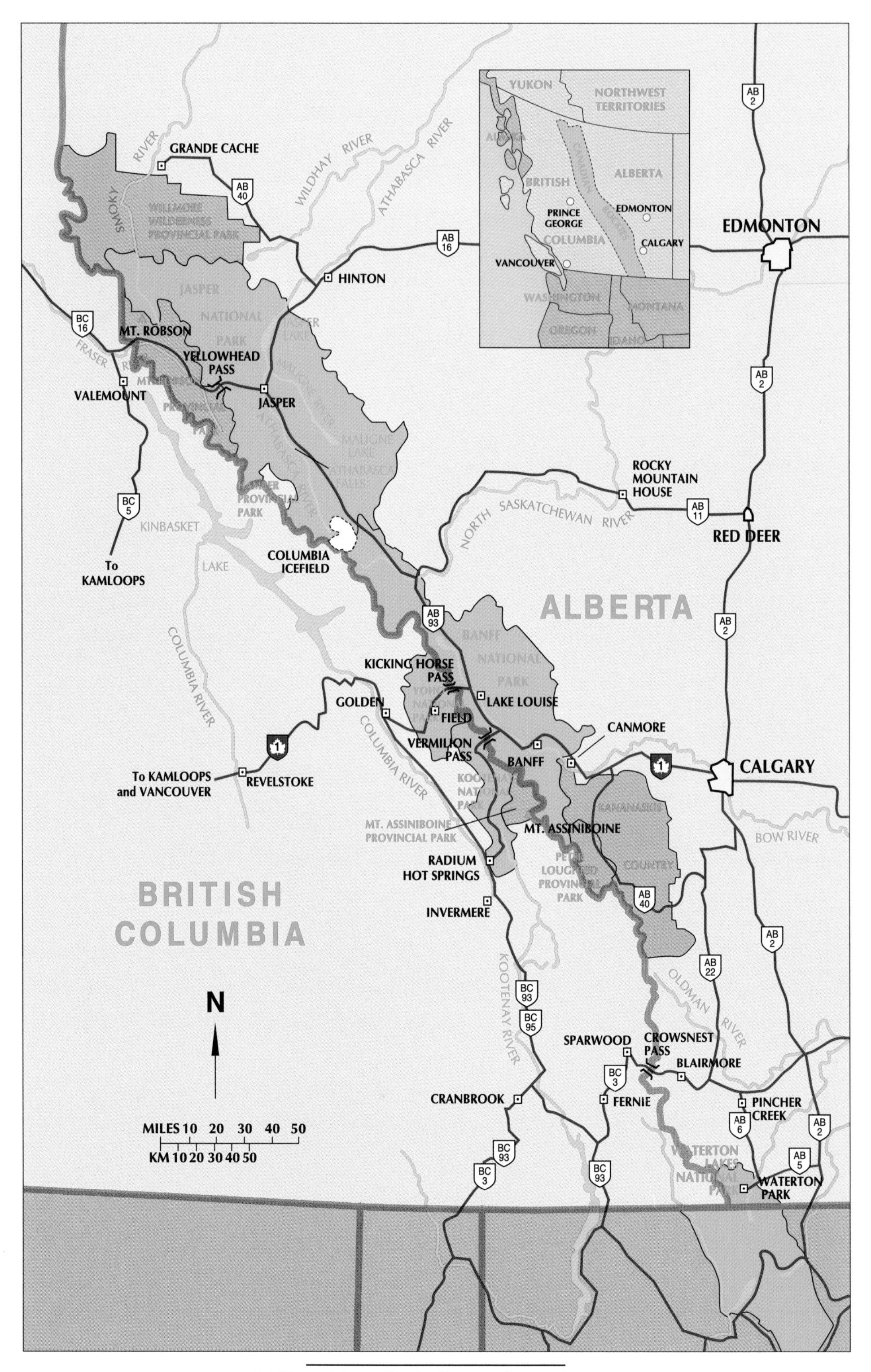

YUKON
NORTHWEST TERRITORIES
ALBERTA
EDMONTON
PRINCE GEORGE
CALGARY
VANCOUVER
WASHINGTON
MONTANA
OREGON
GRANDE CACHE
SMOKY RIVER
WILDHAY RIVER
ATHABASCA RIVER
WILLMORE WILDERNESS PROVINCIAL PARK
AB 40
AB 16
AB 2
HINTON
EDMONTON
JASPER NATIONAL PARK
BC 16
MT. ROBSON
YELLOWHEAD PASS
FRASER
VALEMOUNT
JASPER
MT. ROBSON PROVINCIAL PARK
MALIGNE LAKE
ATHABASCA FALLS
BC 5
KINBASKET LAKE
To KAMLOOPS
COLUMBIA ICEFIELD
ROCKY MOUNTAIN HOUSE
NORTH SASKATCHEWAN RIVER
AB 11
RED DEER
ALBERTA
AB 93
BANFF NATIONAL PARK
COLUMBIA RIVER
KICKING HORSE PASS
GOLDEN
LAKE LOUISE
FIELD
VERMILION PASS
CANMORE
BANFF
CALGARY
To KAMLOOPS and VANCOUVER
REVELSTOKE
MT. ASSINIBOINE PROVINCIAL PARK
MT. ASSINIBOINE
KANANASKIS COUNTRY
BOW RIVER
RADIUM HOT SPRINGS
INVERMERE
BRITISH COLUMBIA
AB 22
OLDMAN RIVER
KOOTENAY RIVER
BC 93
BC 95
SPARWOOD
CROWSNEST PASS
BLAIRMORE
BC 3
FERNIE
CRANBROOK
PINCHER CREEK
AB 6
AB 5
WATERTON LAKES NATIONAL PARK
WATERTON PARK
N
MILES 10 20 30 40 50
KM 10 20 30 40 50

Preface

Welcome to the Canadian Rockies. These mountains are renowned as a destination for hikers. The scenery revealed from the network of more than 4000 km of trails is remarkable.

Most of this trail network explores the backcountry. However, it also includes more than 100 Walks and Easy Hikes on frontcountry trails, close to roadsides and townsites. Although solitude may be difficult to find on these trails, the scenery is often as spectacular as that in the backcountry.

In researching this book, I had the pleasure of hiking all the Walks and Easy Hikes, many of them more than once. In total, they feature virtually every aspect of topography, vegetation, wildlife and climate that make up the Rockies. If you complete every Walk and Easy Hike, you will see: 38 glaciers, 2 icefields, 39 waterfalls, 13 canyons, 4 hot springs, 92 lakes and half a dozen alpine meadows. There are wonderful opportunities for viewing wildflowers, birds and animals.

The Walks and Easy Hikes grant us access to this exceptional landscape. However, the landscape readily shows evidence of our passing. We must learn to tread lightly, and with respect. Please read *A Trail Etiquette,* and do your part to help preserve the parks of the Canadian Rockies.

Throughout this book, "Rockies" and "Canadian Rockies" refer to the area between Waterton Lakes National Park and Mt. Robson Provincial Park. The accepted pronunciation of unfamiliar words is given in parentheses. The stressed syllable is capitalized.

If you have any corrections or suggestions concerning *Walks and Easy Hikes,* please send them to me in care of the publisher. Happy walking and hiking.

Ratings

The Walks and Easy Hikes follow maintained trails. None will present any difficulty to a fit pedestrian or a seasoned walker. For the more casual walker, each outing has been rated using the following system.

Viewpoint: Less than 400 m to a viewpoint at roadside. The walkway is paved, gravelled or wood decked.

Easy: Less than 1.6 km and relatively flat

Moderate: 1.6 km to 3.2 km, with noticeable elevation change

Harder: More than 3.2 km, or shorter with considerable elevation change

The distances given are *one-way,* from trailhead to destination. The distance indicated for a loop trail is the total for the round-trip. Wheelchair accessible trails, and those recommended for families are listed in the Reference section.

Trailhead elevations for the Walks and Easy Hikes range between 1300 m and 2350 m above sea level. The effects of elevation may shorten your breath and create rapid fatigue. If you feel you've taken on more than you can handle in terms of distance to be travelled or elevation to be gained, simply turn around and retrace your route to the trailhead.

"Lighting" indicates the optimum time for viewing the trail's featured scene on sunny days. However, mountain weather can produce spectacular lighting at any time. Don't be discouraged if your schedule does not coincide with the recommended time.

A Trail Etiquette

We each walk the trails of the Rocky Mountain parks for different reasons. Some of us do so for exercise, others for the view. Still others are motivated by interests in plants, birds, animals or geology. Whatever our motivation, we must share the trails with each other. We must also tread lightly, so as not to damage what we have come to see. The following trail etiquette respects the rights of others to an enjoyable hiking experience, and ensures protection of the natural environment.

1. Pass each other without stepping off the trail. Avoid shortcutting on switchbacks. Do not walk around wet or snowy areas. In other words: *please stay on the trail.* Walking off-trail results in the trampling of surrounding vegetation, and can create erosion problems. Twenty pairs of feet walking on untrammeled ground will create a permanent trail. At high elevations, it may take decades for damaged vegetation to recover.

2. Report trail problems: chronic wet or muddy areas, broken steps or guardrails, downed trees, slumps, washed-out bridges etc. The staff at park information centres will record and act on this information.

3. Do not feed, entice or harass wildlife. This is for your protection, as well as theirs. Report significant wildlife sightings to a park information centre.

4. Do not remove, deface or disturb any natural or historical object—flower, tree, rock, fossil, dropped antler etc. It is an offence to do so under the National Parks Act.

5. Be aware of trails shared with horses and bicycles. Cyclists should dismount to pass you. When you meet a horse party, make verbal contact with the lead rider, and quietly step to the downhill side of the trail. Do not speak or move until the last horse in the party is well past you.

6. Do not take your dog onto the trail.

7. Take all your litter back to the trailhead with you. Pick up any litter left by persons less considerate than yourself, and pack it out also. Recycle paper, plastic, glass and cans. Deposit the remainder in the receptacles provided.

8. It is best not smoke while using trails. Cigarette butts and spent matches are among the most common types of litter. If you must smoke, pack out your cigarette butts.

9. Most of the popular trails have outhouses at the trailhead. Please use them.

10. Do not enter a trail or area marked with a closed sign.

11. On trails where interpretive brochures are provided, return the brochures if you do not wish to keep them.

12. Black bears and grizzly bears may be encountered throughout the Rockies. Read Parks Canada's pamphlet *You Are in Bear Country.* Take extra care when a bear caution sign is posted for a particular trail or area.

13. Respect the rights of others to solitude. Hike in small groups.

14. There are no campgrounds on the Walks and Easy Hikes. If you would like to camp on a trail, consult a park information centre to find out where this is permitted, or refer to the Altitude SuperGuide *Classic Hikes in the Canadian Rockies.*

What to Wear and Carry

The hiking season in the Rockies is generally late May to early October at lower elevations, and late June to mid-September, higher up. Please enquire about trail conditions at a park information centre, especially if you will be hiking early or late in the season.

You can wear street shoes for some of the shorter walks, but for most outings, sturdy running shoes or lightweight hiking boots are recommended. On wet days, rubber boots can be handy. If you are blister-prone, experiment with different thicknesses of socks, or a combination of a thin inner sock and a thicker outer sock.

Mountain weather is characterized by changeability. A sunny morning can become a wet, miserable afternoon, and vice versa. In addition, some of the trails make their way in and alongside canyons, where cold, damp air prevails. If embarking on one of the longer Walks and Easy Hikes, you should carry a minimum of a rain jacket and a sweater as extra clothing. On hikes to higher elevations, take a warm hat and gloves as well. Your rain jacket can also serve as a windbreaker. Rainfall in the Rockies is usually very cold. A full rainsuit, warm hat and gloves will be required on rainy days. An umbrella will suffice when showers are intermittent.

The effects of sunlight are increased in the mountains. Skin burns more rapidly because of the thinner atmosphere. Wind can also produce skin burns, and contributes to dehydration. Apply a good sunscreen on sunny days, and wear sunglasses and a light-coloured sun hat. Drink lots of water. Avoid beverages that contain caffeine or alcohol, as these contribute to dehydration.

Carry your clothing, water bottle, snacks, sunscreen, insect repellent and first aid kit in a small day pack. The pack can be shared by different hikers. You will tire less easily if your camera, binoculars or video unit are carried over the shoulder in a bag or on a strap, rather than in your hand. Because these trails are popular, you should not drink any water from trailside streams or lakes. Bring your drinking water with you from your hotel, home or campground.

Banff National Park

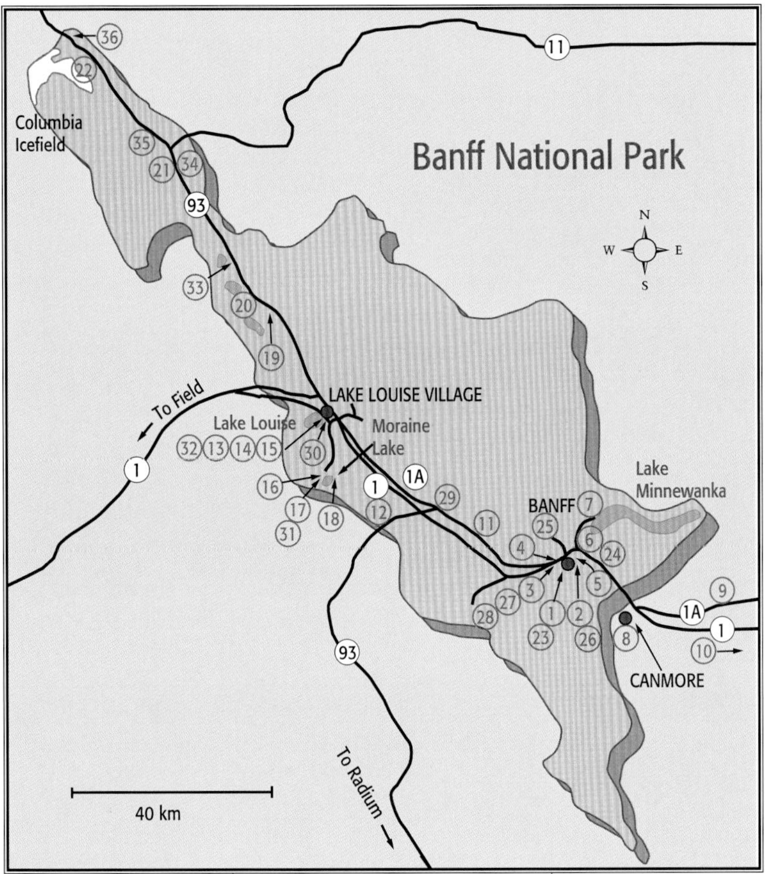

Banff was established in 1885 as Canada's first national park, to preserve a small area near the Cave and Basin hot springs. Together with Jasper, Yoho and Kootenay national parks, Banff is now part of a protected area that includes 20,160 km^2 of the Canadian Rockies.

Most of the Walks and Easy Hikes near Banff townsite are located in the Bow Valley, amid the gray limestone peaks of the front ranges. Two of the trails take you easily to mountain tops. Others explore the extensive wetlands immediately west of the townsite. Elk, bighorn sheep, mule deer, beaver and black bear are the common large mammals that you may see from these trails.

Lake Louise to Columbia Icefield

The Walks and Easy Hikes between Lake Louise and Columbia Icefield, beginning on page 49, feature the trademark views of the Canadian Rockies: glacier-capped peaks, flower-filled meadows, and blue-green glacial lakes. Wildlife is common along the Icefields Parkway, the access road to many of the trailheads.

Most of these trails are snow-covered for much of the year. If you are visiting early or late in the hiking season, please check trail conditions at the park information centre in Lake Louise.

Bow Falls have been eroded by the Bow River into the contact between two rock formations. The trail to the falls follows the Bow River from Banff townsite.

1. Bow Falls

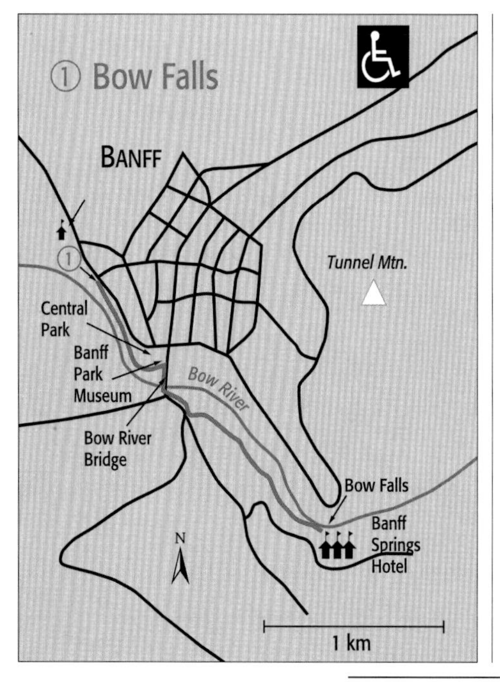

Banff residents and visitors are fortunate that the Bow River flows through town. The walk along the riverbank to Bow Falls offers escape from the busy streets nearby, and features tranquil views of this picturesque river. You can visit the Banff Park Museum in Central Park on your way to the falls.

The Bow River is the longest river in Banff National Park. From its headwaters at Bow Lake, 90 km to the north, it drains an area of 2210 km^2. After flowing through Banff, the Bow eventually

Route Information

Trailhead: The boat house at the corner of Wolf Street and Bow Avenue in Banff townsite

Rating: moderate, 2.1 km. Wheelchair accessible

Lighting: morning and early afternoon

joins the South Saskatchewan River in southern Alberta. The river's name comes from the Cree words *manachaban sipi:* "the place from which bows are taken." Natives made hunting bows from Douglas fir saplings found on its banks.

Severe flooding of the Bow River near Banff townsite has been reported 11 times since 1894, when a flood washed out the railway line and stranded guests at the Banff Springs Hotel. Stoneys from Morley were brought to Banff to entertain the idle tourists. This was the origin of the celebration of native culture known as Banff Indian Days, held annually until 1979.

The large coniferous trees along the riverbank and in Central Park are white spruce—the climax species in the succession of wetland to floodplain forest. Banff's first non-native dwelling was built nearby in 1874, when American trapper and prospector Joseph Healy wintered here. Look for the wildflower, shooting star, on the riverbanks in June.

The Banff Park Museum was constructed in 1903. It is a National Historic Site, and is the oldest natural history museum in western Canada. It features many of the mammals and birds that live in the park. The museum grounds were formerly the site of a zoo and an aviary.

From the museum, turn south (right) on Banff Avenue, and cross the Bow River bridge. Constructed in 1923, it replaced a succession of bridges and ferries at this location. The bridge was refurbished in 1990. The sculptures and much of the original "river stone" work were retained. These features are best appreciated from river level.

Across the bridge, descend west (right). Turn east (right) onto the walkway that passes beneath the bridge, and follow the path along the riverbank.

The Bow River has not always followed this course through Banff. Before the last advance of the Wisconsin Glaciation, the river may have flowed between Tunnel Mountain and Cascade Mountain. When the ice age glaciers receded, the river's course was blocked with moraines. A large lake formed west of the present townsite. Its waters eventually spilled through the gap between Tunnel Mountain and Mt. Rundle, at the present site of Bow Falls. The area west of Banff is still wetland—a legacy of the ancient lake. Ancient river terraces or levées, are scattered throughout the town.

The trail climbs to a viewpoint above Bow Falls, and then descends to river level. Bow Falls are being eroded into the contact between two rock formations. Looking upstream, the rocks of the west (left) bank are 245 million years old, and those of the east (right) bank are 320 million years old. The jagged formation of the west bank extends into the riverbed, creating the rapids. Slightly downstream from the falls, the Spray River enters the Bow River. From here, you may ascend to the Banff Springs Hotel, or return along the riverbank to your starting point.

Black-billed Magpie

On your way to Bow Falls you are likely to see black-billed magpies. The Latin genus and species name of this bird is *Pica,* which means "black and white"—an accurate description of its attractive plumage. The long tail feathers are highlighted with iridescent green.

This large and vocal member of the crow family is found year-round in Banff. The magpie is not overly selective about what it eats; garbage is a favourite food. As with other members of the crow family, the magpie will also eat the young and eggs from other birds' nests. Its diet is 60 percent meat. In recent years, magpies have developed a new food source—dead bugs on the fronts of vehicles. At the parking lot in Banff's Central Park, you can watch magpies perched on automotive bumpers—their local bar and grill. The great horned owl is the magpie's principal predator.

Magpies are known to mate for life, and usually nest near water. Their homes are a bulging assembly of sticks, set in the crotch of a tree trunk.

The summit of Tunnel Mountain offers a paramount view of the Bow Valley near Banff townsite.

2. Tunnel Mountain

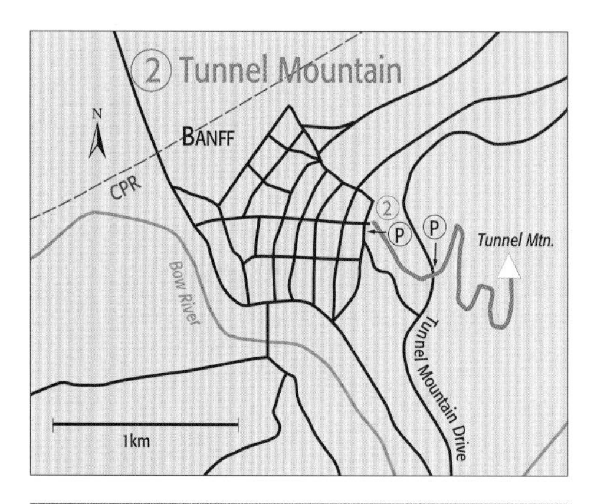

Route Information

Trailhead: In Banff townsite, at the parking area on the south side of St. Julien Road, 350 m south of Wolf Street. You can reach the trailhead easily by walking east from town on Wolf Street or Caribou Street.
Rating: harder, 1.8 km
Lighting: anytime

With an elevation of 1692 m, Tunnel Mountain is the lowest feature to which the name "mountain" is applied in the Rockies. Although it is a steep climb, the well-beaten path to the summit hardly qualifies as mountaineering. From trail's end, you enjoy unrestricted views over the Bow Valley.

In 1882, Major Rogers, a surveyor for the CPR, determined that Tunnel Mountain blocked the Bow Valley. He thought that a tunnel would be required for the rails to proceed. His superiors were skeptical. A follow-up investigation found ample room for the railway in the valley between Tunnel Mountain and Cascade Mountain. The tunnel was never built, but the mountain's name has endured.

The trail climbs steadily on the southwest slope of the mountain, crossing Tunnel Mountain

Drive after 300 m. The forest here is open lodgepole pine and Douglas fir. In the undergrowth are bearberry, twinflower, common juniper, harebell and brown-eyed Susans. Through the trees, you can see the Banff Springs Hotel. The original hotel was constructed by the CPR in 1888. Most of the building we see today dates to 1928. The slopes behind the hotel rise to the ridge of Sulphur Mountain.

Tunnel Mountain is an extension of Mt. Rundle. The gap between the two was originally eroded by glaciers. Since then it has been enlarged by the Bow River. Tunnel Mountain's shape is characteristic of a common mountain type in the front ranges of the Rockies—the overthrust mountain. The steeply tilted slope you have been climbing, ends on a northeast-facing cliff. If you look across the gap to Mt. Rundle, you will see that it too is an overthrust mountain.

Looking east from Tunnel Mountain's summit, the mountains of the Fairholme Range are prominent. These mountains extend along the east side of the Bow Valley, from Lake Minnewanka to Exshaw. Mt. Rundle (2949 m) rises to the south. It was named for Methodist missionary, Robert T. Rundle. In 1844 and 1847 he preached to Stoney natives near the present site of the Banff airstrip. To the north is Cascade Mountain (2998 m), highest near Banff. To the west, beyond the roof tops of Banff townsite, are the Vermilion wetlands. On the western skyline are the peaks of the Massive Range.

Given the view, you won't be surprised to learn that a fire lookout once occupied this spot. After it was visited by King George VI in 1939, it became known as "Royal Lookout." It was one of seven lookouts in a system that covered Banff National Park.

Douglas Fir

The steep, sunny, southwest-facing slopes of Tunnel Mountain are ideal habitat for the Douglas fir, the climax tree species of the montane ecoregion. The thick, corky bark of the mature tree allows it to withstand most ground fires and infestation by insects. The fires remove competing vegetation, creating open parkland dotted with stately firs. Douglas firs in such settings may be 600 years old.

The Douglas fir is not a true fir, but is a member of the pine family. There are two varieties: coastal and interior. Although the two cross-pollinate, the interior or "blue Douglas fir" is most common in the Rockies. It is near the eastern limit of its range here. Large specimens are 30 m to 40 m tall and 1 m in diameter, often with a gracefully curving trunk. In Pacific rainforests, the coastal variety attains heights of 80 m and diameters in excess of 4 m.

The tree was named for David Douglas, a Scottish botanist who collected in the Rockies in 1826 and 1827. Timbers sawn from Douglas firs are prized for their strength and colour. Intensive harvesting of Douglas firs in the commercial forests of BC guarantees that old-growth stands of this tree will soon be non-existent outside protected areas.

Hot water that seeps from the Cave and Basin springs has a moderating effect on the nearby Vermilion wetlands. Along the Marsh Trail boardwalk you will see species of plants, fish, birds and reptiles that are exotic to the Rockies.

3. Marsh Trail

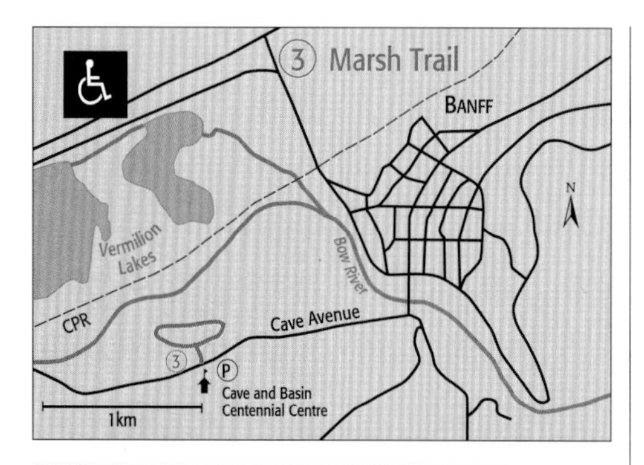

Route Information

Trailhead: Follow Banff Avenue south to the Bow River bridge. Turn west (right) and follow Cave Avenue 1 km to the Cave and Basin Centennial Centre. The trail begins at the west end of the pool.

Rating: easy, 500 m loop, boardwalk. Wheelchair accessible

Lighting: anytime

Of the 60 known hot springs in Canada, eight are near Banff townsite. Most of their combined outflow of more than 3800 litres per minute drains into the Vermilion wetlands, where the hot water changes the local environment. The Marsh Trail boardwalk follows the edge of this wetland, offering the opportunity to view plants and wildlife that are exotic to the Canadian Rockies. The area is good for birdwatching. A viewing blind is provided.

The hot water that emerges at the Cave and Basin springs does not originate underground. It all was originally surface water that managed to filter through cracks into the bedrock. The temperature underground typically increases 1°C for every 33 m descent. Approximately 3 km below the surface, water reaches the boiling point and becomes pressurized. It returns to the surface along other crack systems. Near Banff townsite, the hot spring water surfaces along the Sulphur Mountain Thrust Fault.

In its journey, the heated water dissolves minerals from the surrounding bedrock. A few minerals (uranium and radium) make the waters slightly radioactive. In late-Victorian times, people thought this was therapeutic. Sulphur di in the water, and sulpha tabolized by algae in th combine to give the cha tic "rotten egg" smell. I eral content, the hot springs at Banff are similar to those at Bath, England.

Most of the rock in this area is limestone and dolomite. So these hot springs carry calcium carbonate, an element of lime, in solution. When gases in the water are released at the spring outlets, this lime-rich solution precipitates as a crumbly rock known as tufa (TOO-fah). The tufa deposits at the Cave and Basin are 7 m thick.

The hot spring water prevents most of the wetlands near the Cave and Basin from freezing in winter. Some migratory birds stay year-round: killdeer, snipe, American robin, and mallard duck. Six species of orchids bloom in spring on the banks above the wetlands, where you may also see the non-poisonous wandering garter snake. The wetlands are frequented by coyotes, and by elk in late spring.

Minnows and sticklebacks are native to these warm waters. In less enlightened times, aquarium buffs imported their favourite fish and plants to the marsh, with disastrous results (see box). In 1991, the author noted that someone had added a small turtle to the shallows. Please remember that it is illegal to tamper with the ecosystem in a national park.

Mallard duck

Banff Longnose Dace

In the past, as many as eight species of fish have lived in the shallow, warm waters near the Marsh Trail. Of these, only two were native: the Banff longnose dace and the brook stickleback.

In 1983, both native species were present. However, their populations soon declined. It was feared that introduced species threatened the native fish with extinction. Sadly, in 1990, the Committee on the Status of Endangered Wildlife in Canada declared the Banff Longnose dace extinct—a victim of human interference in a unique and supposedly protected ecosystem.

The Fenland Trail loops through a shaded spruce forest along the banks of Forty Mile Creek, and provides the opportunity to see elk, beaver, deer, and songbirds.

4. Fenland Trail

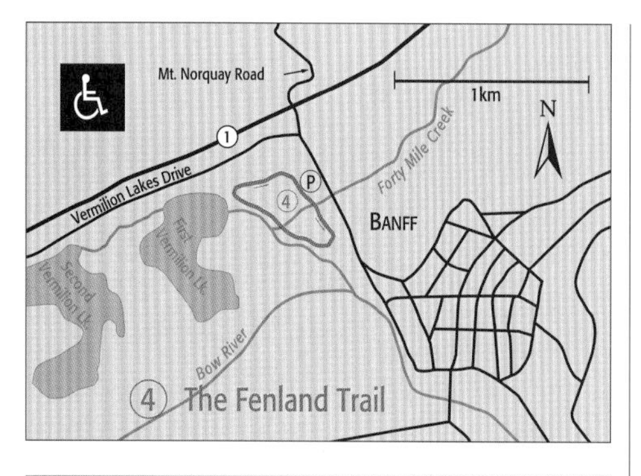

Route Information

Trailhead: Follow Gopher Street north from Banff. Cross the railway tracks. The trailhead is on the left in 300 m. You may also reach the trailhead by walking north from the boathouse at the corner of Wolf Street and Bow Avenue. Walk the loop clockwise.
Rating: easy, 1.5 km loop. Wheelchair accessible. A brochure may be available at the trailhead.
Lighting: anytime

A "fen" is a lowland covered wholly or partially by water. The self-guiding Fenland Trail explores a shaded white spruce forest along the banks of Forty Mile Creek—an area typical of the wetlands west of Banff townsite. These wetlands are being slowly transformed from open water to montane spruce forest, in a natural process called succession.

Parks Canada's brochure describes ten interpretive stops:

1. The wetlands near Banff townsite were a natural barrier against fires that swept the Bow Valley after construction of the CPR in the 1880s. This mature white spruce forest was spared by fire, and is ancient compared to most other forests in this valley.

2. Black bears are adept tree climbers. A

mother bear will often send her cubs up trees when she feels they are threatened. The scarred bark of trembling aspens reveals dark claw marks left by climbing bears.

3. The view at this stop demonstrates how wetlands in the fen are shrinking, whereas the forest is becoming more extensive.

4. Many of the wetlands near Banff townsite have been created or modified by the handiwork of beavers. The mound of sticks and mud is a beaver lodge.

5. Beavers create canals in their shallow ponds. These deeper channels provide escape routes from predators: coyote, wolf and bear.

6. Spring flood waters undermine the banks of Forty Mile Creek, causing trees to topple. The disturbed soils wash into the nearby fen. These soils create more habitat for vegetation, speeding up the fen's transition into forest.

Red osier dogwood

7. The Vermilion wetlands are among the best bird-watching locations in the Rocky Mountain parks. Bald eagle, osprey, red-winged blackbird and a variety of waterfowl are common.

8. Forty Mile Creek is a natural moat, making the interior of the fen less accessible to predators. Cow elk raise their young here in spring, and bull elk herd their harems during the autumn rut.

9. The buds of willows, aspen and red osier dogwood are an important food source for elk, deer and moose.

10. The stumps reveal that the white spruce trees of this area were attractive building timbers in Banff's early days. Hay crops were harvested from the nearby marshes until 1910. The level of the First Vermilion Lake was controlled by a concrete dam until 1985. Impacts like these are no longer tolerated near the Fenland, as nature's balance is being restored.

Elk

The elk, or wapiti, is the most plentiful large mammal in the Rocky Mountain parks. Estimates for Banff give a population of 3200 elk in summer, and 1600 in winter. The adult bull elk stands 1.5 m tall at the shoulder. Its coat is light brown, darker on the neck and legs, with a shaggy fringe on the underside of the neck. The animal is further identified by its tawny or white rump patch. *Wapiti* (WAH-pih-tee) is a Shawnee word that means "white rump."

Elk eat grasses, buds and tender vegetation. The males have antlers that can reach 1.8 m in width. It is dangerous to approach within 30 m of elk during their autumn courtship, or when a female is caring for young in the spring. The animals are very protective and will use their antlers and sharp hooves to attack a human intruder. The Fenland Trail is sometimes closed in late spring to protect elk and people.

The Tunnel Mountain Hoodoos have been sculpted by rainwater, wind and snowmelt from debris flow deposits.

5. Tunnel Mountain Hoodoos

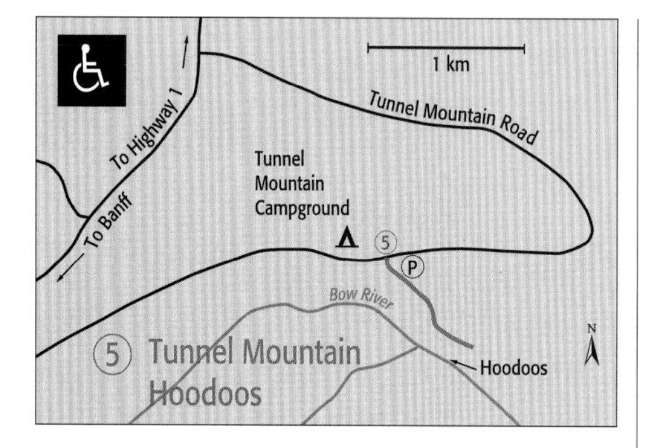

Route Information

Trailhead: 6.2 km east of Banff on Tunnel Mountain Road, opposite Tunnel Mountain campground
Rating: easy, 500 m. Wheelchair accessible
Lighting: afternoon and evening

The paved Tunnel Mountain Hoodoos trail leads along the east bank of the Bow River to viewpoints that overlook the hoodoos and the Bow Valley. The trail also provides excellent views of Mt. Rundle and Tunnel Mountain.

During the Wisconsin Glaciation, an ice age that lasted from 75,000 to 11,000 years ago, there were three distinct advances of glacial ice from the high country of the Rockies towards the foothills. The first two advances extended beyond the present location of Banff, carving the Bow Valley into its U-shape.

For many years, geologists thought that the Tunnel Mountain Hoodoos had been eroded from deposits of glacial moraine left behind on the floor of the Bow Valley, when the ice-age glacier that had occupied it retreated. However, more recent research indicates that the material in the hoodoos, although moraine-like in content, was deposited by debris flows.

At the end of the Wisconsin Glaciation, the massive Bow Valley glacier was slowly retreating. The glaciers that occupied smaller side valleys were retreating more rapidly. Meltwater from these side valley glaciers could not readily drain into the Bow Valley, because the Bow Valley glacier blocked the water's course. As a result, the meltwater from the side valley glaciers pooled into lakes.

When the Bow Valley glacier retreated past the mouths of the side valleys, the natural dams were lost and the water that had been impounded surged from the side valleys as debris flows. The debris flows deposited rubble and sediment onto the floor of the Bow Valley. Because limestone is one of the most common rock-types in the Rockies, these gravelly deposits contained a high concentration of lime. As the deposits dried and hardened, they became natural concrete.

The Bow River exposed the debris flow deposits in its riverbanks. Over a period of thousands of years, rainwater, runoff and wind eroded furrows into the deposits. Additional erosion enlarged these furrows until freestanding pillars developed. Called hoodoos, these pillars were originally protected by capstones – large boulders that had been carried in the debris flows. Now missing their capstones, the Tunnel Mountain Hoodoos will eventually weather away until they collapse.

Douglas fir

Stoney natives thought that the Tunnel Mountain Hoodoos were giants turned to stone, or teepees that housed "bad gods." There are other hoodoo formations nearby in the Bow Valley. You can see them from Highway 1 between Banff and Canmore.

Douglas fir and limber pine grow along this trail. Limber pine has long, curved needles in bundles of five. Its trunk and branches are frequently contorted. The tree is locally common on cliff edges and in other windy locations in the montane ecoregion, south of Saskatchewan River Crossing.

Chinook Winds

The chinook (shih-NOOK) is a warm winter wind that blows eastward at the mountain front. Chinook is a Native word that means "snow eater." Chinooks have been known to raise the temperature as much as 40°C in a few hours. At Pincher Creek, one chinook raised the temperature 21°C in 4 minutes.

A chinook originates when warm air from a Pacific storm system meets a cold air mass east of the Rockies. The storm system has shed most of its moisture on the western slopes of the Rockies, and the resulting dry air is heated by an increase in air pressure as it sweeps down the eastern slope.

Chinooks generally last from a few hours to a few days, but occasionally endure longer. There are roughly 20 chinook days a year near Banff. Chinooks melt the snow, making the front range valleys of the Rockies prime winter habitat for elk, deer and bighorn sheep—and for their predators: wolf, coyote and cougar.

The coal mining town of Bankhead flourished at the base of Cascade Mountain in the early 1900s. The photograph shows the tipple, where the different-sized pieces of coal were sorted. Photograph by Elliott Barnes, courtesy of the Whyte Museum of the Canadian Rockies

6. Bankhead

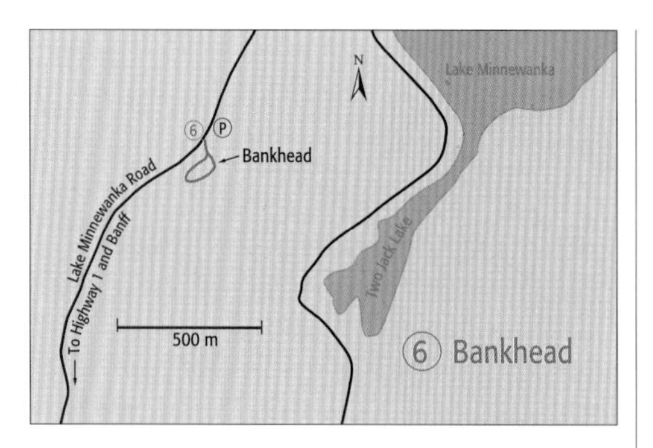

Route Information

Trailhead: Follow Banff Avenue 3 km east from town to Highway 1. Keep straight ahead on the Lake Minnewanka Road for 3.3 km. The trailhead is on the southeast (right).

Rating: easy, 1.1 km loop. A brochure may be available at the trailhead.

Lighting: anytime

The Bankhead loop explores the industrial area of a coal mining community that flourished in the early 1900s. You can see artifacts associated with the mine. Coal cinders are frequently underfoot.

Coal was discovered east of Banff in 1883. The Canadian Anthracite Coal Company began mining at a location near the Canadian Pacific Railway line in 1886. Not wanting to depend on an outside supplier for its locomotive coal, the CPR obtained its own license to mine coal in 1903.

Named after a Scottish town, the Bankhead mine was intended only to serve the railway's needs. However, the coal shortage of 1906-07 created a huge, national demand for coal. The CPR expanded operations rapidly and built a townsite adjacent to the mine.

Mine production peaked in 1911; estimates vary from 250,000 to 416,000 tonnes of coal. The town's population also reached maximum the same year. Officially recorded as 900 persons, some reports indicate that 2000 people lived at Bankhead. Most of the miners were immigrants: German, Italian, Swedish, Polish and Chinese. The town featured a coal-burning power plant that also supplied electricity to Banff.

Although resource extraction industries have been viewed as undesirable in national parks since the National Parks Act was passed in 1930, park managers in the early 1900s encouraged developments at Bankhead. The park superintendent praised Bankhead in 1911: "With its beautiful homes and its teeming industrial life, it has already become a popular stopping place for tourists."

Bankhead's coal was extracted in an unusual fashion. The horizontal coal seams lay in the mountainside above the valley floor. Reaching the seams necessitated burrowing upwards on a slight angle. Coal was then knocked downwards into rail cars that gravity assisted in returning to the mine entrance. Three mining levels were developed. A total of 320 km of mining, transportation and ventilation tunnels was excavated.

Narrow-gauge trains transported coal from the mine to the tipple, where the coal was sorted. To prevent ignition of combustible gases in the mine tunnels, the trains were powered by compressed air. Known as "dinkys," the trains pulled 30 boxcars, each of which held 2 tonnes of coal.

From a combustion point of view, Bankhead's coal was desirable, high quality semi-anthracite. However, 35 percent of the coal was little more than dust by the time it reached the mine portal. To salvage this coal, the CPR imported pitch from Pennsylvania to manufacture briquettes. Despite the expense, this process proved successful.

As with most mining towns, Bankhead's history was one of boom and bust. A decade of labour troubles forced closure of the mine in 1922. Despite having produced more than 2,600,000 tonnes of coal, the mine never reopened. The miners moved on. Many of the town's buildings were moved to Banff, Canmore and Calgary. By 1928, Bankhead was a ghost town.

A Rival Community to Banff

During its heyday, Bankhead rivalled Banff as the most thriving community in the Rockies. Residents of Bankhead enjoyed many conveniences: rail service, a hotel, school, two dairies, skating rinks, court, churches, tennis courts and a library. Some homes had running water, sewers and electricity—before these amenities came to Banff.

The train station at Bankhead was a whistle stop. One night when the train carrying the CPR payroll passed through, a clerk threw the payroll bag in the general direction of the station. He missed. Concerned mine officials found the payroll the next day, in a snowbank 400 m from the station.

One aspect of civilization that Bankhead lacked was a cemetery. Most residents thought that bad luck would befall the family of the first person to be buried in a new cemetery, so burials were made in Banff—much to the consternation of park officials. When a Chinese labourer at Bankhead was murdered in 1921, it was thought that he had no family, so he was interred as the first, and only, burial at Bankhead's cemetery. When word of his death eventually reached his homeland, the labourer's family requested that his remains be shipped to China. This request was fulfilled in 1939, and Bankhead's cemetery was closed.

The trail to Stewart Canyon skirts the north shore of Lake Minnewanka, the largest body of water in Banff National Park. The lake is a hydroelectric reservoir. Dams have raised the lake's natural level 25 m, and added 8 km to its length.

7. Stewart Canyon

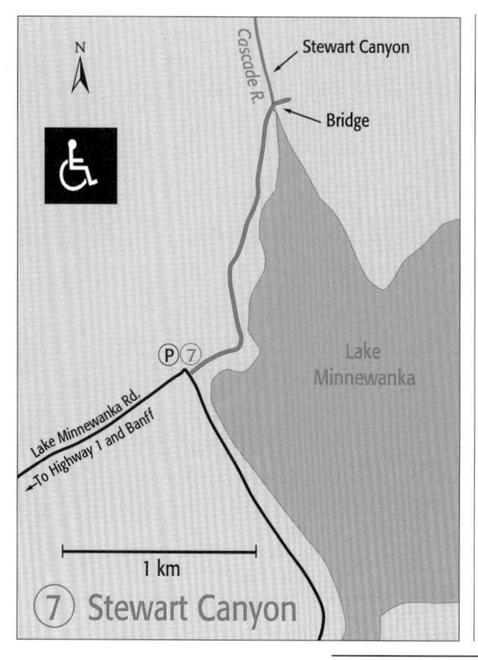

The Stewart Canyon trail is an ideal walk for families. It follows the north shore of Lake Minnewanka to a bridged canyon where the Cascade River enters the lake. The pleasant, shaded trail leads through a mature lodgepole pine forest, with scattered Douglas fir. The parking lot area is summer home to a flock of

Route Information

Trailhead: Follow Banff Avenue 3 km east from town to Highway 1. Keep straight ahead on the Lake Minnewanka Road for 5.9 km to Lake Minnewanka. Park on the north (left).

Rating: easy, 1.7 km. The first 700 m are wheelchair accessible.

Lighting: anytime

bighorn sheep.

With an area of 12.95 km^2, Lake Minnewanka is the largest lake in Banff National Park. The lake we see today is a hydroelectric reservoir. When the Bankhead mine developed nearby in 1903, it provided coal-fired electricity for its own needs and for Banff townsite. A miner's strike in 1912 temporarily disrupted Banff's electricity supply. The town desired a more reliable source, and decided to dam the outlet of Lake Minnewanka in order to generate hydroelectricity.

The initial dam raised the lake level 3 m. The dam was enlarged in 1922. In 1941, a much larger hydroelectric facility was constructed. The new dams raised the lake level a further 22 m, submerging the village of Minnewanka Landing, and lengthening the lake by 8 km. Today, divers often explore the ruined village on the lake bottom.

Minnewanka means "lake of the water spirit." According to Stoney legend, the spirit in the lake is malevolent, and belongs to a being—half fish, half human—that can move the lake waters at will. Natives would neither swim or canoe in the lake. Earlier this century, Minnewanka was commonly called Devil's Lake.

The Cascade River originally flowed west of Lake Minnewanka, and received the lake's outflow via Devil's Creek. When the lake level was raised, the mouth of the river was submerged in the lake, and Devil's Creek disappeared. At the east end of the lake, the flow of the Ghost River was dammed and reversed, so it would also feed into Lake Minnewanka.

Stewart Canyon is a strike canyon. The Cascade River is eroding a fault in the bedrock, where two thrust sheets meet. The canyon was named for George Stewart, the first superintendent of Banff National Park. The oldest archaeological site in Banff National Park is nearby—a native hunting camp that dates to 11,500 years ago.

Bighorn Sheep

The bighorn sheep is the symbol of Banff National Park, and is the park's second most abundant large mammal. Many visitors confuse bighorn sheep with mountain goats. To simplify identification, remember: sheep are light brown with brown horns, and goats are white or cream-coloured, with black horns.

The bighorn ram stands about 1 m tall at the shoulder, and when mature, has a set of thick horns that spiral forward. These horns are never shed. It is possible to determine the approximate age of a ram by counting the annuli, or rings on one of its horns. Each annulus contains a dark and light band, together representing one year of growth. The female sheep (ewe) grows horns too, however these are less spectacular, and curve backwards.

The rams flock together in high places during summer and early autumn. The dominant ram must constantly defend his place. Usually, this is done without battle in what is called the "present" (pree-ZENT)—when two rams turn their heads sideways, to allow each to inspect the horns of the other. When rams duel, they charge headlong at each other and meet with a mighty crash. Thick armour bones beneath the horns usually prevent serious injury. However, duels to the death do take place.

Grasses are the most important foods for bighorn sheep. Grizzly bears, wolves and cougars are the animal's principal predators. They may achieve success by forcing sheep to run over a cliff. Poaching, and deaths from collisions with trains and vehicles claim more animals than natural causes.

Bighorn sheep are generally accustomed to humans, and will often allow us to approach closely. This puts both humans and sheep in peril. With their horns and sharp hooves, sheep are capable of inflicting serious injury. If a sheep approaches you, scare it away.

The Grassi Lakes are on the lower flank of Mt. Rundle, west of Canmore. On the way to the lakes, you obtain a spectacular overview of the Bow Valley.

8. Grassi Lakes

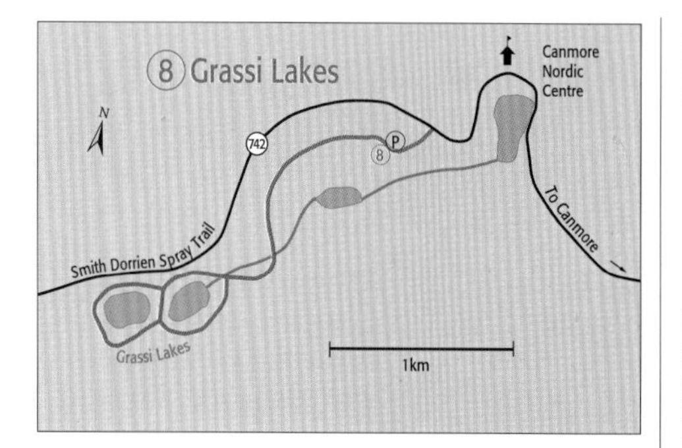

Route Information

Trailhead: From Canmore, follow signs for the Canmore Nordic Centre to the Smith-Dorrien/Spray Road. The Grassi Lakes turnoff is 1 km beyond the Nordic Centre, on the south (left).
Rating: harder, 1.75 km
Lighting: anytime

The trail to Grassi Lakes climbs west out of the Bow Valley onto the lower slopes of Mt. Rundle, and provides a spectacular overview of the Canmore area. The beautiful blue and green waters of the lakes commemorate Lawrence Grassi, miner and trail builder. In the 1920s, Grassi and fellow workers from the nearby Georgetown coal mine built this trail to fill idle time during a strike. The trail features a rock staircase, and formerly included a log ladder, to surmount a rock step. These devices were Grassi trademarks. He also used them on trails that he constructed in the Lake O'Hara area of Yoho National Park. Originally named Twin Lakes, the lakes were renamed in Grassi's honour in 1938. Grassi died in 1980, at age 90.

Initially the trail climbs gently through an

open forest of lodgepole pine. The undergrowth includes the shrubs buffaloberry, common juniper, Labrador tea, and prickly wild rose—Alberta's flower emblem. Adding splashes of colour are the wildflowers: arnica, harebell, twinflower and western wood lily.

Soon, the trail begins a steeper climb toward the 100 m-high waterfall that drains the lakes. Benches provide resting points. The interpretive signs at trailside describe the Spray hydroelectric project. The Spray River was dammed in the late 1940s. Some of its waters were diverted east into the Bow River. The signs neglect to mention a very significant impact of this project: the area of the Spray development was formerly protected within Banff National Park, but was removed in 1930 to allow the watercourse diversion and flooding to take place. At the waterfall, the trail draws alongside the cliff edge (use caution), and grants views east to the limestone peaks of the Fairholme Range across the Bow Valley.

Labrador tea

Despite the many dams, reservoirs and penstocks in this area, the Grassi Lakes are natural features of the landscape. They are fed by water that seeps from the bedrock above. The beautiful colours of the lakes are characteristic of cold, clear water. Rocks on the lake bottoms are covered in dense blooms of algae. The American dipper (also called water ouzel) lives here. The dipper is the only aquatic songbird in North America. It stays in the mountains year-round, feeding on larvae and insects in the water, and nesting on rocks nearby. Its down-like feathers are coated with a thick oil that repels water and helps keep the bird warm during winter. The dipper has flaps that cover its nostrils, allowing it to remain submerged for more than a minute.

The limestone cliffs above the lakes are remains of an ancient marine reef. It is thought that the caves in these cliffs were used for shelter by natives as recently as the late 1700s.

Western Wood Lily

The western wood lily is one of the prettiest wildflowers in the Rockies. It is locally common on grasslands and in low elevation pine forests. The stem of this flower may be 50 cm tall, and the flower as much as 10 cm across. The petals are deep orange, speckled inside with black dots on a yellow background. The flower blooms from early June until mid-July, and is the floral emblem of Saskatchewan. The tiger lily is a different species.

The western wood lily suffers a fate of many attractive plants. Its flower is commonly picked by admirers, and like most wildflowers that grow from bulbs, the plant usually dies as a result. Please leave this beautiful flower for others to enjoy.

You can explore Grotto Canyon from within, by walking off-trail along the streambed. The canyon walls are 60 m high.

9. Grotto Canyon

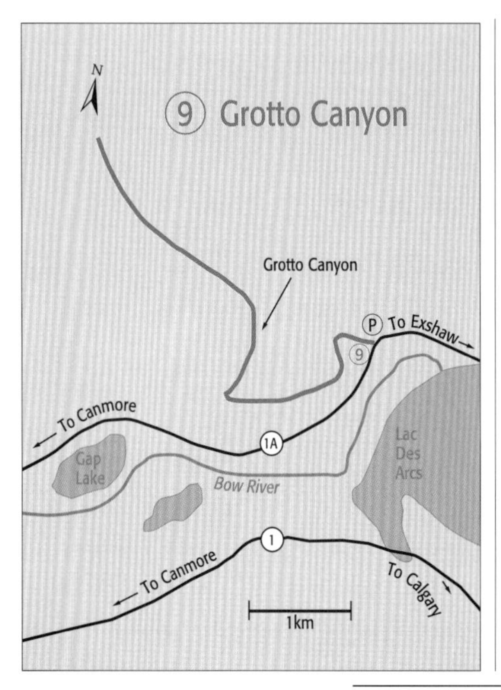

Although many walks in this book feature limestone canyons, Grotto Canyon is the only one you explore by walking on the canyon floor. This is also the only outing in this book that ventures off maintained trail. Sturdy footwear is recommended. Avoid this hike during heavy rains.

The first 600 m of trail is along an old roadbed, carpeted with the minuscule evergreen wild-

Route Information

Trailhead: Grotto Mountain picnic area on Highway 1A, 12 km east of Canmore, 16 km west of the junction with Highway 1X (Bow Valley Provincial Park)
Rating: harder, 2.5 km
Lighting: anytime

flower, yellow mountain avens. This plant is common in gravelly areas. Its nodding, yellow flowers are replaced in July by twisted seed pods that resemble those of dandelion. The roots of mountain avens fix nitrogen from the atmosphere into the soil.

The rubble along the roadbed is material eroded upstream in the canyon and deposited here during flash-floods. It has created a landform called an alluvial fan. The shape and height of this fan is evident near the canyon mouth. Look toward the Bow Valley for a good view of Gap Lake, Mt. Lougheed and Pigeon Mountain.

After turning north (right) toward the canyon, you are greeted by a blast of cold air, chilled by the canyon walls. This is the end of well-defined trail. In the canyon you will be walking on water-worn rock slabs, rubble and boulders.

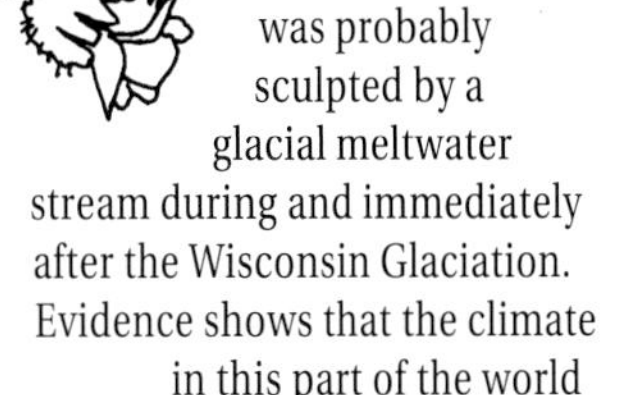

Yellow mountain avens

Grotto Canyon is dry most of the time. How did the canyon become so deep, with so little water flowing through it? The original canyon was probably sculpted by a glacial meltwater stream during and immediately after the Wisconsin Glaciation. Evidence shows that the climate in this part of the world was relatively warm from 8000 to 5000 years ago. The warmth caused glaciers on upper mountain sides to melt rapidly. Water erodes limestone easily. With a constant flow of water at high volume, the remaining depth of this canyon could have been cut in a few thousand years. Today, the major erosional forces at work are frost shattering of the cliffs, and flash-floods of sedimentary debris after heavy rains.

In terms of the hiking experience, the confines of Grotto Canyon are more typical of Utah than the Rockies. After walking about 1 km, the canyon branches. The right branch climbs to a small waterfall. The left branch winds toward a more open valley, where limber pine and Douglas fir grow. In this valley is a large hoodoo formation that contains a cave. Grotto means "cave," but the canyon does not take its name from this feature. Eugene Bourgeau of the Palliser Expedition named the mountain west of the canyon in 1858, after he explored a massive cave in its slopes.

Grotto Canyon is popular with rock climbers. In winter, waterfall ice climbers practice their craft on frozen seeps along the canyon walls.

Pictographs

There are several panels of rock art in Grotto Canyon. The illustrations are pictographs, created with a crude paint that may contain ochre. The shaded locations of the pictographs have preserved them for perhaps 500 to 1000 years. Recently they have suffered heavily at the hands of careless visitors. For this reason, the author has chosen not to include specific descriptions of their locations.

Mt. Yamnuska (yam-NUSS-kuh) is prominent in the view from the interpretive trails in Bow Valley Provincial Park. Yamnuska is a rendition of a Stoney word that means "flat-faced mountain."

10. Montane Trail

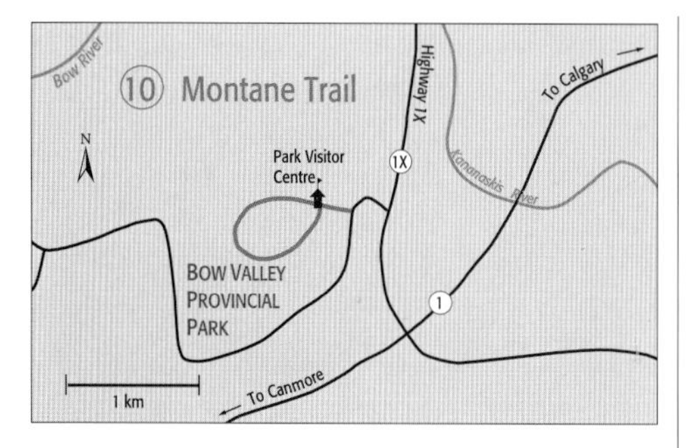

Route Information

Trailhead: Follow Highway 1 to the junction with Highway 1X, 80 km west of Calgary, 28 km east of Canmore. The Bow Valley Provincial Park Visitor Centre is 1 km north, on the west (left). The trail begins at the rear of the building.
Rating: easy, 2.2 km loop
Lighting: anytime

Bow Valley Provincial Park is located where the front ranges meet the foothills. As at Waterton Lakes National Park, the transition is marked by a tremendous variety of plant and animal life. The pockets of forest contain species native to the mountains, and the meadows contain flora and fauna commonly found in the foothills and on the prairies. Of the half dozen interpretive walks in the park, the Montane Trail best displays this diversity.

The montane ecoregion occupies major valley bottoms in the Rockies. The climate is characterized by wind, extremes of temperature, and relatively low annual precipitation. The windiness at the mountain front is accentuated by winter chinooks. The montane provides important habitat for most larger mammals, especially in winter. Significant as it is, the montane comprises only 5 percent of the area of the Rocky Mountain parks. Most development in these parks has taken place in the montane, with severe impacts on wildlife habitat.

On the Montane Trail you will see extensive evidence of the area's glacial past. During the Wisconsin Glaciation, between 75,000 to 11,000 years ago, massive rivers of ice, 1000 m thick, flowed east from the Rockies onto the plains. When they melted, these glaciers left behind many landforms made of boulders, sand and gravel, creating the undulating landscape of Bow Valley Provincial Park.

Sinuous ridges of gravel called eskers were formed by streams that flowed beneath glacial ice. Part of the Montane Trail is along the crest of an esker. Cone-shaped piles of rubble called kames were deposited by meltwater flowing from the surface of the ice. Detached blocks of glacial ice melted into the rubble, creating kettle ponds. Oval-shaped mounds called drumlins, and other irregular clumps of moraine also dot the area.

The mule deer is the most common of the two deer species in the Rockies. The area traversed by the Montane Trail is ideal deer habitat.

The glacial landforms serve as windbreaks, controlling the growth of forest. The windswept ridges have few trees. The protected hollows support groves of trembling aspen, white spruce and lodgepole pine.

The grassy meadows along the Montane Trail are frequently swept by hot ground fires. The fires eliminate tree growth, and rejuvenate the grasses. The glacial landforms keep these fires localized, helping sustain the mosaic of forest and meadow. Wildlife such as elk and deer benefit by having open areas for grazing, and forest nearby for shelter.

The McConnell Thrust Fault

Many who approach the Rockies from the east marvel at the front ranges, which rise dramatically 1000 m above the foothills. During mountain building, crustal forces compressed the sedimentary rock formations that comprise the Rockies, until some buckled and broke. Great sandwich layers of rock, called thrust sheets, slid upwards and northeast over the underlying rock layers. The boundary between the thrust sheet and the underlying layers is called a thrust fault.

You can see the McConnell Thrust Fault at the base of Mt. Yamnuska. Here, layers of 540 million year old limestone have been thrust upward and northeast for 16 km, and have come to rest atop undisturbed shales that are 90 million years old.

Limestone is tougher than shale. Hence the cliff of Yamnuska has endured, whereas the exposed shales of the adjacent foothills have weathered away, creating the exaggerated vertical relief at the mountain front.

The McConnell is the most easterly thrust fault in the front ranges. Richard McConnell was an assistant to George Dawson of the Geological Survey of Canada, in 1880.

The Lower Falls in Johnston Canyon mark a point where Johnston Creek has encountered a resistant layer of dolomite in the limestone bedrock.

11. Johnston Canyon

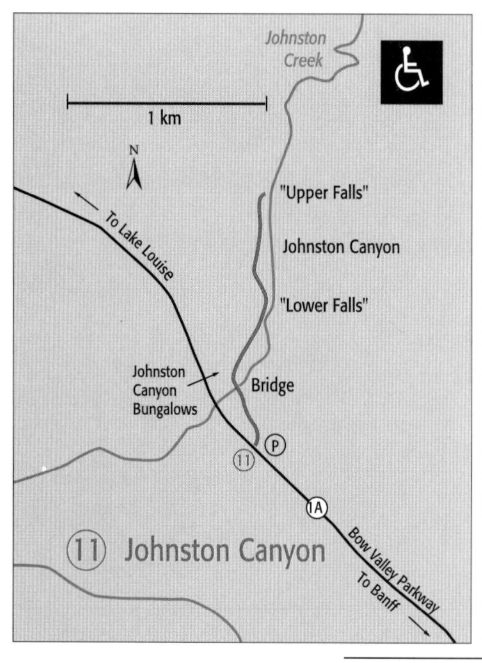

Of the seven trails in this book that lead to limestone canyons, the Johnston Canyon trail provides the most interesting walking experience. A suspended walkway takes you into the heart of the canyon, and provides views of waterfalls, and a close-up perspective on the effects of flowing water.

Johnston Creek has not always flowed through this canyon. At the end of the Wisconsin

Route Information

Trailhead: East side of the Bow Valley Parkway (Highway 1A), 23.6 km west of Banff, 6.5 km east of Castle Junction

Rating: Lower Falls, easy, 1.1 km; Upper Falls, moderate, 2.7 km

Lighting: early afternoon

Glaciation, 11,000 years ago, the creek flowed east of here alongside Mt. Ishbel, and emptied into the Bow River down the valley. About 8000 years ago, a massive landslide broke free from Mt. Ishbel. The Hillsdale Slide blocked the course of Johnston Creek, forcing it to seek another outlet. Eventually the creek took advantage of a bedrock fault and eroded the canyon.

You walk to the Lower Falls along a walkway within Johnston Canyon.

There are seven waterfalls in Johnston Canyon. Each marks the location of a relatively resistant outcrop of dolomite rock in the limestone bedrock. The dolomite lip of a waterfall endures as the limestone beneath is eroded into a plunge pool by the incessant pounding of the water. Eventually, the lip is undercut by the plunge pool and collapses. The falls then migrate slightly upstream. The highest waterfall and deepest point in Johnston Canyon is the 30 m Upper Falls.

Limestone erodes relatively easily in water because rainfall and runoff are naturally slightly acidic. This chemical erosion, coupled with abrasion by sediments in the water and frost-shattering of the canyon walls, has created interesting formations in the canyon. One of these is the natural tunnel at the Lower Falls. As with other limestone canyons in the Rockies, Johnston Canyon exhibits potholes and abandoned channels. There is even an abandoned waterfall.

In the canyon, lodgepole pines and a few Douglas fir trees grow on south-facing slopes. The colder, wetter north-facing slopes support Engelmann spruce and subalpine fir. Red squirrel, American dipper, porcupine and common raven are residents of the canyon. You will sometimes see mule deer and black bear near the parking lot. The canyon is one of two known nesting sites in Alberta for the black swift. Johnston Canyon was named for a prospector from nearby Silver City, a railway and mining boom town of 1883–85

Travertine

Travertine (TRAH-vur-teen) is banded limestone created by chemical and biological action. Algae that live on the walls of Johnston Canyon remove carbon dioxide from the water during photosynthesis, and deposit a film of calcium carbonate as a waste product. The calcium carbonate eventually builds up into crumbly limestone. A similar process took place in ancient seas hundreds of millions of years ago, and created much of the limestone rock in the Rockies.

Small travertine deposits occur in many canyons in the Rockies, but the travertine wall at the Upper Falls in Johnston Canyon is the most extensive. There are 25 species of algae here. The formation of this travertine is assisted by the spray from the waterfall, and by spring water that seeps from several outlets on the canyon wall. If you look at the base of the wall, you will see that the travertine overhangs the creek.

An early autumn snowfall blankets the mountains above Boom Lake.

12. Boom Lake

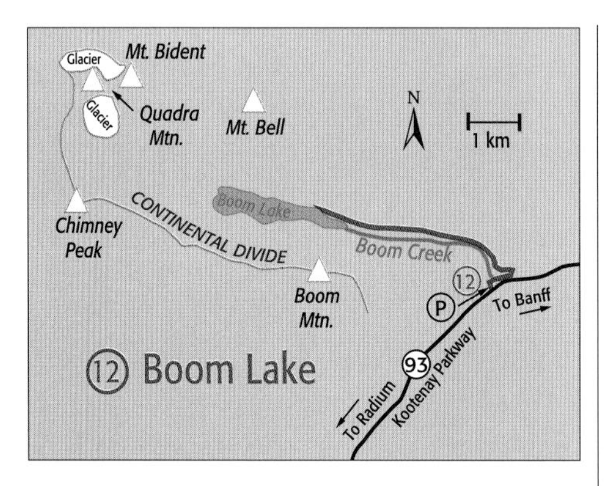

Route Information

Trailhead: Boom Creek picnic area on north side of the Kootenay Parkway (Highway 93 South), 7 km west of Castle Junction, 97.7 km east of the junction with Highway 95
Rating: harder, 5.1 km
Lighting: morning

The Boom Lake hike is a long but undemanding stroll through an ancient subalpine forest. The destination is a superb backcountry lake in a wilderness setting, the match of any in the Rockies. The shores of the lake are a wonderful place to wile away the hours. However, be forewarned: the area is frequented by grizzly bears.

After crossing Boom Creek on a bridge, the broad trail (formerly a tote road to a mine) commences its gradual climb. Keep straight ahead at the Taylor Lake junction at km 2.3. The trail continues its rolling ascent for another 2 km, and then descends gradually, becoming narrower, rocky and rooted for the last 200 m. It emerges on the north shore of Boom Lake about 600 m west of the outlet. Rockslide debris makes travel along the lakeshore difficult.

Boom Lake

Boom Lake is 2.7 km long, 30 m deep, and 366 m wide. With an area of roughly 1 km^2, it is the tenth largest lake in Banff National Park. Its water is remarkably clear given its proximity to glacial ice. Measurements have documented a reduction of silt in the water during the 20th century—indicating that the glaciers that feed Boom Lake are dwindling.

Boom Lake is home to cutthroat trout. The log booms are natural formations created from avalanched trees swept into the lake. The trees then drifted toward the outlet and became lodged on submerged moraines. The prominent snow-clad and ice-clad mountains northwest of the lake are Mt. Bident (3084 m) and Quadra Mountain (3173 m). People familiar with these mountains as viewed from the Moraine Lake Road or from Consolation Lakes may have difficulty recognizing them here. The basin beneath is heaped with moraines, indicating the extent of glacial ice less than two centuries ago.

The trail to Boom Lake is located just a few kilometres east of the continental divide, an area of high precipitation. Engelmann spruce and subalpine fir comprise the damp, mature subalpine forest here. Some of the spruce trees measure 1 m in diameter at the base, and are 40 m tall, indicating ages of perhaps 350–450 years. The spire-like form of the subalpine fir, with its downsloping branches, helps shed the heavy snow load. Labrador tea, dwarf birch, feathermosses, and fungi are prominent in the undergrowth.

This forest, with its deadfall and tree lichens, represents the climax vegetation for this area. It provides ideal habitat for mice and voles, which are standard fare for the American marten, the most widespread carnivore in the Rockies. Moose use this forest for cover, and ruffed grouse and pileated woodpeckers may be seen. Varied thrush, hermit thrush and golden-crowned kinglet are common songbirds. The bark of some Engelmann spruce trees is reddish-purple, where three-toed woodpeckers have removed the brown outer scales in quest of grubs and insects.

The damp and decay of this forest is in contrast to the dry lodgepole pine forest you saw at the trailhead. The pines were seeded naturally after the 1968 Vermilion Pass Burn. Spruce and fir will probably replace the pines within 130 years. This process of transformation in the forest is called succession. Each forest type favours certain species of vegetation and wildlife. The mosaic of new and old, burned and unburned, creates the diversity of habitats required to maintain all species in the forest ecosystem.

Pikas—EEEEP!

So goes the call of the pika (PEE-kah or PIE-kah), one of two members of the rabbit family in the Rockies. The quartzite boulderfields along the shore of Boom Lake are perfect terrain for this tiny (less than 20 cm long) rock rabbit. The pika has a gray coat and a minuscule tail. It has been affectionately described as "a tennis ball with ears." Pikas live in colonies. You will probably hear a pika long before you see it. The shrill call warns its fellows of your presence.

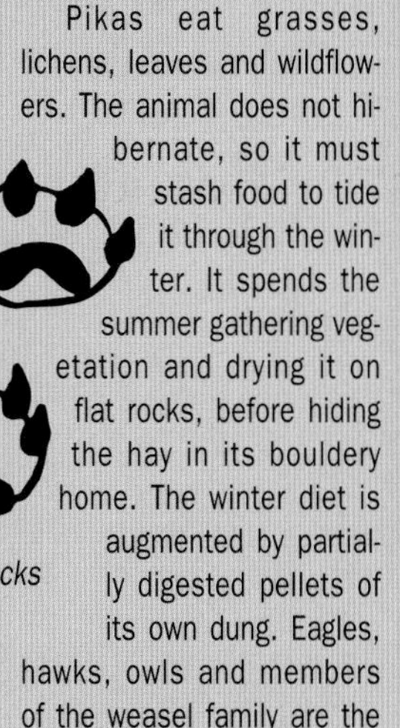

Pika tracks

Pikas eat grasses, lichens, leaves and wildflowers. The animal does not hibernate, so it must stash food to tide it through the winter. It spends the summer gathering vegetation and drying it on flat rocks, before hiding the hay in its bouldery home. The winter diet is augmented by partially digested pellets of its own dung. Eagles, hawks, owls and members of the weasel family are the pika's principal predators.

The ice-draped flank of Mt. Victoria provides the backdrop for the world famous view at Lake Louise.

13. Lake Louise Shoreline

1km
Chateau Lake Louise
1A
Mirror Lk.
Lake Agnes
Lake Louise
Louise Creek
13 P
N
13 Lake Louise Shoreline

Route Information

Trailhead: From Lake Louise Village, follow Lake Louise Drive, 5.5 km to the public parking lots at the lake. Paved walkways lead to the lakeshore and the trailhead at the outlet of the lake.
Rating: moderate, 1.9 km. Wheelchair accessible. The first 300 m are paved.
Lighting: sunrise and morning

The shoreline trail at Lake Louise probably sees more foot and wheelchair traffic than any other place in the Rockies, except Banff Avenue. What is so alluring about Lake Louise is the symmetry of the scene. Mt. Victoria, 10 km distant, and its reflection, are framed perfectly by the converging lines of cliffs and slopes at the far end of the lake. At least one world traveller has ranked "Lake Louise at sunrise" among the top ten of the world's natural wonders.

A developed trail exists along the northwest edge of the lake only (viewer's right). This gravelled trail eventually leads to the Plain of Six Glaciers, but those looking for a shorter outing will find that the boat landing or the delta at the far end of the lake make good places to turn around.

In 1882, pioneer guide and outfitter Tom Wilson was led to Lake Louise by Edwin Hunter, a Stoney native. The Stoneys called the lake, "Lake of the Little Fishes." Wilson called it Emerald Lake. Two years later, the name was changed to Lake Louise to honour Louise Caroline Alberta, the fourth daughter of Queen Victoria, and wife of the Governor-General of Canada. The province of Alberta is also named for her.

Wilson's visit brought the lake to the attention of the CPR. In 1888, Wilson cut a trail to the lake. In 1890, the railway constructed its first chalet at the lake, and began to advertise the rustic shelter to clients who were well-heeled and willing to rough it a bit. From this building, which housed fewer than a dozen guests, the chalet underwent continual transformation, yielding the 515-room Chateau Lake Louise a century later.

Lake Louise occupies a glacially-carved valley adjacent to the continental divide. The lake is 2.4 km long, roughly 500 m wide, and 90 m deep. Its elevation is 1731 m—slightly more than a mile above sea level. The surrounding mountains shade its waters for much of the year, and the lake's surface is frozen from November until June. The maximum water temperature of 8°C is reached in early August. It's no wonder the fishes are little!

You can read interpretive panels that describe the human and natural history of Lake Louise, near the lake's outlet, and along the boardwalk to the boathouse. The plaque that commemorates the designation of the Rocky Mountain parks as a World Heritage Site was unveiled by the Duke of Edinburgh during a royal visit in 1985.

The Subalpine Forest

The forest adjacent to Chateau Lake Louise has been greatly altered during the last century. However, just a short walk from the Chateau, you enter undisturbed subalpine forest that is centuries old.

The most common trees in this forest are Engelmann spruce and subalpine fir. The Engelmann spruce has scaly, reddish-brown bark. The smooth, silvery bark of subalpine fir is often covered in resin blisters, which, when broken, give the forest its sweet fragrance. Its shape is spire-like, to help shed the heavy snow load. The branches are draped with tree lichens. A carpet of rootless plants called feathermosses thrives on the damp forest floor, along with the wildflowers, dwarf dogwood and arnica.

The subalpine forest is often called "the snow forest." More than 4 m of snow falls here each year. Common wildlife includes: masked shrew, pack rat, least chipmunk, red squirrel, American marten, snowshoe hare, beaver, lynx, mule deer, wolverine, porcupine, great horned owl, spruce grouse, Clark's nutcracker and gray jay.

Mt. Victoria rises above a chaos of glacial ice and rubble at the far end of the valley that contains Lake Louise. From the gravelly plain adjacent to Lower Victoria Glacier, many glaciers are visible.

14. Plain of Six Glaciers

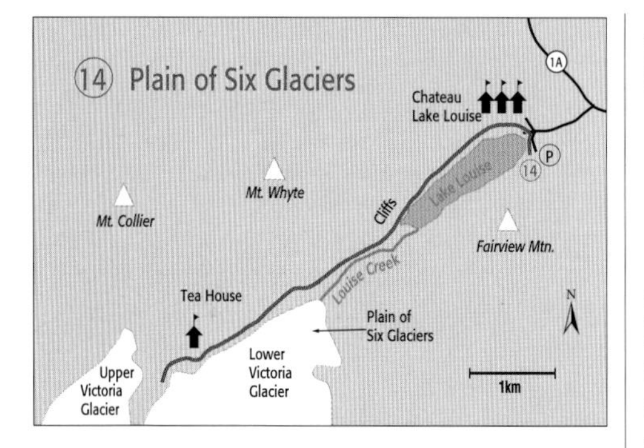

Route Information

Trailhead: From Lake Louise Village, follow Lake Louise Drive, 5.5 km to the public parking lots at the lake. Paved walkways lead to the lakeshore and the trailhead, at the lake's outlet.
Rating: harder, 5.3 km
Lighting: morning

The hike to the Plain of Six Glaciers is a continuation of the Lake Louise Shoreline walk, and delivers you to the jumble of ice and rock at the foot of Mt. Victoria. It is the longest outing in this book, and is also one of the most popular. Sturdy footwear is recommended, and you should be prepared for changeable weather.

At the southwest end of Lake Louise, the trail passes beneath 100 m-high cliffs that are popular with rock climbers. The rock here is colourful Gog quartzite. It underlies most of the mountains in the area. The trail draws alongside the delta at the lake's inlet. You may see beavers here in the morning and early evening.

You gain most of the elevation on this hike in two short climbs. The first of these takes you through subalpine forest, and across openings of several large avalanche paths on the lower slopes of Mt Whyte. In the valley bottom to your left is a jumble of gray boulders—rockslide debris. Farther up the valley, the trail traverses a low cliff edge. Use care here if the rock is wet. If the exposure of the traverse is not to your liking, you can bypass this section by dropping to the moraine on your left. Look for wild onion, shooting stars, star-flowered Solomon's seal, and false Solomon's seal nearby.

The "plain" is a 1 km-long, gravel outwash area in the forefield of the Lower Victoria Glacier. From it, six glaciers are visible: Lower Victoria, Upper Victoria, Aberdeen, Lefroy, "Upper Lefroy" and "Popes." (A seventh glacier, that does not flow into this valley, is visible on the north peak of Mt. Victoria.) During the Wisconsin Glaciation, the combined flow of the six glaciers carved the valley that contains Lake Louise. Since then, the ice has shrunk greatly in length and mass. Lower Victoria Glacier has receded 1220 m in the last 160 years.

The second climb is on switchbacks just before you reach the teahouse. Look for mountain goats and porcupines here. The Plain of Six Glaciers teahouse is at 2135 m. It was constructed in 1924 by Swiss Guides employed by the CPR. The teahouse served as a hiker's destination and as a staging point for mountaineers. Today, lunch, refreshments and snacks are available in season. Overnight accommodation is no longer offered.

Those with sturdy footwear and warm clothing can extend this hike 1.6 km beyond the teahouse, to a spectacular viewpoint on a moraine that overlooks the Lower Victoria Glacier.

Glacier Types

Glacial ice forms in areas where more snow accumulates in winter than melts in summer. The shape of a glacier depends on its location and on features of the surrounding landscape. *Icefields* form on flat areas at high elevation. *Outlet valley glaciers* flow from icefields into valleys below. *Alpine valley glaciers* occupy high mountain valleys and are not fed by icefields. *Cirque glaciers* occupy and erode bowl-shaped depressions in mountainsides. A small cirque glacier is called a *pocket glacier. Catchment glaciers* form at high elevations, where indentations in a mountainside trap windblown snow. If the indentation is deep, the glacier may be called a *niche glacier.*

Any of these glacier types can also be called a *hanging glacier* if the ice terminates on a cliff. A *rock glacier* is a lobe-shaped accumulation of rock that insulates permanent ice within. With the exception of icefields and outlet valley glaciers, you can see all these glacier types from the Plain of Six Glaciers trail.

Lake Agnes is a glacial tarn, nestled in a cirque valley high above Lake Louise. The steep hike to the lake is one of the most popular excursions in the Rockies. The lake is walled by ragged cliffs; a striking contrast to the open prospect across the Bow Valley. This view looks towards the teahouse from the west end of the lake.

15. Lake Agnes

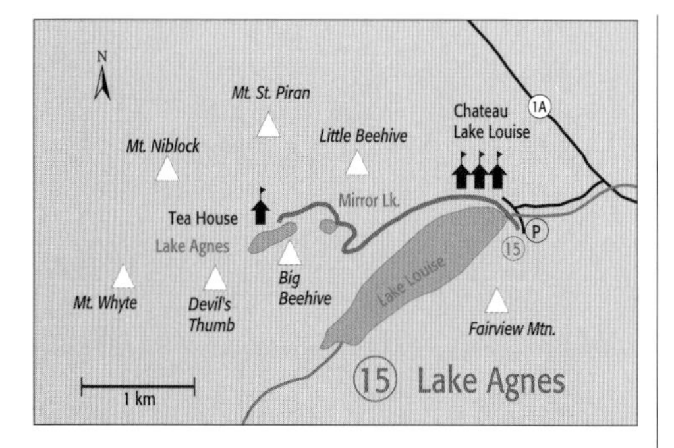

Route Information

Trailhead: From Lake Louise Village, follow Lake Louise Drive, 5.5 km to the public parking lots at the lake. Paved walkways lead to the lakeshore and the trailhead, at the lake's outlet. Walk along the lakeshore to the trail junction west of the Chateau. The Lake Agnes trail branches uphill to the north (right).
Rating: harder, 3.4 km
Lighting: morning

The Stoney guide who led Tom Wilson to Lake Louise in 1882, told him of two other lakes on a nearby mountainside. "The goat's looking glass" was a small lake where goats combed their beards and studied their reflections in the tranquil waters. Higher was another lake, subsequently named Lake Agnes for the wife of Canada's first prime minister.

The lakes soon became known as "the lakes in the clouds." One of the first tasks of Willoughby Astley, manager of Chalet Lake Louise, was cutting a trail to reach them. Today, many visitors are soon humbled by the unrelenting climb that resulted from Astley's work, and also by the effects of the elevation. Take it easy on this hike, and allow a half-day for the round trip.

The first 2 km of the trail to Lake Agnes is

through dense subalpine forest. The most common trees are Engelmann spruce and subalpine fir. The tree branches are draped with lichens, and feathermosses cover the damp forest floor. At km 1.6, the trail makes a 180° switchback turn on a narrow avalanche path. You can see Lake Louise below, and the delta at the lake's inlet. The massive quartzite cliffs across the lake are the lower flanks of Fairview Mountain. At this point you are slightly less than halfway to your destination—both in distance, and in elevation to be gained.

Golden-mantled Ground Squirrel

The golden-mantled ground squirrel is one of the most common small mammals in the Rockies. This resident of the subalpine forest has a body about 20 cm long. Its coat is light gray on top, cream underneath, and reddish-brown on the head and shoulders. The 10 cm-long tail is black. Two white stripes, bordered with black, extend from the shoulders to the rear legs. The eye is encircled with white. The only other animal that looks like this is the least chipmunk, which is about two-thirds the size, and has four grayish-white stripes that extend from the nose to the rear legs.

As with most rodents, the golden-mantled ground squirrel is hyperactive, flitting about the forest floor gathering leaves, seeds, flowers and fungi. Unfortunately, at the teahouse, it also has the habit of jumping onto tables and eating unattended muffins. It will dunk its head in a pitcher of milk for a drink. Although amusing, this behaviour is ultimately harmful, and should not be encouraged. It is also not in the best interest of unsuspecting people, who may take a bite of banana bread after one of these flea-infested critters has left its tracks in the butter. Please be responsible with your food and keep it away from wildlife.

Golden-mantled ground squirrels spend the months of September to May in dormancy, rousing every few days to nibble on food stashed in their burrows.

After the next prominent turn, the forest at trailside becomes thinner, marking the transition to the upper subalpine ecoregion. The trail crosses a metre-wide cut in the forest. This formerly contained a wooden pipeline, used when Lake Agnes was the water source for the Chateau. This pipeline saw service until 1984. A section of it is still imbedded in the trail.

At the horse-hiker barrier, turn west (left). From here to Lake Agnes, the trail is shared with horse traffic. In a few minutes, you reach "the goat's looking glass"—Mirror Lake. The quartzite buttress of Big Beehive forms the lake's backdrop. Although mountain goats now prefer to avoid this busy area, the mountainsides nearby are still home to approximately 50 of these animals. The lake has no surface outlet.

The main trail to Lake Agnes continues to the north (right) from Mirror Lake. Soon you cross an opening in the forest. This is the base of a 1 km-long avalanche path on Mt. St. Piran (pih-RAN). Avalanches of snow sweep this section of the mountain annually. If you look downhill from the trail, you will see a jumble of dead trees and branches—testimony to the power of moving snow. Mt. St. Piran was named for the English birthplace of Chalet manager Willoughby Astley. Looking south from higher on the avalanche path, the glaciated peaks of Mt. Aberdeen and Mt. Temple are visible. Mt. Temple (3543 m) is the highest peak near Lake Louise, and the third highest in Banff National Park.

The final approach to Lake Agnes and the teahouse is made by two flights of stairs. Many hikers arrive breathless after the climb. The elevation of Lake Agnes is 2118 m. Since leaving the shore of Lake Louise, you've gained 387 m, roughly the equivalent to a 130-storey building.

Walter Wilcox, one of the first explorers in the Lake Louise area, called Lake Agnes "a wild tarn imprisoned by cheerless cliffs." Despite the number of visitors to the lake in the present day, his description still holds merit. It is also technically accurate. Lake Agnes is a glacial tarn that occupies the highest in a series of cirque valleys that descends to Lake Louise. The glacier that carved these cirques has long since disappeared, but at few other locations in the Rockies is the amphitheatre-like form of a cirque so evident.

From east to west (left to right), the mountains that form the backdrop at Lake Agnes are: Big Beehive, Devil's Thumb, Mt. Whyte, Mt. Niblock and Mt. St. Piran. Sir William Whyte was second vice-president of the CPR, and John Niblock was a superintendent of the railway in the mountain region. Lake Agnes was one of their favourite fishing holes. Fishing is not allowed at the lake today.

Earlier this century, the CPR constructed three teahouses in the Lake Louise area, to encourage use of the trails. The Lake Agnes teahouse was the first of these, and is believed to have been built in 1901. The present building is a privately owned reconstruction, completed in 1981. Lunch, refreshments and snacks are available in season, which generally runs mid-June to Thanksgiving. Please enquire at the park information centre if you're hiking early or late in the season, and counting on the teahouse being open.

Many rodents inhabit the vicinity of the teahouse: Columbian ground squirrels, red squirrels, least chipmunks and golden-mantled ground squirrels. Hoary marmots and pikas live in the boulderfields along the lakeshore. The sky over the teahouse is busy with the comings and goings of Clark's nutcrackers and gray jays. Although it is tempting to feed these birds and animals, please refrain from doing so.

If you think the hike to Lake Agnes is steep, imagine what the downhill trip would be like wearing a pair of cross-country skis! The wild run down from the teahouse is a favourite with local skiers in winter. In most years, it is possible to skate on the frozen lake's surface before the first heavy snows of autumn.

Clark's Nutcracker and Gray Jay

Clark's nutcracker

Gray jay

The Clark's nutcracker is the more numerous of the two common birds at Lake Agnes. Its plumage is medium gray on the body, with attractive black and white flashes on the wings. The long black beak is designed for extracting the seeds from pine cones, and for burrowing into rotten wood to extract ants and larvae. Berries comprise the rest of its diet. A member of the crow family, the bird was named for Captain William Clark of the Lewis and Clark Expedition.

If you've made the mistake of enticing one of these birds with a crumb or two, the welcome will soon wear thin. The Clark's nutcracker has poor table manners, and will quickly and loudly announce your vulnerability to a host of its cohorts. Soon you will have a convention of nutcrackers on your plate. Please allow these birds to fend for themselves in the forest nearby.

The other common gray, black and white bird that you will see at Lake Agnes is the gray jay, also known as the whiskey-jack. It is smaller and quieter than the Clark's nutcracker, and has a smokier-coloured coat, a short blunt beak, and a white forehead.

The Wenkchemna Peaks form a stunning backdrop in this view from the rockpile at Moraine Lake.

16. Moraine Lake Rockpile

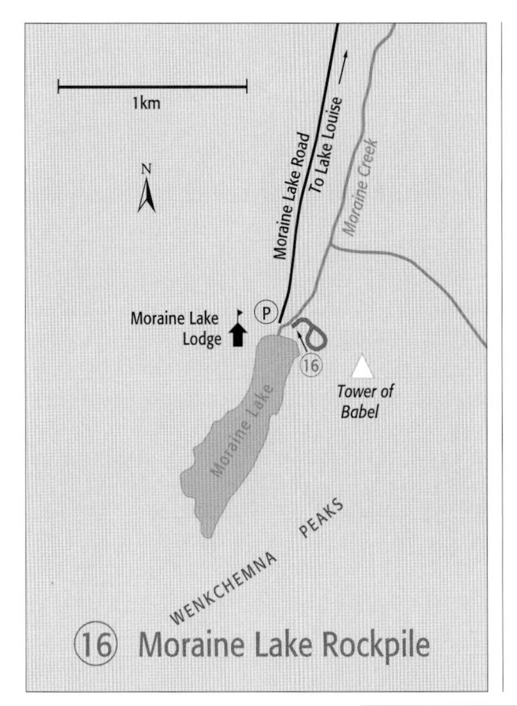

The best view at Moraine Lake is from the top of the rockpile at its outlet. From the parking lot, cross the bridge over the outlet stream, and follow the interpretive trail to the top of this knoll. The colour of the lake is accentuated from this viewpoint, and the Wenkchemna Peaks stand in solemn splendour, an icy wall along the south side of the valley.

When American explorer Walter Wilcox made

Route Information

Trailhead: From Lake Louise Village, follow Lake Louise Drive 3 km to the Moraine Lake Road. Turn south (left). Follow this road 12 km to its end at Moraine Lake. The trailhead is at the southeast corner of the parking lot.

Rating: easy, 250 m

Lighting: morning

the first visit to Moraine Lake in 1899, he assumed that the lake was dammed by a glacial moraine, and named it accordingly. The name "Rockslide Lake" may have been more accurate. The rockpile at the lake's outlet is probably the debris from one or more rockslides. Some geologists think that this debris came to rest atop glacial ice, and was deposited here when the ice receded. This would make the rockpile both rockslide debris and moraine.

Hoary marmot

Most of the blocks in the rockpile are quartzite, sandstone and siltstone that belong to the Gog group of formations. These sedimentary rocks were created from particles deposited on the floors of shallow inland seas between 570 million years ago and 540 million years ago. Gog quartzite is one of the hardest and most common rocks in the Rockies. In some areas, the Gog group is 3 km thick.

Rockslides are often home to the tiny pika of the rabbit family, and to the rodents: least chipmunk, golden-mantled ground squirrel, and hoary marmot. The crevices between the boulders make natural denning and food storage sites for these animals.

Moraine Lake is fed by waters from Wenkchemna Glacier, whose rubble-covered surface is concealed from view at the southwest end of the lake. Explorer Samuel Allen named many of the peaks in the valley in 1893 and 1894, using the Stoney words for the numbers one to ten. Wenkchemna means "ten." The valley became known as the Valley of the Ten Peaks. In 1979, the name Wenkchemna Peaks was officially adopted.

Today, only peaks number four, nine and ten—Tonsa, Neptuak and Wenkchemna—retain Allen's Stoney names. Five of the peaks have been named for mountaineers (Fay, Little, Perren, Allen, Tuzo); one for its physical appearance (Deltaform); and another for an Alberta politician (Bowlen). The Wenkchemna Peaks were featured on the Canadian twenty dollar bill from 1969 to 1993.

Ripple Rock

It is difficult for most of us to comprehend that the massive Rockies were created from tiny sediments deposited in ancient seas. In a few locations, graphic evidence of the Rockies' marine origin has been recorded in the rock.

As you ascend the staircase to the rockpile, you will notice a prominent example of ripple rock. Anyone who has spent time at a beach knows that beach sands frequently take on a rippled effect from the constant action of wavelets. Here, preserved in 560 million-year-old rock, is an indication that the same process was at work before the Rockies were uplifted. These beach sands became lithified when other sediments rapidly accumulated above them. Geologists know that this kind of rippling takes place only in shallow waters. So, they can roughly describe the environment where the sediments that comprise this rock were deposited.

Since this example of ripple rock was brought to public attention, it has been heavily damaged. Sedimentary rock of this type is very fragile. Please do not touch.

The rugged, glaciated crests of Mt. Bident and Quadra Mountain rise above Lower Consolation Lake in this view, taken shortly after sunrise.

17. Lower Consolation Lake

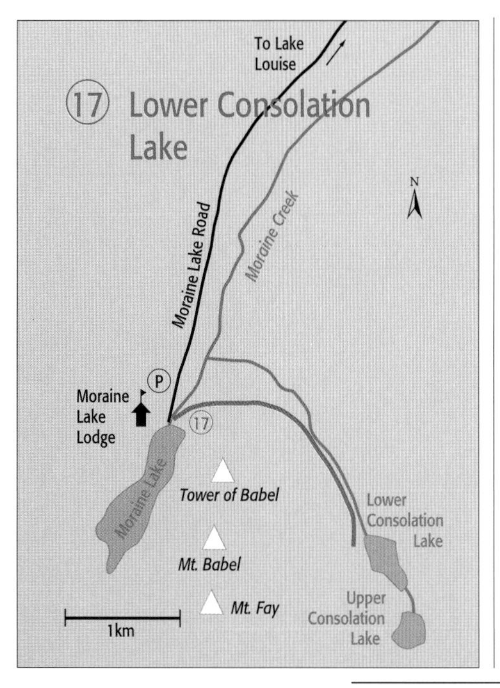

Explorer Walter Wilcox described the view at Lower Consolation Lake as "one of the most beautiful pictures I have ever seen in the Rockies." After his visit to Moraine Lake in 1899, Wilcox made a side trip to Consolation Lakes. To Wilcox, the Moraine Lake area had appeared sombre enough to merit the name Deso-

Route Information

Trailhead: From Lake Louise Village, follow Lake Louise Drive 3 km to the Moraine Lake Road. Turn south (left). Follow this road 12 km to its end at Moraine Lake. The trailhead, shared with Moraine Lake Rockpile, is at the southeast corner of the parking lot.

Rating: moderate, 2.9 km

Lighting: early morning or late afternoon

Rock Lichens

Rock lichens (LIKE-enz) are rootless, leafless plants that consist of fungi and algae. The fungi houses the algae, and the algae produces food for both. The by-product of this relationship is humic acid, which accelerates the chemical breakdown of rock, and the formation of primitive soil.

Rock lichens grow in colonies, radiating outwards in a circular fashion at an incredibly slow and consistent rate. It is thought that some rock lichen colonies in the Rockies may have begun life at the end of the Wisconsin Glaciation, 11,000 years ago! Please try to avoid walking on them if you hop across the boulders.

Two common rock lichens in the Rockies are the orange *Xanthoria elegans* (zan-THOR-ee-uh), and the green and black *Rhizocarpon geographicum* species—also called map lichens (photo). Lichens were formerly widely used in the creation of dies. Litmus, a substance derived from lichens, is today used in the manufacture of litmus paper. Lichens grow well only in unpolluted environments. Their presence indicates that air and water qualities are being maintained.

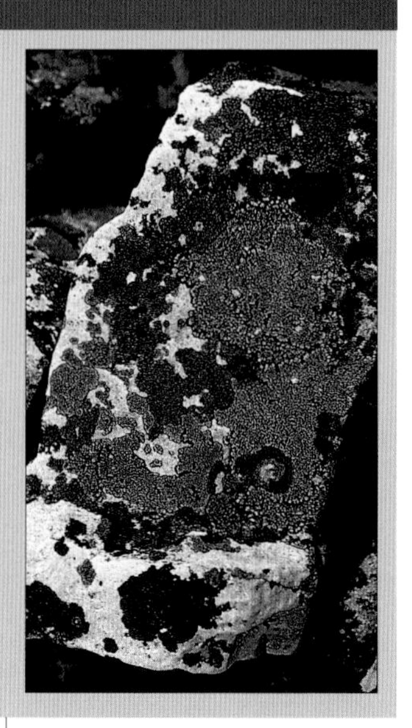

lation Valley. The valley into which this trail leads was perceived more favourably, and was the scenic "consolation" on the trip.

The trail to Lower Consolation Lake contours around the base of the Moraine Lake Rockpile and passes through a quartzite boulderfield. Here, you walk on a natural rock causeway across the outlet of Moraine Lake. For the next 2 km, the trail climbs gradually through subalpine forest. It then swings southeast along Babel Creek into the Consolation Valley. At km 1.6, the Taylor Lake trail branches left. Keep straight ahead. Here the forest floor is carpeted with grouseberry, and spruce grouse may be seen.

For the last 500 m to the outlet of the lower lake, the trail borders a subalpine wet meadow. This meadow is a frost hollow. Cold air collects here and stunts vegetation so that trees will not grow. Elephant head, fleabane, bracted lousewort, red-stemmed saxifrage and colourful Indian paintbrush are among the flowers you will see.

The trail ends near the shore of the lower lake. At the far end of the valley, the glacier-draped crags of Mt. Bident ("two teeth") and Quadra Mountain ("four summits") thrust towards the sky. The larch-covered slopes of Panorama Ridge flank the east side of the valley. To the west are the colossal cliffs of Mt. Babel and Mt. Fay. In the foreground are the lichen-covered, quartzite blocks that dam the placid waters of Lower Consolation Lake. Hoary marmots frequent this area.

The Consolation Lakes are tarns that occupy depressions gouged out of the bedrock by glacial ice. The upper lake is slightly higher in elevation and concealed from view, a kilometre of rough and wet boulder hopping, up the valley.

Indian paintbrush

Larch trees, subalpine meadows and a panoramic view of the Wenkchemna Peaks await you after the steep climb to Larch Valley.

18. Larch Valley

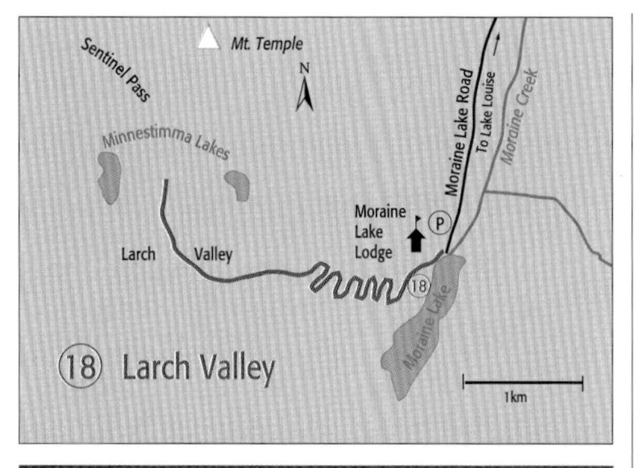

Route Information

Trailhead: From Lake Louise Village, follow Lake Louise Drive 3 km to the Moraine Lake Road. Turn south (left). Follow this road 12 km to its end at Moraine Lake. The trail begins on the lakeshore in front of the lodge.

Rating: harder, 3.2 km

Lighting: anytime

The trail to Larch Valley branches north (right) from the shore of Moraine Lake, just beyond the lodge. In the next 2.5 km, the trail gains 352 m of elevation, making it one of the steepest excursions in this book. Your rewards are splendid views of the Wenkchemna Peaks, and a walk in a forest of Lyall's larch. This trail is so popular and crowded in September, you might want to consider going somewhere else to appreciate the larches.

The first kilometre of steady uphill prepares you for the really hard work on this hike—ten switchbacks (one for each of the ten peaks?)—that deliver you to the mouth of Larch Valley and a well-placed bench. Take time to catch your breath and look around. You will notice a gradual transition from subalpine to upper subalpine forest as you gain elevation. You can see Moraine Lake through the trees.

The Larch Valley trail branches north (right) at the top of the switchbacks, and climbs gradually through a treeline forest dominated by Lyall's larch. Beyond the footbridge, there is an opening in the forest. This meadow is a frost hollow. If you look closely at the trees on the edge of the adjacent forest, you will see that frost has stunted the growth of their branches. The meadow is home to a colony of Columbian ground squirrels. The small mounds have not resulted from their burrowings. They are frost hummocks—soil features created by repeated freezing and thawing of the soil.

Above the treetops, there is a panorama of the Wenkchemna Peaks. Explorer Samuel Allen named these mountains in 1893 and 1894, using Stoney words for the numbers one to ten. He assumed that there are ten peaks in the valley. In reality, there are eighteen. From east to west (left to right), the peaks in view are today named: Mt. Babel, Mt. Fay (with the prominent glaciers), Mt. Bowlen; "Peak 3 1/2"; Tonsa, Mt. Perren, Mt. Allen, Mt. Tuzo, Deltaform Mountain, and Neptuak Mountain. Mt. Little ("Peak 2"), is concealed behind Mt. Bowlen. Wenkchemna Peak is concealed to the north of Neptuak Mountain.

The trail resumes its climb and soon passes treeline. The flower-filled meadows feature a number of lakelets. Samuel Allen named them Minnestimma Lakes—Stoney for "sleeping waters." Many hikers have lunch here before returning. Please keep to beaten paths to prevent damage to the surrounding vegetation. Ahead, the trail continues steeply to Sentinel Pass, the highest point reached by trail in the Rockies. Sentinel Pass is an outing for experienced hikers only.

Lyall's Larch

Lyall's larch is an uncommon coniferous tree that grows near treeline in the southern Rockies. Like the more common tamarack, the needles of Lyall's larch turn golden and fall off in late summer and early autumn. The tree sheds its foliage to conserve energy through the seven months of winter at these elevations. After shedding, the tree goes dormant, with the buds for next year's growth already in place.

Lyall's larch frequently forms pure stands in the treeline forest south of Bow Pass. When mature, it is 5 m to 10 m tall, with a ragged top. Bright green needles grow from black knobby twigs that are covered in dark, woolly down. The wood burns easily, but because the tree grows at high elevations and on rocky terrain, it is seldom consumed by fire. Some trees in Larch Valley may be more than 400 years old. The tree was catalogued by Eugene Bourgeau of the Palliser Expedition. He named it for David Lyall, Scottish naturalist and surgeon to the British Boundary Commission of 1872–76.

Bow Lake is the third largest lake in Banff National Park. Fed by meltwater from Bow Glacier, it is the principal headwaters of the Bow River.

19. Bow Lake

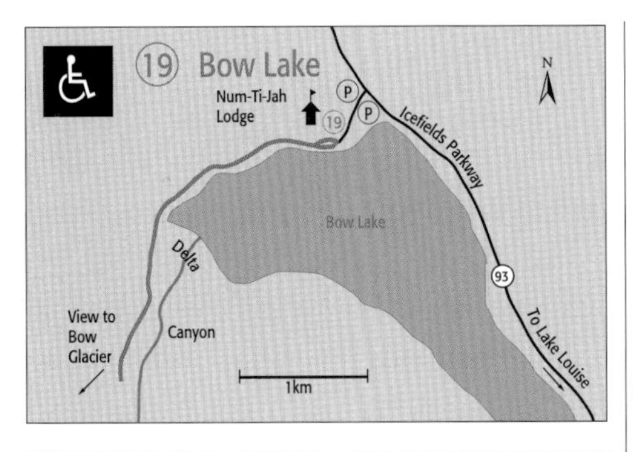

Route Information

Trailhead: West side of the Icefields Parkway, 37 km north of Lake Louise. Follow the Num-ti-Jah Lodge access road west for 400 m, and park in the public parking lot. The trailhead is across from the public rest room.
Ratings: Num-ti-Jah loop, easy, 400 m, wheelchair accessible; Bow Glacier trail, harder, 3.4 km
Lighting: morning

The area near Bow Lake presents a walking option and a hiking option. Casual walkers can make a 400 m loop to the lakeshore and lodge, returning to the parking lot along the road. Those who would like a longer outing may continue west along the lakeshore from the lodge, eventually reaching an unmarked viewpoint that overlooks the forefield of Bow Glacier. Both outings feature splendid views of Bow Lake and Bow Glacier.

With an area of 3.64 km^2, Bow Lake is the third largest lake in Banff National Park. It is also the headwaters of the Bow River. The lake is fed by meltwater from Bow Glacier, one of six outlet valley glaciers of the 40 km^2 Wapta Icefield.

Pioneer guide and outfitter Jimmy Simpson, spent the winters of the early 1900s hunting and trapping in the remote country north of Bow Lake.

He found the area much to his liking. In 1920, he began building a simple log cabin on the lakeshore, the forerunner of today's Num-ti-Jah (numm-TAH-zjaah) Lodge. The lodge's name is a Stoney expression for the American marten, a member of the weasel family found in the surrounding subalpine forest. Simpson's rustic cabin became popular with mountaineers. With construction of the Icefields Parkway in the 1930s, Simpson expanded the lodge to capitalize on his opportunity for commercial success.

Beyond the lodge, the Bow Glacier trail skirts the lakeshore for 1.5 km to the delta at the main inlet. Climbing away from this gravelly area, you gain the edge of a canyon. This canyon is noted for its "natural bridge"—a massive boulder lodged across the opening.

A few hundred metres beyond, you reach the crest of a terminal moraine. This moraine marks the greatest advance of Bow Glacier during the Little Ice Age. One hundred and fifty years ago, the entire area between here and the cliffs was covered by glacial ice. The prominent waterfall on the lower cliff drains from a concealed tarn called "Iceberg Lake." Travel beyond this viewpoint is not recommended. The trail is faint and the icy streams are not bridged.

Jimmy Simpson built a cabin on the shore of Bow Lake in 1920—the forerunner of today's Num-ti-Jah Lodge.

Deltas

Most streams and rivers in the Rockies originate in glaciers. Their waters contain much rubble and sediment. Where the angle of a stream bed is relatively steep, this material can be transported by the water. But where the angle lessens, large particles drop out of the flow, creating a rocky, fan-shaped landform. If this landform occurs on the side of a valley, it is called an alluvial fan. If it occurs on the shore of a lake, it is known as a delta.

Bow Lake features two prominent deltas. The most obvious is the one on the west shore of the lake, where meltwater from Bow Glacier enters the lake. The constant build-up of gravels, and the shifting of the meltwater streams, precludes the growth of much vegetation.

Less obvious is the delta where the lodge sits. The stream that created this delta is now a mere trickle, and no longer transports glacial sediments. Vegetation has managed to stabilize the underlying gravels. It is thought that this delta was created thousands of years ago, by a meltwater surge from a glacier near Bow Pass. This glacier has since disappeared.

Peyto Lake is the fifth largest lake in Banff. The lake was named for Bill Peyto, pioneer outfitter and trailguide.

20. Bow Summit

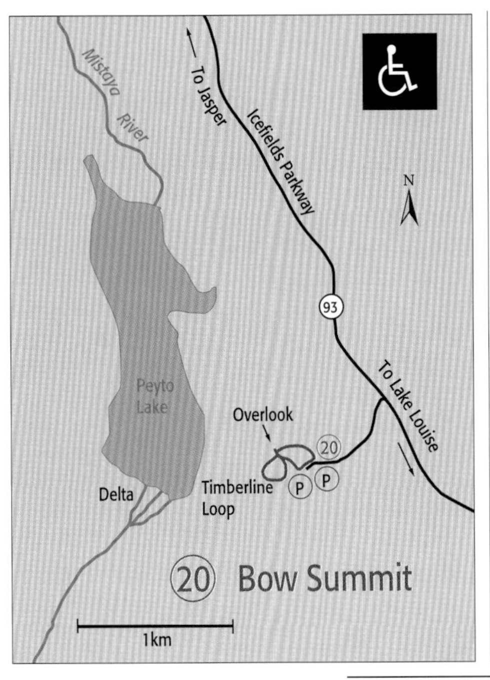

The short walk to the Peyto (PEE-toe) Lake overlook at Bow Summit, takes you through the treeline forest of the upper subalpine ecoregion—the land of wind flowers and wind timber. It ends at one of the most spectacular viewpoints in the Rockies.

At an elevation of 2069 m, Bow Pass is the

Route Information

Trailhead: West side of the Icefields Parkway, 42 km north of Lake Louise. Turn west onto the access road, and park in the first parking lot on the north (right).

Rating: easy, 350 m, paved. If you continue to the upper parking lot, the path to the viewpoint is wheelchair accessible and 100 m.

Lighting: anytime

highest point in Canada crossed by a paved road that is open all year. The first thing you will notice as you step out of your vehicle, is that it is colder here than it was at Lake Louise or in Banff. The high elevation of Bow Pass would normally account for a temperature 1.5°C cooler than at Lake Louise. However, the chilling mass of nearby Wapta Icefield makes Bow Summit even colder. Do not be surprised if the day has a wintry feel, even in mid-summer. Dress warmly, especially if it is windy.

Glacier lily

Bow Summit is not a mountain top, but a height of land that separates waters that flow south to the Bow River, from those that flow north to the Mistaya (miss-TAY-ah) River. In describing this watershed divide, the words "summit" and "pass" are used interchangeably. Located on a shoulder of Mt. Jimmy Simpson, the slopes of Bow Summit are buffeted by glacially cooled winds that deliver 6 m of annual snowfall, and cause repeated freezing and thawing.

The Treeline Forest

The forest at Bow Summit is coniferous: Engelmann spruce, subalpine fir, and whitebark pine. On the lower slopes near the parking lot, the trees are widely scattered and of normal height. But on the upper slopes, stunted tree islands are all that can grow. Why? These upper slopes are more than twice as windy as those 100 m lower. Wind dries vegetation, making growth difficult and slow. The gnarled and twisted trees that result are known by the German expression kruppelholz, which means "crippled wood."

Subalpine fir has silvery

Colour of Glacial Lakes

What is the most frequently asked question in the Canadian Rockies? ...*Why is the lake that colour?*...The answer: Glaciers created the lakes, and glaciers give them their colours.

Glaciers grind up bedrock, creating rubble and sediments of all sizes. The sediments are transported by glacial meltwater. Where the meltwater enters a lake, the stream velocity decreases. The larger sediments drop out of the flow, building a delta. The smaller sediments disperse into the water. Eventually, most of these sediments settle to the lake bottom, leaving only the tiniest particles suspended in the water. These particles, called rock flour, distribute themselves evenly throughout the lake.

The minute dimension of rock flour enables it to reflect the blue and green spectra of light. Thus, glacial lakes take on the rich and remarkable hues for which the Rockies are renowned. Lake colours become more pronounced as the glacier melt season progresses and the density of rock flour in the water increases. Viewing from above enhances the effect. Mineral content of the water is not a significant factor in the colour.

At Peyto Lake, you can often see muddy sediment plumes just beyond the delta. These plumes indicate where the meltwater stream disperses its sediment load into the lake.

bark. This tree is more tolerant of harsh conditions than Engelmann spruce. Thus, firs are usually more numerous in the kruppelholz. They are able to take root either from seeds, or by "skirting"—sending down shoots from their branches. Subalpine firs spend much of the year covered in snow. They develop snow mould—a black growth that covers the lower branches.

The upright Engelmann spruce have a more scaly, reddish-brown bark, and grow from seeds that develop in the sheltered centres of the mats of subalpine fir. The spruce frequently display branches only on their eastern sides. They arc said to "flag" the prevailing wind.

Despite waxy needles and thick sap, the new kruppelholz growth of each summer cannot withstand the cold winds of the following winter. Only branches that are insulated within the snowpack are spared this natural pruning. The kruppelholz firs have adapted to this harsh reality by growing horizontally so that their branches will remain protected within the snow. Dense, twisted mats of fir result.

Snowdrifts accumulate in the lee of the kruppelholz stands. These drifts endure most of the summer. As they slowly melt, they provide a constant water supply for moisture-loving wildflowers, in an area where only one quarter of the precipitation falls as rain.

Grizzly bear tracks

The Subalpine Meadows

Bow Summit is renowned for its mid-summer wildflower display. One of the first flowers to bloom is the glacier lily. Its nodding, yellow flower often pokes through receding snowbanks. The protein-rich corm or bulb of the glacier lily is a favourite food of bears. Other common wildflowers in these meadows are: valerian, yellow columbine, Indian paintbrush, bracted lousewort, fleabane, arnica, ragwort, white globeflower, mountain heather and everlasting. Varieties of anemone (an-EMM-owenee), including western anemone and Drummond's anemone, also grow here. Anemone means "wind flower." These members of the buttercup family thrive in this windy location.

The average annual temperature at Bow Summit is -4°C. Glacier lily, anemone and other upper subalpine wildflowers manage their rapid bursts of early summer growth because

Kruppelholz

The upper slopes of Bow Summit feature stunted tree islands of Engelmann spruce and subalpine fir, known as kruppelholz ("crippled wood" in German). In winter, exposed tree branches freeze and die. Kruppelholz firs survive by growing more horizontally than vertically. This allows them to remain insulated within the snowpack, protected from the wind for much of the year. The under-snow branches become afflicted with black-felt snow mould. The firs provide shelter for the taller spruce. The photo shows several spruce trees growing from within a mat of fir.

their bulbs and root systems store energy gathered from sunshine the previous summer. At Bow Summit, these perennial flowers have only six weeks to flower and seed. Without such adaptation, a few successive shorter-than-average summers would kill them off. The blooms are usually at their peak in the third week of July.

Peyto Lake Overlook

From the overlook at trail's end, you obtain the most spectacular trailside view of a glacial lake in the Rockies. Three hundred metres below, Peyto Lake, fifth largest in Banff National Park, stretches before you. The lake is 3 km long and 1 km wide. It is fed by meltwater from Peyto Glacier, an outlet valley glacier of the Wapta Icefield.

On the opposite side of the lake is Caldron Peak, and to its left (south), the turreted form of Peyto Peak. The toe of Peyto Glacier is concealed from view in a canyon farther south (left). The glacier has receded 2 km in the last 100 years. The massive delta at the lake's inlet has been built from glacial debris deposited by the meltwater stream. The lake's outlet is dammed by forested mounds of moraine.

Peyto Lake is named for "Wild" Bill Peyto, noted trail-guide and later park warden. An immigrant from England, Peyto arrived in the Rockies in the early 1890s. He readily adapted to the backwoods life—hunting, trapping and staking mineral claims. He began work as a trail-guide in 1893. Peyto guided several important mountaineering expeditions, including the one that discovered Columbia Icefield in 1898. During Walter Wilcox's expedition that camped at Bow Lake in 1896, Peyto stole away after chores to this viewpoint for some peace and quiet. When Wilcox later saw the lake, he named it "Peyto's Lake."

"Wild" Bill Peyto began work in the Rockies as a trail guide in 1893. He later became one of the first park wardens in Banff.

The viewpoint area is populated by least chipmunks, golden-mantled ground squirrels, and a few pikas. The meadows at Bow Summit are inhabited by Columbian ground squirrels, and the chatter of red squirrels greets you from the treetops.

If you would like to spend more time in the upper subalpine, the Timberline Trail is recommended. As you leave the Peyto Lake overlook, you have a choice of three paths. The left-hand path returns to the lower parking lot; the centre path to the upper parking lot; and the right-hand path leads to the 600-m Timberline Trail. Interpretive panels on this loop trail explain more about the harsh life of vegetation in the upper subalpine ecoregion.

Mistaya Canyon has been eroded into a limestone step at the mouth of the Mistaya Valley. The deep canyon displays interesting features of erosion.

21. Mistaya Canyon

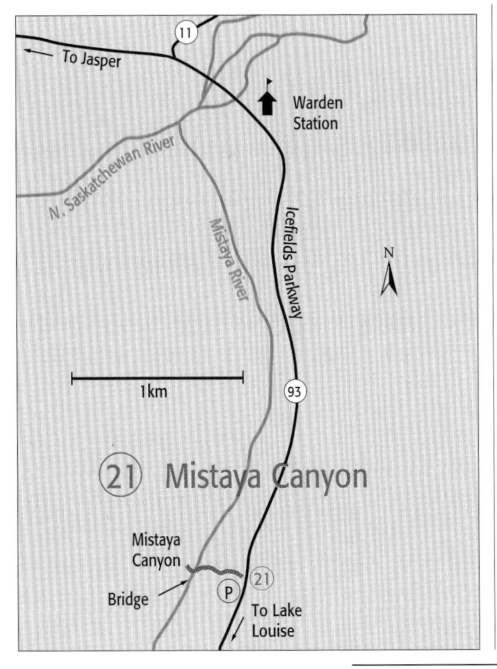

The trail to Mistaya (miss-TAY-yah) Canyon follows an old road bed to a sturdy bridge over the Mistaya River. It is an excellent excursion for families who want to take a break while driving the Icefields Parkway.

During the Wisconsin Glaciation, the North Saskatchewan Valley was eroded more deeply than the Mistaya Valley. When the ice age ended, the Mistaya River plunged over a high waterfall into the North Saskatchewan River. Since then, the

Route Information

Trailhead: West side of the Icefields Parkway, 72 km north of Lake Louise, 5.5 km south of the junction with Highway 11
Rating: moderate, 450 m
Lighting: afternoon

Mistaya River, full of abrasive glacial sediment, has eroded a narrow canyon into the limestone step at the mouth of the valley.

From the bridge over the canyon, you can see an unusual feature. The canyon opening makes a series of short, symmetrical dogleg turns. The river has followed a joint set, a system of parallel cracks in the bedrock. You can also see potholes and a natural arch. On their hunting trips into the mountains, Stoney natives would cross the Mistaya River here, on bridges felled across the canyon.

Upstream from the canyon, Mt. Sarbach (SAR-back) is prominent in the view. This 3155 m peak was named for Peter Sarbach, the first Swiss Guide to climb in Canada. He led the mountain's first ascent in 1897.

You would normally expect to find a damp forest in the vicinity of a canyon. However, the wall of mountains that borders the western edge of the Mistaya Valley creates a rain shadow. Thus the forest at trailside is dry, and is dominated by lodgepole pine, with an undergrowth of buffaloberry and juniper.

Buffaloberry

Mistaya is a Stoney word that means "grizzly bear." Explorers originally knew the tributaries of the North Saskatchewan by logical but confusing names. The Mistaya River was the Little Fork, the Howse River was the Middle Fork, and the stream that issues from Saskatchewan Glacier was the North Fork. Adding confusion, the Alexandra River was known as the West Branch of the North Fork! After a few years, the Little Fork became known as Bear River. Explorer Mary Schäffer renamed it Mistaya in 1907, in order to avoid confusion with the many other Bear creeks and Bear rivers in the Rockies.

Black Bear

Although Mistaya means "grizzly bear," you are more likely to see a black bear near Mistaya Canyon. The open, dry forest here supports an abundance of the shrubs, berries and flowers that are the black bear's favourite foods. In the Rockies, the black bear's diet is 75 percent vegetarian. The red and amber coloured fruits of buffaloberry are one of the most important food sources.

The adult male black bear is slightly less than 1 m tall at the shoulder, and weighs approximately 170 kg. Its coat is not always black. Cinnamon coloured bears are common. When the coat is black, there is often a small white patch on the chest.

Female black bears mate every other year. The litter is normally two cubs, born in the den during winter dormancy. The black bear is an adept tree climber, and will use this tactic to escape its two enemies—humans and grizzly bears.

Recent study has reversed a long-standing conception regarding bear populations. It is now thought that due to a lack of favourable habitat, there are fewer black bears than grizzly bears in the Rockies. A population of 50 to 60 black bears is estimated for Banff National Park. Some wildlife biologists fear that this population is too small to guarantee the local viability of the species.

The view from Parker Ridge features the 9 km-long Saskatchewan Glacier, Castleguard Mountain, and the southeastern edge of Columbia Icefield.

22. Parker Ridge

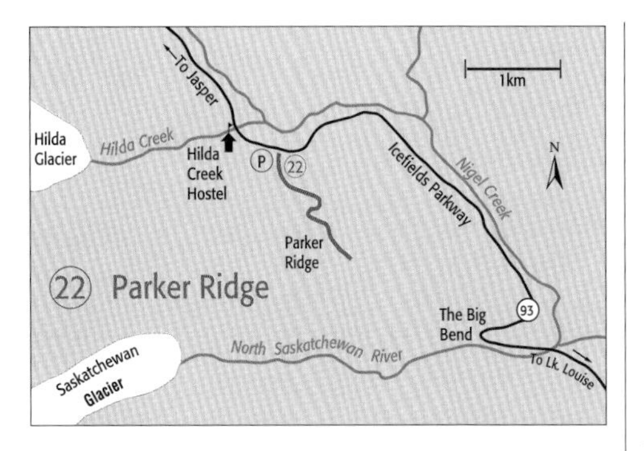

Route Information

Trailhead: South side of the Icefields Parkway, 118 km north of Lake Louise, 9 km south of the Columbia Icefield Information Centre
Rating: harder, 2.4 km
Lighting: morning

The Parker Ridge trail climbs steeply through the transition between upper subalpine forest and alpine tundra, and provides quick access to a ridgetop environment. From the ridge, you obtain a panoramic view of Saskatchewan Glacier and the southeastern fringe of Columbia Icefield. The ridge is often cold and windy. Carry warm clothing, including gloves and a hat.

The Parker Ridge trailhead is located in a tree-line forest. High elevation, cold glacial air, near constant winds, poor soils, avalanches and a northeast-facing slope combine to hinder the growth of vegetation. Leaving the parking lot, the trail crosses a subalpine meadow. This meadow is a frost hollow, typical of areas adjacent to glaciers. Cold air from Hilda Glacier collects here, creating a local growing season so short that mature trees cannot develop.

Across the meadow, the climb begins. The trail enters a small but ancient forest. At one point you squeeze between two massive Engelmann spruce trees that are probably at least 400 years old. But most of the vegetation here is in kruppelholz form. The gnarled, dense, evergreen mats with silvery bark are subalpine fir trees. Although they appear to be shrubs, these are mature trees, many decades old.

On your way to the ridge top you will see dozens of signs that indicate where shortcut trails have been closed. By the late 1970s, heavy traffic and uneducated hiking practice had combined to transform the slopes of Parker Ridge into a maze of trails. Vegetation was trampled and erosion was widespread. The trail was rehabilitated in a costly project. Seeds from Parker Ridge were grown in greenhouses, and the resulting plants were transplanted back to the ridge. Please help protect the area and this investment by keeping to the gravelled path.

The treeless areas on the northeast slope of Parker Ridge are either avalanche-swept rock, or tundra. The tundra is composed of sedges, white mountain avens, mountain heather, snow willow, arctic willow, and everlasting. Vegetation grows close to the ground to reduce wind exposure. Thick, waxy leaves help retain the moisture gathered by extensive root systems. In some areas, the thin rocky soils support little but rock lichen colonies and a few alpine grasses.

More than 6 m of snow falls at Parker Ridge each year. Because of the shaded, northeast aspect and cold temperatures (due to high elevation and the nearness of Columbia Icefield), this snow endures into the summer. Needless to say the slopes of Parker Ridge are popular with skiers in winter and spring, but don't be surprised if you see some die-hards carving turns on a Parker Ridge snowpatch in mid-summer—to the possible detriment of the underlying vegetation.

After a steady climb, the trail gains the open ridge at an elevation of 2271 m. From here, follow the beaten path 500 m east (left) to a viewpoint that overlooks Saskatchewan Glacier. With a length of 9 km, this outlet valley glacier of Columbia Icefield is one of the longest in the Rockies. It drops 750 m from the icefield rim to terminate in a marginal lake, the principal headwaters of the North Saskatchewan River. Unlike Athabasca Glacier, Saskatchewan Glacier has no icefalls and very few large crevasses. Of interest is a medial moraine, a strip of dark rubble that runs lengthwise on the glacier's surface. This moraine forms where two tributary glaciers merge. Saskatchewan is a Cree word that means "swift current." Mt. Saskatchewan is the high, craggy peak protruding above the rounded summits, 8 km south of Parker Ridge.

Immediately south (left) of the head of the Saskatchewan Glacier is Castleguard Mountain. South of this mountain is the entrance to Castleguard Cave, one of the largest cave systems in Canada, and the

Horn Mountains

The summits of the higher mountains in the Rockies protruded above ice-age glaciers. Since the retreat of these ice sheets, alpine glaciation has continued on the upper reaches of the mountains, frequently creating a mountain shape known as a horn.

When cirque and niche glaciers form on adjacent mountain sides, they erode downwards into the rock, creating depressions

that are separated from each other by sharp crested ridges called aretes (ah-RETTS). If two or more sides of the mountain are eroded in this fashion, the pyramid-like, horn shape will result.

The most famous horn mountain in the world is the Matterhorn on the border of Switzerland and Italy. Many other well known mountains, including Mt. Everest, are also horn mountains. When viewed from the Parker Ridge trailhead, Mt. Athabasca and its outlier, Hilda Peak, are fine examples.

third deepest in Canada and the US. Eighteen kilometres of passages have been discovered and explored. Some of these follow ancient glacial drainages beneath Columbia Icefield, and terminate in dead-ends choked with glacial ice. If the day is clear, the view beyond Castleguard Mountain will include the icy summit of Mt. Bryce (3507 m), 19 km distant.

If you look uphill along the crest of Parker Ridge, you will notice that the outlying ridge is rounded in appearance, becoming much more rugged towards Mt. Athabasca. The rounded parts of the ridge were completely covered by the ice of the Great Glaciation. The higher, jagged areas were not. If you choose to explore along the ridge to the cairned high point (2350 m), please stay on the beaten path. The ridge crest features kruppelholz forms of whitebark pine, a common tree in windy locations. You may also see coral-like fossils called *Syringopora*. Please do not remove them.

Mountain goat, white-tailed ptarmigan, gray jay, Clark's nutcracker, pika and raven are the most commonly observed wildlife on Parker Ridge. If you are fortunate, you may also see grizzly bear, wolverine and golden eagle. The ridge was named for Herschel Parker, an American mountaineer who made several first ascents of mountains near Lake Louise at the turn of the century.

Mountain Goat

Parker Ridge is home range for a herd of mountain goats. These animals are easily differentiated from bighorn sheep. The goat has a white or cream-coloured coat, and black horns that are never shed. The bighorn sheep has a light brown coat with a tawny rump patch, and brown horns.

Mountain goats live on upper mountainsides, occasionally venturing to mineral licks in the valley bottoms. Grassy ledges and slopes that offer quick escape to nearby cliffs are their favourite habitat. Grasses comprise three quarters of their diet. Not a true goat, the mountain goat is more closely related to mountain antelopes of Asia.

To a causal observer, male (billy) and female (nanny) goats appear similar. The best indicator that a mountain goat is female is if a kid is tagging along. The offspring, born in June, stay with the mother for a year.

The mountain goat is the master of alpine ridge, cliff edge and mountain top. Nature has equipped this animal with remarkable hooves, tendons and muscle power that allow it to range over the steepest terrain with ease. The split hoof is a soft pad surrounded by a hard, bony shell. The soft pad grips like a suction cup on steep slabs, and the bony exterior can be used to lever upwards on tiny ledges. The strong muscles and tendons allow the mountain goat to leap from ledge to ledge, and cushion the shock upon landing. The mountain goat is able to turn around on narrow ledges by standing on its front legs, and walking its rear legs around on the cliff above.

Goats are well adapted and spend much time in hazardous areas, but they seem nonchalant about certain dangers. The author has seen a goat bedded down on a snow cornice, overhanging a 1000-m cliff. Avalanches, rockfall and starvation account for most of the natural mortality. Cougar and golden eagles are the main predators. They occasionally achieve success in attacks from above. It is common to see the nanny goat standing over her young to protect against this threat.

It is estimated that there are 860 mountain goats in Banff National Park, 340 in Yoho, and 300 in Kootenay. Both Kootenay and Mt. Robson parks use the mountain goat as their emblems.

Other Walks and Easy Hikes in Banff National Park

23. Banff Cemetery

Trailhead: From the corner of Banff Avenue and Buffalo Street in Banff townsite, walk 300 m east along Buffalo Street.
Rating: easy, 500 m
Lighting: anytime

Banff's cemetery was established in 1890, and is the internment place for more than 2000 former residents. These include many who played major roles in the history of the Rockies: Tom Wilson, Bill Peyto, Jim Brewster, Byron Harmon, R.G. Brett, Peter and Catharine Whyte. Please be respectful during your visit.

Please see map on page 11

24. Johnson Lake

Trailhead: Follow Banff Avenue 3 km east from town to Highway 1. Keep straight ahead on the Lake Minnewanka Road. Turn south (right) in 1.2 km for Two Jack Lake and Johnson Lake. In 3.3 km turn south (right) again. Follow this road 2.3 km to Johnson Lake.
Rating: easy, 2.4 km loop
Lighting: anytime

Johnson Lake is an artificial reservoir, and is a popular swimming hole with Banff locals. The loop trail around its shores features fine views of Cascade Mountain and Mt. Rundle, and the opportunity to see elk and deer.

25. Stoney Squaw

Trailhead: Follow Gopher Street north out of Banff. Cross Highway 1 and ascend the Mt. Norquay Road to the first parking lot at the ski area, 6 km from Banff.
Rating: harder, 2.1 km
Lighting: anytime

The Stoney Squaw trail climbs onto the 1868 m forested summit of this modest mountain, and provides a grand view of the Bow Valley near Banff townsite. The mountain was named for the heroine of a Stoney legend, which tells of an injured man who lay at the mountain's base while his wife tended to him and hunted on the slopes above.

26. Vista Trail

Trailhead: Sulphur Mountain gondola, 3.5 km south of town on Mountain Avenue. Board the gondola (fee charged). The trail begins at the upper terminal.
Rating: easy, 500 m
Lighting: anytime

The Vista Trail provides a panoramic view of the Bow Valley, Spray Valley and Banff townsite. The trail heads north along the crest of Sulphur Mountain to the site of an old observatory, at an elevation of 2281 m. Norman Sanson, curator of the Banff Park Museum from 1896–1942, was a regular visitor to the observatory. In all, he made more than 1000 trips to this ridge top to gather weather information, without the benefit of a gondola. The north peak of Sulphur Mountain is now named for him. The observatory has been restored.

27. Discovery Trail

Trailhead: Follow Banff Avenue to the south end of the Bow River bridge. Turn west (right) and follow Cave Avenue 1 km to the Cave and Basin Centennial Centre. The trail begins at the staircase to the south (left) of the building.
Rating: easy, 400 m loop
Lighting: anytime

The self-guiding Discovery Trail tells the story of the discovery of the Cave and Basin hot springs, and their subsequent development. The trail visits the upper entrance of the Cave springs, and crumbly outcrops of tufa—rock deposited by the hot spring water. You may complete this walk with a visit to the Cave pool and additional interpretive displays, both accessed from within the Cave and Basin Centre (fee charged).

28. Sundance Canyon

Trailhead: Follow Banff Avenue to the south end of the Bow River bridge. Turn west (right) and follow Cave Avenue 1 km to the Cave and Basin Centennial Centre. Continue west on the paved path.
Rating: harder, 5.1 km. The first 3.8 km is wheelchair accessible.

The Cave pool at Cave and Basin

Lighting: morning

Sundance Canyon is located 3.8 km along a paved bike path from the Cave and Basin Centennial Centre. En route to the canyon there are fine views along the Bow River, particularly of the dogtooth spire of Mt. Edith to the north. Sundance Canyon has been eroded into a bedrock fault at the mouth of a hanging valley. Hike clockwise on the 2.5 km canyon loop. Two viewpoints overlooking the Bow Valley are featured in the descent. The canyon was named for the ritual sundance of Stoney natives, said to have been performed nearby.

29. Silverton Falls

Trailhead: East side of the Bow Valley Parkway (Highway 1A) at the Rockbound Lake trailhead, 29.5 km west of Banff, 200 m east of Castle Junction
Rating: moderate, 900 m
Lighting: late afternoon

Follow the Rockbound Lake trail for 350 m. Take the south (right) trail branch, and follow this to Silverton Creek. Do not cross the creek! Instead, face downstream from the bridge and take the unmarked trail that ascends the slope to the north (right). This trail climbs to an unfenced viewpoint that overlooks the uppermost of a half dozen cascades. Use caution. "Silverton" refers to Silver City, the mining and railway boom town that flourished nearby in the Bow Valley from 1883 to 1885.

30. Bow River

Trailhead: Lake Louise campground
Rating: easy/moderate/harder, loops of 2.5 to 7.2 km are possible. Portions are wheelchair accessible.
Lighting: anytime

This interpretive trail along the banks of the Bow River near Lake Louise Village is ideal for outings from the campground. The river is bridged in four places, allowing loop walks of various lengths. You may visit the historic Lake Louise train station. Mt. Temple is prominent in the view south.

31. Moraine Lakeshore

Trailhead: From Lake Louise Village, follow Lake Louise Drive 3 km to the Moraine Lake Road. Turn south (left). Follow this road 12 km to its end at Moraine Lake. The trail begins in front of the lodge.
Rating: easy, 1.5 km
Lighting: morning

This trail follows the forested shore of Moraine Lake to its inlet, providing views of the Wenkchemna Peaks.

32. Fairview Lookout

Trailhead: From Lake Louise Village, follow Lake Louise Drive, 5.5 km to the public parking lots at the lake. Paved walkways lead to the lakeshore. The Fairview Lookout–Saddleback Pass trailhead is adjacent to the World Heritage Site monument, near the lake's outlet.
Rating: moderate, 2.9 km loop
Lighting: afternoon

Follow the Saddleback Pass trail for 200 m and turn west (right). The Fairview Lookout trail ascends steadily through subalpine forest to a viewpoint that overlooks Lake Louise. Although the growth of trees is gradually blocking the view of the Chateau, interpretive panels provide interesting information on the hotel's history. It is easier to retrace your route to the Chateau than to complete the loop trail, which descends steeply from the viewpoint to the lakeshore. The latter option is rocky in places, and is subject to flooding when the lake level is high.

33. Upper Waterfowl Lake

Trailhead: West side of the Icefields Parkway, 56 km north of Lake Louise, 1.5 km south of Waterfowl Lake campground, 20.7 km south of the junction with Highway 11
Rating: easy, 200 m
Lighting: morning

Take the trail that descends west from the north edge of the parking lot. After 40 m, you cross the bed of the "Wonder Road," forerunner of the Icefields Parkway. The trail reaches the shore of Upper Waterfowl Lake at a wet meadow that supports sedges, a favourite food of moose. You may see this animal here in early morning and evening.

Across the lake rise the peaks of the continental divide. Howse Peak, with its two niche glaciers, is prominent, as is Mt. Chephren (KEFF-ren) and the Whyte Pyramid.

Howse Peak, reflected in Upper Waterfowl Lake

34. Warden Lake

Trailhead: Icefields Parkway, 75 km north of Lake Louise, 2 km south of the junction with Highway 11. Park opposite the warden station. The trailhead is on east side of Icefields Parkway, just south of the warden station. Use caution crossing the road.
Rating: moderate, 2.2 km
Lighting: anytime

The hike to Warden Lake is along an old jeep road, the original highway from Red Deer into the mountains. It follows the banks of the North Saskatchewan River, which was designated a Canadian Heritage River in 1989. Warden Lake is the second and the largest lake reached by this trail. The lakes are kettle ponds. The backdrop at Warden Lake is Mt. Murchison. You may see moose and waterfowl here.

35. Howse Valley Viewpoint

Trailhead: Picnic area on the west side of the Icefields Parkway, 76.4 km north of Lake Louise, 300 m south of the junction with Highway 11
Rating: 250 m loop. Wheelchair accessible
Lighting: late afternoon

This trail loops through a lodgepole pine forest to the crest of a river terrace that overlooks three valleys: the North Saskatchewan, the Mistaya, and the Howse. The pine trees seeded naturally after the Survey Peak burn of 1940, the last major wildfire in Banff National Park.

The view southeast is dominated by Mt. Murchison, which Stoney natives believed was the highest peak in the Rockies. To the south is the Mistaya Valley. In the distant west is Mt. Forbes, the second highest mountain in Banff National Park. The Howse Valley stretches away to the southwest. It was part of the original fur trade route across the Rockies. You may inspect the plaque unveiled when the North Saskatchewan River was proclaimed a Canadian Heritage River in 1989.

36. Panther Falls

Trailhead: East side of the Icefields Parkway, 113 km north of Lake Louise; 13.5 km south of the Columbia Icefield Information Centre. Park at the uppermost of the two viewpoints at the top of the Big Bend Hill.
Rating: moderate, 450 m
Lighting: morning

This unmarked trail departs from the south edge of the parking lot, and switchbacks down into Nigel Creek canyon. After traversing beneath a cliff, the last 50 m of trail crosses an exposed sideslope to an unfenced viewpoint at the base of the 60 m high falls. This is a hazardous area. Use caution.

Jasper National Park

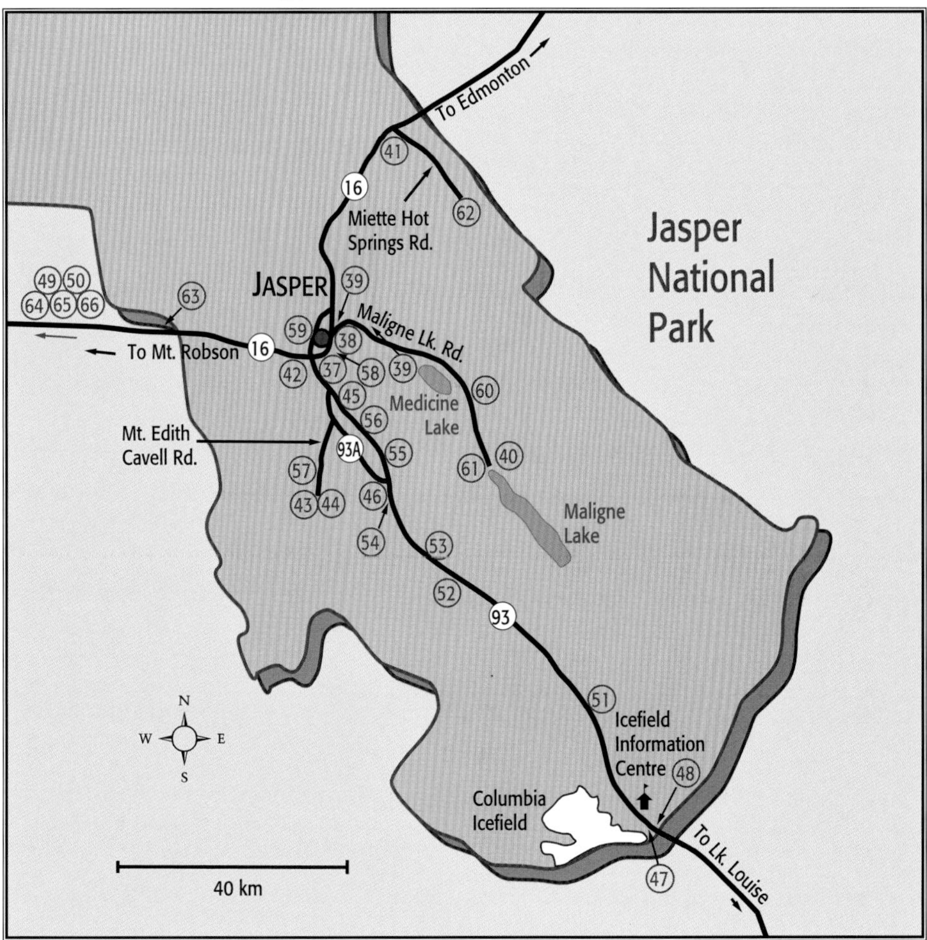

Established in 1907, Jasper is the largest of the Rocky Mountain parks. It includes 10,878 km^2 of foothills, front ranges and eastern main ranges—larger than the combined area of Banff, Yoho and Kootenay. The Walks and Easy Hikes in Jasper feature human history, tranquil lakes and ponds, glaciers, Columbia Icefield, alpine meadows and a mountain summit. Many of the trails are in prime wildlife habitat. You may see elk, deer, black bear, grizzly bear, bighorn sheep, mountain goat, moose, coyote, wolf and mountain caribou. Jasper was named for Jasper Hawse, the manager of a North West Company fur trade outpost in the Athabasca Valley, in 1817.

Mt. Robson Provincial Park

The Jasper Walks and Easy Hikes include Mt. Robson Provincial Park. Mt. Robson was the second provincial park established in BC, in 1913. The park's chief attraction is Mt. Robson, "The Monarch of the Rockies." Its 3954 m summit rises more than three vertical km above the Robson Visitor Centre.

The Walks and Easy Hikes in the park feature human history, the Fraser River, and the lush vegetation that results from the higher precipitation on the western slopes of the Rockies.

Pyramid Mountain provides the backdrop for Jasper townsite in the view north from Old Fort Point. The point is located where the Miette Valley and Athabasca Valley merge.

37. Old Fort Point

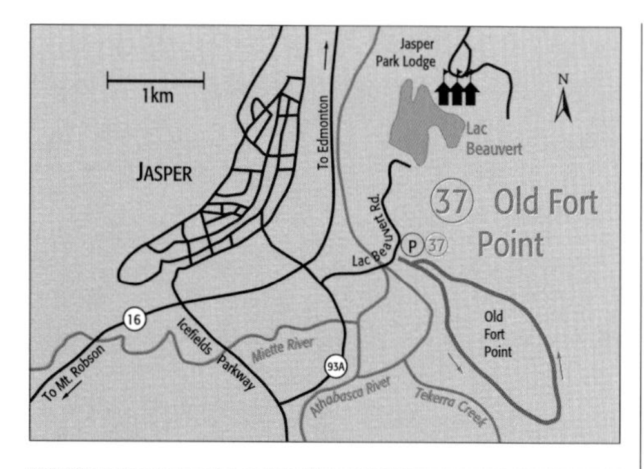

Route Information

Trailhead: Follow Highway 93A south from the intersection of Hazel Avenue and Connaught Drive in Jasper townsite. Cross Highway 16. Turn east (left) onto the Lac Beauvert Road. Follow this for 1 km. Cross the bridge over the Athabasca River and park on the south (right).

Rating: harder, 4.5 km loop

Lighting: anytime

The trail to Old Fort Point climbs steeply to the crest of a rocky knoll south of Jasper, and provides an overview of the townsite and the Athabasca Valley. The name of the knoll commemorates a possible location of Henry House, the first fur trade outpost in the Rockies.

During the winter of 1811, David Thompson, an explorer and fur trader with the North West Company, established a fur trade route across Athabasca Pass. While he was gone, Thompson had one of his men, William Henry, build an outpost near present day Jasper townsite. Henry House was the first, permanent Euro-Canadian habitation in the Rockies.

For decades, historians have disputed the exact location of Henry House. They have studied the original accounts and diaries of Thompson and other explorers. Unfortunately, these accounts offer contradictory information as to the precise location. They also indicate that there may have been several "Henry Houses," constructed over the span of a few decades.

Recently, it has been suggested that the name, Old Fort Point, is a corruption of Old *Ford* Point. A ford is a natural shallow, or a series of islands that allows relatively easy crossing of a river. If this theory is true, then Old Fort Point may not have had any connection with the location of Henry House.

It is best to hike the Old Fort Point loop in a counter-clockwise direction, beginning at the staircase adjacent to the parking lot. In this fashion, the first kilometre of the hike is steep, but the remainder involves a gradual descent. At the top of the staircase, you may inspect the plaque unveiled when the Athabasca River was proclaimed a Canadian Heritage River in 1989. The Athabasca River is 1230 km long. It rises at the north edge of Columbia Icefield and flows to the Arctic Ocean by way of the Slave and Mackenzie river systems. Together with its tributaries, the Athabasca drains most of the area of Jasper National Park. Athabasca is a Cree name that means "place where there are reeds"—a reference to the delta at the river's mouth in Lake Athabasca.

From the heritage river plaque, the trail continues its steady climb onto the crest of Old Fort Point, revealing a splendid 360° panorama of the Athabasca and Miette valleys, and Jasper townsite. The point is sparsely vegetated with Douglas fir, juniper and grasses. The view would have made it a good location for an outpost. But hauling water up the slope from the river would have been a chore!

After you leave the high point, the trail descends into a grove of trembling aspen, and loops northward to the parking lot through a damp pine forest. There is a maze of trails in this area. Follow signs for trail #1 or #1A at all junctions.

Roche Moutonnée

Roche Moutonnée (detail from a painting)

Old Fort Point is a roche moutonnée (ROSH moot-on-AY). This French expression means "fleecy rock." A roche moutonnée is a relatively resistant rock outcrop—in this case gritstone of the Miette formation. The shape of a roche moutonnée indicates the direction that glacial ice flowed during past ice ages. The smooth, streamlined slope faced into the flow of ice, and the jagged, cliff-like side faced away. The streamlined slope of Old Fort Point faces the Athabasca River. Glaciers that flowed north in the Athabasca Valley, and east from the Miette Valley, merged here.

Annette Lake is one of many kettle ponds on the east bank of the Athabasca River near Jasper. From the shores of the lake, you can see many of the mountains near the townsite. Here, Signal Mountain is seen at sunrise.

38. Annette Lake

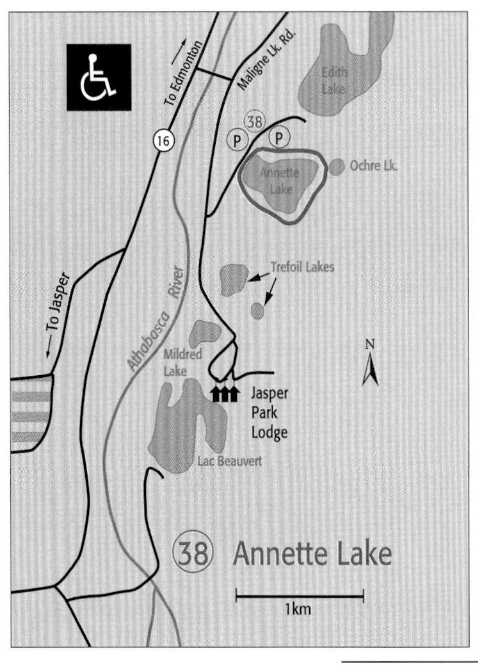

The paved trail around Annette Lake is one of the few trails in the mountain national parks designed to allow wheelchair access. Trail construction was made possible by a grant from the Clifford E. Lee Foundation in 1981, the International Year of Disabled Persons.

Route Information

Trailhead: Follow Highway 16 east from Jasper for 3.7 km to the Maligne Lake Road. Turn east (right). In 500 m turn south (right) onto to the Jasper Park Lodge road. Follow this for 1.4 km. Turn east (left) and drive another 600 m to the second parking area.

Rating: easy, 2.4 km paved loop. Wheelchair accessible

Lighting: anytime

Annette Lake

There are more than 800 lakes and ponds in Jasper National Park. Many occupy glacially-scoured hollows in bedrock. Others are beaver ponds or backwaters of rivers like the Athabasca. Annette Lake and the other lakes near Jasper Park Lodge are kettle ponds. They were created when large blocks of ice detached as glaciers retreated at the end of the Wisconsin Glaciation, 11,000 years ago. As the ice blocks slowly melted, they created depressions in the underlying glacial rubble. Silts then accumulated in the bottoms of the depressions, plugging cracks in the rubble, allowing the lakes to form. It is thought Annette Lake resulted from the joining of three kettle ponds.

Where does the water in Annette Lake come from today? Not from glacial melt. Rainfall, runoff and springs account for most of the inflow. However, studies of the Maligne Karst System (see page 69) have shown that some of the water that disappears underground at Medicine Lake, emerges at Annette Lake and other lakes near Jasper Park Lodge. Annette Lake has no surface outlet.

There are many kettle ponds in the Rockies. Most will eventually fill with aquatic vegetation. Soils will collect among the growth, allowing trees to take root. Then the lake bottoms will be reclaimed as part of the surrounding forest.

At its northeastern end, the trail separates Annette Lake from the swampy waters of Ochre Lake. The bottom of Ochre Lake is quicksand. For your safety, please keep away.

From the south shore of Annette Lake, the view north shows the division between the front ranges and the eastern main ranges. The gray, steeply-tilted limestone peaks of the front ranges are to the east (right). The reddish, more angular, quartzite peaks of the eastern main ranges are to the west (left). The thrust fault that separates the front and main ranges is slightly west (left) of the massive cliff of the Palisade.

You may see elk near Annette Lake. Loons nest on the shore. On hot summer days Jasper locals flock to the lake to take a dip. The surface water may reach 20°C—hot for the Rockies! The lake was named for Annette Rogers, the wife of an early superintendent of Jasper National Park.

Roche Bonhomme

Roche Bonhomme (ROSH bun-OMM) is a 2495 m summit in the Colin Range northeast of Jasper, and is prominent in the view from the townsite. The name means "good fellow rock" in French. The arrangement of slabby rock layers near the mountain crest, bears a striking resemblance to the face of a man, looking skyward. See if it reminds you of anyone you know.

Many of the French names in the Athabasca Valley were given by the voyageurs of the fur trade between 1811 and the 1840s. The name, Roche Bonhomme, first appeared in print in the book *Ocean to Ocean*, published in 1873.

Maligne Canyon is one of the most interesting limestone canyons in the Canadian Rockies. Its maximum depth is 55 m, yet in places it is scarcely a metre wide.

39. Maligne Canyon

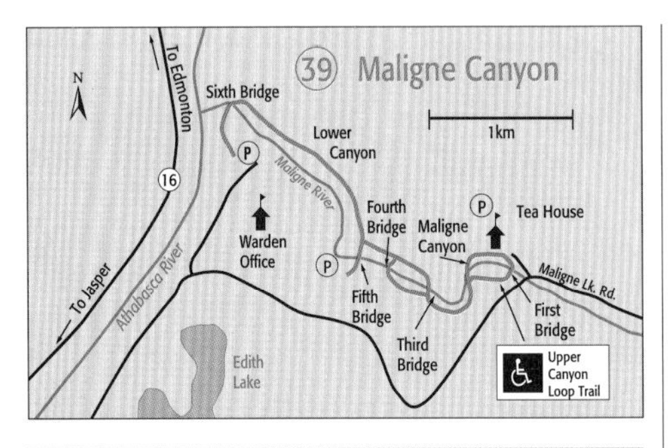

Route Information

Trailheads: Follow Highway 16, 3.7 km east from Jasper to the Maligne Lake Road. Turn east (right). There are three trailheads for the canyon.
Sixth Bridge (turnoff at km 2.3), Fifth Bridge (turnoff at km 3.1), and Maligne Canyon (turnoff at km 6.3).
Ratings: Sixth Bridge, harder, 3.7 km; Fifth Bridge, moderate 2.7 km; Maligne Canyon, easy, 0.8 km loop. Wheelchair-accessible between the parking lot and Second Bridge
Lighting: early afternoon

When asked to compare canyons in the Rockies, one early visitor to Maligne Canyon remarked: "Any other canyon is like a crack in a tea cup."

The three trailheads at Maligne (muh-LEEN) Canyon allow you to choose different experiences. The short loop from the teahouse is on a paved path, and provides quick access to the canyon's highlights. The longer, uphill walks from the Fifth Bridge and Sixth Bridge are on rougher trails, but allow a greater appreciation of the canyon's features.

The blueprint of the Rockies was revealed 11,000 years ago, at the end of the Wisconsin Glaciation. The major valleys had been more deeply eroded by the glaciers than their tributary valleys. Thus, the floors of the tributary valleys were left hanging above the main valleys.

The Maligne is a hanging valley. Initially, the Maligne River plunged into the Athabasca Valley as a waterfall. But over the course of thousands of years, the Maligne River has taken advantage of cracks in the limestone bedrock near the mouth of its valley, and has eroded the 2 km-long Maligne Canyon. With a maximum depth of 55 m near the Second Bridge, Maligne is one of the most spectacular limestone canyons in the Rockies.

How the Canyon Was Formed

Maligne Canyon is being eroded into a natural joint set in the limestone, by three processes: abrasion by silt-laden glacial meltwater, dissolution of the limestone bedrock by naturally acidic rainwater, and the collapse of the canyon walls caused by the sheer hydraulic force of the water torrent. The highest waterfall, 23 m, is just above the First Bridge. Here, the entire volume of the river is forced through a narrow breach before it plunges over the precipice.

The upper canyon is being eroded into tough 360-million-year-old limestone of the Palliser Formation. In many places, the canyon is scarcely a metre wide. This narrowness indicates that the limestone is hard, and that erosion has been rapid. In this case, "rapid" erosion is 0.5 cm per year. Downstream from the Fourth Bridge, the lower canyon is being eroded into softer, younger shales of the Banff Formation. The canyon is wider as a result.

Life: Past and Present

The narrow, vertical world of the canyon is home to pack rats, mice and ravens, whose nests are visible in places on the canyon walls. Maligne Canyon is one of two known nesting sites in Alberta for the black swift. You may also see the American dipper.

The airborne spray from the waterfalls coats the canyon walls and edges. Moisture-loving plants grow within the canyon, and white spruce and Douglas fir trees cling to the rim.

The limestone rocks of Maligne Canyon contain many fossils: snail-like gastropods, clam-like brachiopods, squid-like cephalopods, crinoids (related to starfish), and corals. You can see two prominent examples of fossils in the upper canyon, between the teahouse and the First Bridge. Please do not touch them.

The Maligne Valley

The Maligne Valley is a strike valley. The Maligne River follows a major fault in the earth's crust. This fault marks the division between the 360-million-year-old limestones of the front ranges to the east, and the 570-million-year-old quartzite of the eastern main ranges to the west. (Please note: this is not the age of the mountains, but of the rocks that comprise them.) The front range peaks of the Colin Range and Queen Elizabeth Ranges were uplifted 85 million years ago, and feature steeply tilted, sawtooth mountain shapes. The quartzite summits of the Maligne Range were uplifted 120 million years ago. They were totally enveloped in glacial ice during the Great Glaciation, hence their rounded shapes.

If you look carefully at some of the boulders at trailside, you will notice that they are different from the rock in the canyon walls. These boulders are glacial erratics—rocks transported by the glaciers, and deposited here when the ice receded. By studying erratics, glaciologists can determine a past glacier's point of origin.

The Maligne Karst System

Maligne Canyon is undeniably spectacular, but the Maligne Valley contains an even more remarkable feature—an underground river system that may be the largest in the world. Rainwater and runoff naturally contain carbonic acid, which dissolves limestone. Cracks in the bedrock are enlarged into deep fissures. When connected, these fissures become subterranean waterways, known as karst.

To fully appreciate the nature of the Maligne Karst System, we must trace the Maligne River from its headwaters at the Brazeau Icefield, 80 km south of Maligne Canyon. The glacial meltwater initially collects in Maligne Lake. Then, along with other runoff, it flows on the surface to Medicine Lake, 17 km south of Maligne Canyon. Here, the karst nature of the valley is revealed.

The level of Medicine Lake fluctuates dramatically during the year. The lake bottom contains a series of holes, karst features known as sinks. These sinks allow the lake water to drain underground at a rate of 24,000 litres per second. During the snowmelt of spring and early summer, the sink holes cannot drain the lake fast enough. So, the lake level rises. In some years Medicine Lake overflows at its northern end. By late summer, as the snowmelt season ends, the capacity of the sink holes exceeds the volume of the water flowing into the lake. The water level drops. By autumn, all that remains of Medicine Lake is a braided stream on an expansive mud flat—a good place to look for moose, elk and caribou.

Before the road was constructed along the east shore of Medicine Lake, a boat service shuttled tourists across it. The fluctuating lake level played havoc with the schedule, and unsuccessful attempts were made to plug the sink holes with newspapers, and mattresses.

Most of the water that disappears at Medicine Lake emerges downstream from the Fourth Bridge in Maligne Canyon. You can see the karst outlets, or subemergences, there. Some of the water also feeds lakes near Jasper Park Lodge. The water you see upstream from the Fourth Bridge in Maligne Canyon has not journeyed underground, but has collected in a normal fashion on the surface. So, there are two Maligne Rivers between Medicine Lake and Maligne Canyon—one on the surface, and one underground.

The Maligne karst system is one of the most studied in the world. The underground waterway, although 17 km long and capable of transporting an enormous volume of water, is too narrow to allow access to cavers, even during low water. Dyes have been released into Medicine Lake, and by observing where they emerge, many of the karst outlets have been found. However, the exact nature of the intervening system remains unknown.

The six bridges allow wonderful opportunities to appreciate Maligne Canyon.

Potholes

Potholes are circular depressions drilled into bedrock rock at falls and rapids by the relentless action of water. At first, the water spins sand and pebbles trapped in a slight depression. These particles act like a drill bit. As the pothole develops, boulders fall into the depression, and the pothole becomes larger. If, after centuries, the stream changes course, the pothole may be left high and dry, often with the rounded pebbles and boulders in place. Some potholes eventually fill with silt and thin soils. They become hanging gardens on canyon walls, where ferns, mosses, shrubs, and small trees take root. There are good examples near the teahouse.

Maligne Lake is the largest lake in the Canadian Rockies. It is fed principally by meltwaters from the Brazeau Icefield, and from other glaciers at the southern end of the lake.

40. Maligne Lake

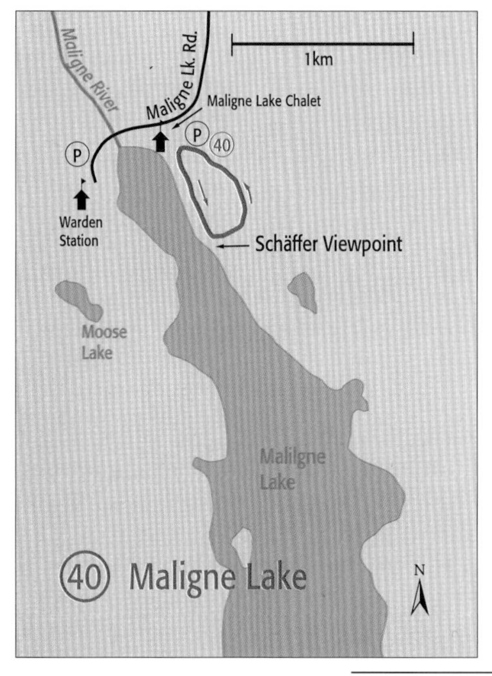

The trail to Schäffer Viewpoint on Maligne Lake follows the lake's east shore to a prominent bay, where interpretive signs describe the lake's exploration in 1908.

Maligne (muh-LEEN) Lake is the largest lake in the Canadian Rockies. It is 22 km long, has an area of 20.66 km^2, and a maximum depth of 96 m. The average width is about 1 km. The lake is fed by

Route Information

Trailhead: Follow Highway 16, 3.7 km east from Jasper to the Maligne Lake Road. Turn east (right). Follow this road 44 km to the parking lots on the east side of Maligne Lake. The trail begins in front of Maligne Lake Chalet, and heads south.
Rating: moderate, 3.2 km loop
Lighting: anytime

meltwater from the Brazeau (brah-ZOE) Icefield, and other glaciers on the mountains in view, 30 km to the south. Maligne is a French word that means "wicked." Father Jean Pierre de Smet gave the name to the river in 1846, when he had trouble crossing it near its mouth at the Athabasca River.

Large lakes usually owe their existence to dams—natural or otherwise. Maligne is no exception. Its outlet is dammed by the second largest measured rockslide in the Canadian Rockies. With an estimated volume of 498,000,000 cubic metres, this rockslide is more than 13 times the size of the famous Frank Slide in Crowsnest Pass.

Until 1908, Maligne Lake was one of the best kept secrets in the Rockies. Henry MacLeod, a surveyor working for the CPR, had reached the lake from the north in 1875. His report was hardly the kind of advertising to inspire further interest. Fed up with the difficult trail from the Athabasca Valley, MacLeod called Maligne, "Sorefoot Lake," and wrote off the valley for further exploration.

However, Stoney natives had long known of Maligne Lake. To them it was Chaba Imne—Beaver Lake. American explorer Mary Schäffer attempted to find the lake in 1907, but failed. Sampson Beaver, a Stoney chief, had seen the lake when he was 14. In 1908, at Schäffer's request, Sampson drew a crude map of the lake from memory. This map provided Schäffer and her party with enough clues to reach Maligne Lake from the south that year. Schäffer's party constructed a raft, christened the *Chaba,* and spent three days mapping the lake and naming many features.

Schäffer returned to the lake in 1911 to make a more accurate map. She published accounts of her packtrain travels in magazine articles, and in her book *Old Indian Trails of the Canadian Rockies.* She was a talented writer and artist, and became a reluctant celebrity. The Stoneys respected her and called her Ya-he-Weha, which means "mountain woman." Schäffer married one of her guides, Billy Warren, and settled in Banff in 1915.

In the view south from Schäffer Viewpoint, Leah Peak (closest), and Samson Peak are on the east (left). Leah was Sampson Beaver's wife. On the west (right) side of the lake are the glaciated peaks of Mt. Charlton and Mt. Unwin. Sidney Unwin was one of Mary Schäffer's guides in 1908. Near these mountains, Maligne Lake's width is reduced to 200 m. This is Samson Narrows, the location of Spirit Island, and destination for the boat tour.

From Schäffer Viewpoint, return to the parking lot along the lakeshore, or follow the loop trail east, and then north.

Moose

The moose is the largest antlered animal in the world, and is circumpolar in distribution. It has a dark chocolate-coloured, or reddish-brown coat, with lighter coloration on the legs. The adult male (bull) sports palmate antlers. It weighs up to 600 kg, and stands 2 m tall at the shoulder. The female (cow) does not carry antlers. A flap of skin called a bell or dewlap, hangs from the throats of both sexes. Aquatic plants are favourite summer foods of moose. In winter, moose move to higher elevations, where they browse on shrubs that protrude above the snowpack.

Despite their ungainly appearance, moose can run up to 55 km per hour, and are capable swimmers. Wolves are the principal predator. Moose are no longer numerous in the Rocky Mountain parks. The overall population may be less than 300. A parasitic liver fluke has taken a heavy toll in recent years, as have deaths on highways and railways. The shores of Maligne Lake, and the numerous lakes and ponds immediately to the north, are among the few remaining good places to see moose, especially in early morning and evening.

Pocahontas was a coal mining town that developed in 1910 near the mouth of the Fiddle River in northeastern Jasper National Park. As with many mining towns, Pocahontas was a boom and bust affair. The mine closed in 1921 and the town folded soon after. Photo courtesy of the Glenbow Archives

41. Pocahontas

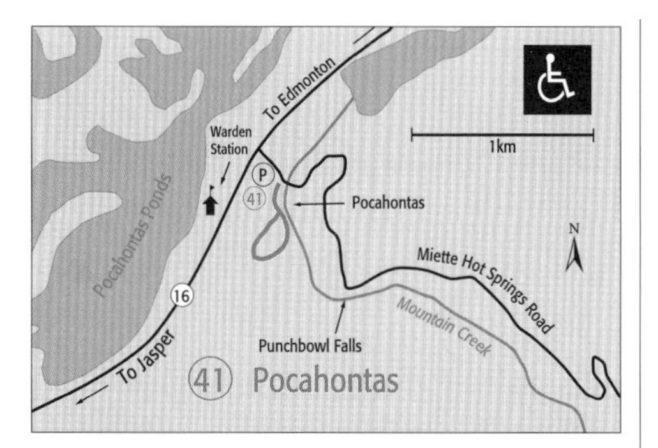

Route Information

Trailhead: Follow Highway 16, 42.9 km east of Jasper townsite to Pocahontas. Turn south (right) onto the Miette Hot Springs Road. The trailhead is 150 m along this road, on the west (right).
Rating: easy, 1 km loop. Wheelchair accessible
Lighting: anytime

The paved Coal Mine Trail at Pocahontas explores the ruins of the industrial and commercial sections of this mining town. As with Bankhead in Banff, the mine and town were established before the National Parks Act prohibited mining and logging.

The Pocahontas mining claims were staked in 1908, when prospector Frank Villeneuve discovered coal on the lower slopes of Roche Miette (ROSH mee-YETT). Villeneuve was in the right place at the right time. A second transcontinental railway, the Grand Trunk Pacific, had been proposed to cross the Rockies at Jasper. The coal-fired locomotives would pass close to the claim. Villeneuve named his mine Jasper Park Collieries. The community that evolved nearby was named

Pocahontas, after the successful coal mining town in Virginia.

Mining began in 1910. A residential upper town and a commercial lower town developed. The upper town, on the east bank of Mountain Creek, reportedly housed more than 2000 people, making it far larger than Jasper at the time. Most of the miners were immigrants from Britain, Italy and eastern Europe.

World War I created a huge market for coal, but affairs at Pocahontas were far from happy. Poor management gave rise to labour unrest. Safety problems were cited in a series of fatal accidents. A second railway, the Canadian Northern, was completed through Jasper in 1913. Soon, both it and the Grand Trunk Pacific were near economic collapse. They amalgamated in 1916. The superfluous railway tracks were torn up and shipped to Europe for use in the war effort. Unfortunately for Pocahontas, the tracks on southeast bank of the Athabasca River were removed, leaving the mine without rail access. Labour unrest continued. The demise of Pocahontas was assured by the general miner's strike of 1919. Thereafter, industry looked elsewhere for coal, and the mine closed permanently in April 1921.

Punchbowl Falls

An inescapable aspect of life at Pocahontas was the steep hill that separated the upper and lower towns. As they went about their business, residents were continually walking up and down the hill, and crossing Mountain Creek. This crossing was usually made at an ornate bridge above Punchbowl Falls.

Most of the rocks near Punchbowl Falls are relatively soft, and easily eroded. However, at the falls, Mountain Creek has uncovered a resistant, conglomerate rock, the 98-million-year-old Cadomin Formation. Conglomerate is a sedimentary rock that contains various sizes of pebbles and fragments eroded from other rocks. It looks like concrete. Unable to erode deeply into this rock, Mountain Creek cascades over it. The pounding water has eroded several plunge pools: bowl-like depressions that give the falls their name. A 3500-year-old native archaeological site has been discovered nearby. You may inspect an outcrop of coal near the falls, which are lit best in the afternoon.

The stark summit of The Whistlers is typical of mountain top environments in the Rockies.

42. The Whistlers

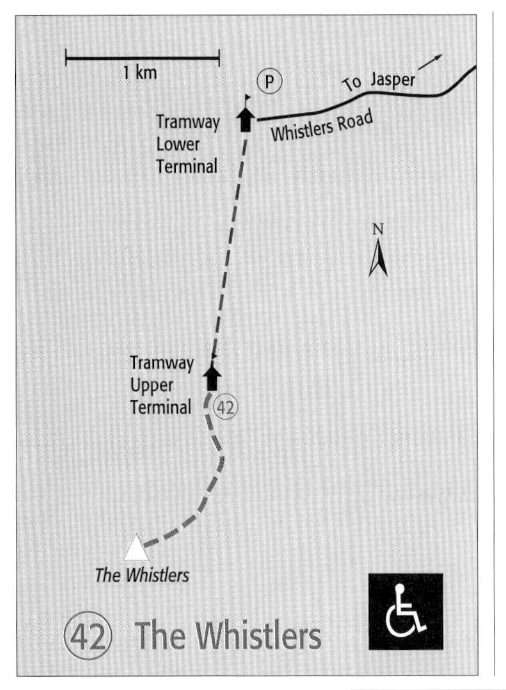

In its seven minute ride, the Jasper Tramway climbs 937 m, whisking you from the montane ecoregion to the stark, mountain top environment of The Whistlers. From the upper terminal, if you are well-shod and warmly-

Route Information

Trailhead: Follow the Icefields Parkway, 2.5 km south from Jasper townsite to Whistlers Road. Turn west (right). Follow this road 4 km to the Jasper Tramway. The trailhead is at the upper terminal of the tramway (fee charged). If you do not want to ride the tramway, hike the steep 7.9 km trail (harder) from the south side of the Whistlers Road, at km 2.7.

Rating: harder, 1.4 km. The boardwalk at the upper terminal is wheelchair accessible.

Lighting: anytime

clothed, you can walk the rocky summit trail. This is the easiest way to a mountain top in the Rockies, and at 2464 m, is the highest point on any trail in this book. The panorama from The Whistlers includes the Miette and Athabasca valleys, Jasper townsite, many lakes, and on clear days, Mt. Robson, the highest peak in the Canadian Rockies, 78 km distant.

Well above treeline, the summit of The Whistlers is the domain of strong winds, harsh sunlight, poor soils and brief summers. Your first impression may be of a barren mountain top. However, The Whistlers supports a surprising array of alpine vegetation.

The harsh conditions have dictated ingenious adaptations. Alpine plants are tiny, and hug the ground to reduce exposure to wind. Leaves are frequently thick and waxy, to retain the moisture gathered by extensive root systems. The blooms do not last long, as energy must be conserved. Some plants are mat-like, and grow outwards in a circular fashion. Frequently, the centres of the mats die off, as the plants prune themselves and direct energy toward new growth. The mats, both dead and growing, help prevent soils from blowing away, and provide opportunity for other vegetation to take root.

The Whistlers shows many characteristics of a glaciated landscape. Its domed summit was completely covered by ice during the Great Glaciation. Huge blocks, known as glacial erratics, were left on the mountain top when the glaciers receded. Several bowl-shaped depressions called cirques were eroded into the mountainsides.

Today, repeated freezing and thawing of moisture trapped in rocky crevices, continues to wedge boulders apart on the mountain top, helping to slowly create new soil. This mineral soil is stabilized and enriched by pioneering plants that fix nitrogen from the atmosphere. Eventually, a small alpine meadow appears.

Unfortunately, construction of the tramway in 1963 introduced an unnatural agent of erosion to The Whistlers—the feet of human visitors. More than 150,000 people now visit the upper terminal each year. Snow patches frequently linger until mid-summer, making it difficult for you to find and stay on the trail. A single footstep off the trail can destroy an alpine plant, obliterating decades of growth in an instant. Please wear appropriate footwear and make every effort to stay on the trail.

Wildlife you may see on this hike includes Columbian ground squirrel, golden-mantled ground squirrel, least chipmunk, pika, white-tailed ptarmigan, hoary marmot and woodland (mountain) caribou.

Hoary Marmot

The Whistlers is named for the piercing whistle of the hoary marmot. Similar in appearance to the woodchuck, this large rodent lives in the quartzite boulderfields on the mountain top. Grasses, leaves, flowers and berries make up its diet. Grizzly bear, lynx and eagles are its predators. The marmot has the perfect answer to the rigours of life in the alpine. When the snow flies and the going gets tough, the marmot goes to sleep. Remarkably, it hibernates nine months of the year.

Marmot track

The winged shape of Angel Glacier adorns the cliffs of Mt. Edith Cavell above the Path of the Glacier trail.

43. Path of the Glacier

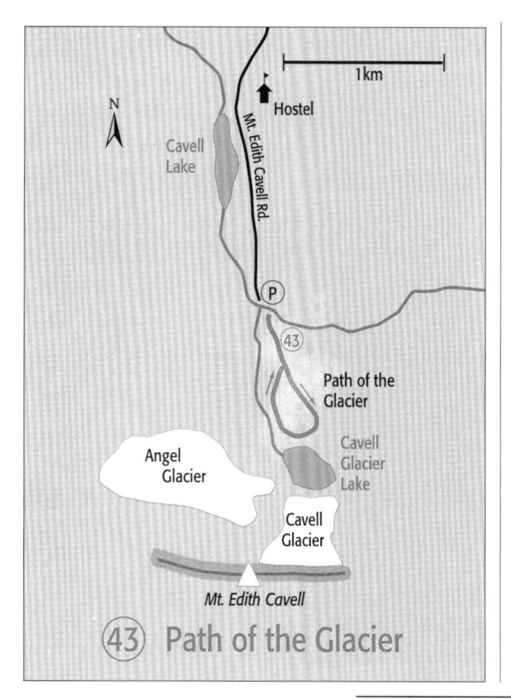

The Path of the Glacier explores the forefield of Cavell Glacier, an area that was covered by glacial ice only a century ago. This rocky trail provides spectacular views of Mt. Edith Cavell, a glacial lake, and Cavell and Angel glaciers.

Route Information

Trailhead: Follow the Icefields Parkway, 7 km south from Jasper townsite to Highway 93A. Turn west (right). Follow this road 5.2 km to the Mt. Edith Cavell Road. Turn west (right), and follow this road 14.5 km to its end at the Mt. Edith Cavell parking lot. Trailers and large RVs cannot negotiate the sharp turns of the Mt. Edith Cavell Road. Use the trailer drop-off on Highway 93A.

Rating: easy, 1.6 km loop

Lighting: morning

The late 1800s saw the end of a period of global glacial advance, known today as the Little Ice Age. During this glacial advance, the ice of the two principal glaciers on Mt. Edith Cavell combined to flow north as far as the present day parking lot. Since the 1880s, the earth's climate has been warming and these glaciers have retreated dramatically.

The initial climb from the parking lot is over a landform known as a terminal moraine, a horseshoe-shaped pile of boulders bulldozed by the advancing Cavell Glacier. From the crest of the moraine, you can look south across the bleak forefield uncovered by the retreating ice. In its advance, the glacier obliterated the vegetation and centuries-old soils of a mature spruce-fir forest. In its retreat, it left behind this landscape of rocky rubble.

The glacial forefield is a harsh home for vegetation. It is cold here, and the slope is north-facing. However, if you look closely, you will see small communities of willows, sedges and hardy wildflowers, especially along the banks of meltwater streams. Despite this growth, less than 1 percent of the forefield is currently vegetated. It will be centuries before a mature forest becomes re-established, unless another glacial advance overruns the area.

For the next 500 m, the trail climbs gradually along the flank of a lateral moraine. After you pass the junction with the Cavell Meadows trail, The Path of the Glacier descends south toward Cavell Glacier and its ice-berg dotted lake. Here, in the near perpetual shade of Mt. Edith Cavell, you are face to face with an ice-age landscape. Cavell Glacier is a cirque glacier, fed by snow and ice avalanches from the north face of Mt. Edith Cavell.

Mountain fireweed

In contrast to the daunting appearance of Cavell Glacier, the winged, sunlit shape of Angel Glacier is a delight. The descending tongue of this glacier broke contact with Cavell Glacier in the early 1940s. Since then, the terminus of Angel Glacier has retreated rapidly up the cliff. The hanging body of ice is fed by a large cirque glacier that is concealed from view. The ice cliffs that comprise "the Angel's wings" exceed 60 m in height.

Mt. Edith Cavell

Natives called Mt. Edith Cavell "White Ghost," probably in reference to the snow-covered mountain's appearance in moonlight. Mt. Edith Cavell (3363 m) was known to the voyageurs of the fur trade in the early 1800s as La Montagne de la Grande Traverse—"The Mountain of the Great Crossing." It was a landmark on their westward journeys. South of the mountain, the voyageurs made a hazardous crossing of the Athabasca River. They then crossed the backbone of the Rockies at Athabasca Pass.

When the Grand Trunk Pacific Railway reached Jasper in 1911, the mountain became known as Mt. Fitzhugh, after the railway's vice-president. In 1916, the name was changed to commemorate Edith Cavell, a British nurse who remained in Brussels after it fell to the Germans in World War I. She was executed for allegedly assisting the escape of Allied prisoners. The mountain was first climbed in 1915. The east ridge (left skyline) is one of the most popular mountaineering routes in the Rockies.

Wildflowers, spectacular views of Angel Glacier, and the 1600 m-high north face of Mt. Edith Cavell are the highlights of the Cavell Meadows trail.

44. Cavell Meadows

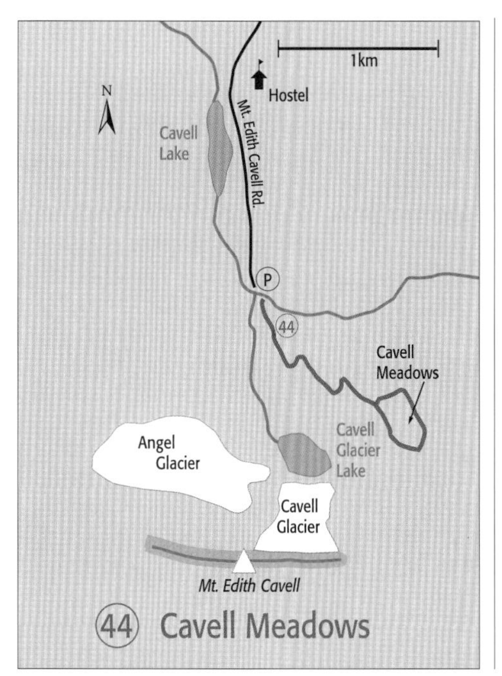

Of the half-dozen trails in this book that lead into the alpine ecoregion, the Cavell Meadows trail does so in the most spectacular setting.

The first 600 m of trail is shared with the Path

Route Information

Trailhead: Follow the Icefields Parkway, 7 km south from Jasper townsite to Highway 93A. Turn west (right). Follow this road 5.2 km to the Mt. Edith Cavell Road. Turn west (right), and follow this road 14.5 km to its end at the Mt. Edith Cavell parking lot. Trailers and large RVs cannot negotiate the sharp turns of the Mt. Edith Cavell Road. Use the trailer drop-off on Highway 93A.

Rating: harder, 3.8 km

Lighting: morning

Woodland caribou

of the Glacier. At the junction, turn east (left). The Cavell Meadows trail climbs steeply over a lateral moraine—a ridge of rock debris deposited alongside Cavell Glacier when it advanced down the valley. The coarse sand underfoot has been eroded from the surrounding quartzite boulders. Least chipmunk, golden-mantled ground squirrel and pika live here.

At the top of the moraine, there is an abrupt transition from boulderfield to forest. This is the trimline of Cavell Glacier, where ice met trees. Some trees near trimline have roots and trunks damaged during the most recent glacial advance.

After paralleling the moraine crest for a few hundred metres, the trail resumes its climb. The forest here is an ancient one, dominated by Engelmann spruce and subalpine fir. In the winter of 1990–91, a snow avalanche from the north face of Mt. Edith Cavell created a wind blast strong enough to topple some of these trees. At trailside, one spruce tree cleared by chainsaw from the avalanche debris shows 232 dark concentric rings. Each ring represents the winter growth of one year. See if you can find a fallen tree that was older.

Two and half kilometres from the trailhead, the forest becomes a patchwork of tree islands, separated by glades of subalpine meadow. Although the elevation here (1860 m) is low for treeline, the glacial chill prevents the growth of dense forest above this point. Soon the trail emerges from the forest, revealing astounding views of Angel Glacier. Keep right at the junctions, and follow the trail through a carpet of wildflowers to a cairned knoll. From here, the trail loops back through the upper meadows to rejoin the approach trail at treeline. Please keep to the beaten path.

The upper meadows are in the alpine ecoregion, and are occasionally visited by woodland (mountain) caribou and grizzly bear. Some hollows here hold snow into late summer. The reddish tinge is "watermelon snow," a one-celled algae, that has a red eye-spot. Some of the steep slopes above the meadows contain called rock glaciers: lobe-shaped accumulations of rock that contain just enough ice to allow the whole mass to creep downhill.

Mountain Heather

Botanists call areas like Cavell Meadows a heath tundra. "Heath" is mountain heather, one of the most common plants in the upper subalpine and alpine ecoregions. Heather frequently forms dense mats, and grows in association with everlasting, mountain avens, crowberry, grouseberry, alpine willow and snow willow. There are four varieties of heather—two white, one pink and one yellow. All have bell-shaped, nodding flowers. Mountain heather is an evergreen member of the family of plants that includes blueberries. However, heather is berry-less.

The lakes in the Valley of the Five Lakes are noted for their blue and green colours.

45. Valley of the Five Lakes

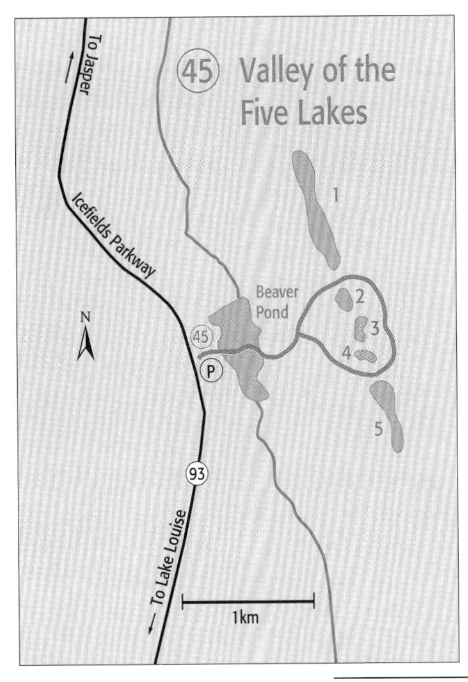

Although not glacially fed, the lakes in the Valley of the Five Lakes possess striking aquamarine and jade hues. The trail leads you through the rolling ridge country of the Athabasca Valley, and offers opportunity to see wildlife: deer, elk, beaver, waterfowl, coyote and bears. The forest is open lodgepole pine, with an undergrowth of buffaloberry, bearberry, twinflower and juniper.

The trail initially crosses a gritstone ridge, and

Route Information

Trailhead: East side of the Icefields Parkway, 11 km south of Jasper townsite, 92 km north of Columbia Icefield Information Centre.
Rating: moderate, 4.6 km loop
Lighting: anytime

then descends to an unnamed creek that has been dammed by beavers. You cross the resulting pond on a boardwalk. Look for the beaver lodges, dome-shaped mounds of sticks and mud. You may see beavers here in early morning or late evening. Sedges and a thicket of moisture-loving shrubs grow at the pond's edge. The author has seen a great blue heron here.

Keep east (straight ahead) at the junction as you climb uphill from the pond. This grassy, sunny slope is another gritstone ridge, and supports a stand of mature, stately Douglas fir trees. Mt. Edith Cavell is prominent in the view west during this climb. On top of the ridge, you enter a grove of trembling aspen trees. The trail soon forks. Take the left branch, and descend from the ridge into a damper lodgepole pine forest.

The Five Lakes owe their existence to the bedrock structure of the Athabasca Valley. Parallel, upturned ridges of resistant gritstone are separated by weaker shales that have been eroded into hollows. The hollows have become home to the Five Lakes, which are separated by natural dams of more resistant rock.

Beavers have created the pond that you cross on the way to the Five Lakes.

There is a maze of trails near the Five Lakes. Use the accompanying map to ensure that you don't become sidetracked. The loop trail leads between lakes one and two, then turns south (right) onto an open sideslope along the east shore of the second lake. The third and fourth lakes are joined by a narrows. It is in the fourth lake that the shades of blue and green are most pleasing.

At the south end of the fourth lake, turn west (right) across one of the rock dams to begin the return section of the loop. On the dam, a side trail to the south (left) provides a good view of the fifth lake, where you may see Common loon and waterfowl.

Miette Gritstone

The bedrock ridges in this part of the Athabasca Valley are comprised of gritstone of the Miette (mee-YETT) group of formations. Gritstone is a coarse, resistant sandstone. The Miette sediments were deposited between 730 million years ago and 570 million years ago, making the resulting rocks the oldest visible in this part of the Rockies.

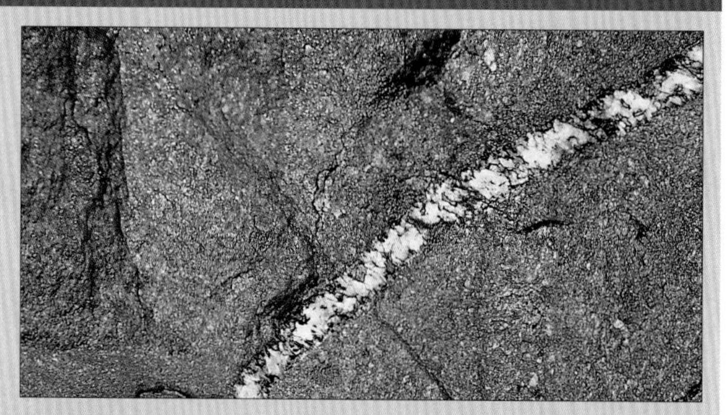

Miette sediments accumulated to a maximum thickness of 8 km. When water seeps into cracks in rock that far underground, it becomes pressurized. Its temperature greatly exceeds the boiling point, and the water is able to dissolve minerals from the surrounding rock and transport them. The white veins you see in Miette gritstone near the Valley of the Five Lakes, are cracks that were filled with liquefied quartz. The rock cooled when thrust to the surface during mountain building, and the quartz solution solidified.

Athabasca Falls is one of the most impressive waterfalls at roadside in the Rockies. The falls mark a location where the Athabasca River encounters a resistant formation of quartzite in the bedrock.

46. Athabasca Falls

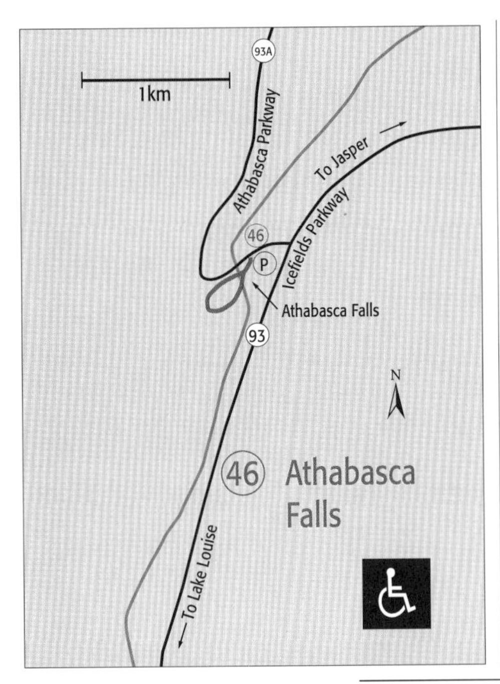

The Athabasca River carries more water than any other river in the Rocky Mountain parks. At Athabasca Falls, the river thunders over a 23 m drop just a few metres from fenced viewpoints.

During the Wisconsin Glaciation, glacial ice filled the Athabasca Valley nearly to the brim. The glaciers flowed north from Columbia Icefield, carving the valley's massive, U-shaped trough. However, the ice was unable to completely

Route Information

Trailhead: On Highway 93A, 500 m west of the Icefields Parkway, 32 km south of Jasper townsite, 71 km north of Columbia Icefield Information Centre
Rating: viewpoint. Wheelchair accessible in part
Lighting: afternoon

smooth out the valley bottom. It was forced upward by resistant rock formations, and then plunged downward once it had flowed past them. At the location of Athabasca Falls, the ancestral Athabasca Glacier encountered a resistant outcrop of Gog quartzite. The glacier skipped over the outcrop and eroded a deep hollow downstream. It is over this glacial rock step that Athabasca Falls now cascades.

Because of the quartzite's toughness, the rock step at Athabasca Falls has been eroded relatively slowly. The falls are therefore broader than most in the Rockies, and the canyon downstream is relatively short. The rock at Athabasca Falls features potholes. In several places the trail follows dry watercourses that were abandoned when the river found a path of less resistance. The most spectacular viewpoints at the falls are on the south side of the river.

Eventually, the brink of Athabasca Falls, and the viewpoints it supports, will be undercut by the river. Then the whole area will collapse, and the falls will migrate slightly upstream. For now, please keep within the paved and fenced viewpoints. This protects the surrounding vegetation from trampling, and also protects you. People have fallen into the abyss and died.

The spray from the falls keeps the area nearby moist and cool, and sustains a canyon forest of lodgepole pine, subalpine fir and white spruce. Feathermosses and lichens thrive in this area, along with shade-tolerant shrubs and wildflowers. There is a stand of moisture-loving black spruce at the Icefields Parkway junction. This tree is uncommon in the Rockies.

From its sources on the northern edge of Columbia Icefield, the Athabasca River flows 1230 km to Lake Athabasca in northeastern Alberta. The 168 km reach within Jasper National Park was designated a Canadian Heritage River in 1989. Athabasca is Cree for "place where there are reeds"—a reference to the delta at the river's mouth. The name was one of the first used by Euro-Canadians in the Rockies, possibly as early as 1790.

Synclines

The mountain east of Athabasca Falls is Mt. Kerkeslin (kurr-KEZZ-lin). If you look at the sedimentary layers in the mountain's northwest face, you will see a shallow, downward fold. This U-shape is called a syncline (SIN-cline).

When the rock that now comprises Mt. Kerkeslin was deep within the earth's crust, it was warm and pliable. The tremendous compressive forces of mountain building were able to warp it into folds. The U-shaped fold of a syncline was usually paired with an arch-shaped fold called an anticline. Rock at the base of a syncline was compressed and rendered more resistant to erosion. Rock at the crest of an anticline was stretched, weakened, and consequently more easily eroded.

Many major valleys in the Rockies, including the Bow and Athabasca, have been eroded by ice and water downward into anticlines, whereas the paralleling mountain ranges have endured atop synclines. The fold in Mt. Kerkeslin marks the northern end of the Castle Mountain Syncline. It begins at Castle Mountain in Banff, and extends for 260 km.

Mt. Kerkeslin was named by James Hector of the Palliser Expedition in 1859. Kerkeslin is a Cree word that means "wolverine." The mountain is 2984 m high. An alpine valley glacier is concealed from view on its northern slopes.

Athabasca Glacier flows from Columbia Icefield to within 1.6 km of the Icefields Parkway. The Forefield Trail allows you to walk to the glacier across an area that was covered by glacial ice less than a century ago.

47. Athabasca Glacier

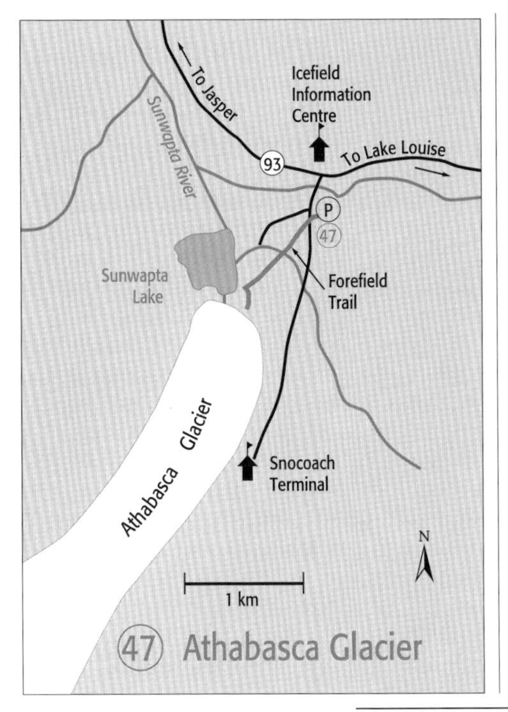

The Athabasca Glacier is the most accessible glacier in North America. Although many people drive to the parking lot closest to the glacier's toe, you can walk to the glacier along the Forefield Trail. This rough trail has been cleared from glacial rubble, so sturdy footwear is recommended. If the day is typical, you will also need a warm hat, gloves, sweater and windbreaker.

Route Information

Trailhead: West side of the Icefields Parkway, 127 km north of Lake Louise, 103 kilometres south of Jasper townsite, 250 m south of Columbia Icefield Information Centre. Follow the glacier access road 200 m to the first parking lot.

Rating: moderate, 2 km

Lighting: morning

After crossing the forefield, this trail connects with the well-beaten path from the second parking lot to the toe of the glacier. For your safety, please keep to the track.

Columbia Icefield—The Ice Factory

The Athabasca Glacier is one of eight outlet valley glaciers that flow from Columbia Icefield. The glacier is 5.3 km long, 1 km wide, and contains an estimated 640,000,000 cubic metres of ice. Impressive as these statistics may seem, they are but an inkling of the vast domain of ice that lies above on Columbia Icefield.

With an area of 325 km^2, Columbia Icefield is the largest icefield in the interior of North America. Nestled on an upland plateau with an average elevation of 3000 m, it is ringed by 13 of the 30 highest mountains in the Rockies. Meltwaters from the summit of Snow Dome on Columbia Icefield flow to three oceans: the Pacific via the Columbia River, the Atlantic via the Saskatchewan river system, and the Arctic via the Athabasca, Slave and Mackenzie river systems. There is only one other tri-oceanic apex in the world, in Siberia.

More than 10 m of snow falls on Columbia Icefield each year, and very little melts. Over time, the fallen snow changes shape from flakes to grains. Then, the grains begin to compact under the weight of snow layers above. Eventually, when a thickness of 30 m of compacted snow has accumulated, its lower layers become glacial ice. The maximum ice thickness on Columbia Icefield is estimated to be 365 m.

Columbia Icefield acts as a huge refrigerator, chilling the air above it. Cold air is more dense than warm air. It flows downhill from the icefield into adjacent valleys and collects in hollows. As you walk the Forefield Trail, you will probably feel the cold air that drains from Athabasca Glacier. This chill, coupled with the ever-changing courses of glacial meltwater streams, makes it difficult for vegetation to grow here. Mats of white mountain avens, clumps of snow willow, alpine willow, sedges and mountain fireweed are all that have taken hold since the ice retreated.

Glacier Movement

Glacial ice naturally flows downhill. Because it is under less resistance and pressure, ice on the surface of a glacier flows faster than ice at the base or sides. Glacial ice is also somewhat plastic, and conforms to irregularities in the bedrock. These properties create crevasses (creh-VASS-es)—fissures in the surface of glacial ice. They extend from side to side, or parallel with a glacier's flow. Near the toe of a glacier, crevasses often splay diagonally. It has been estimated that there are more than 30,000 crevasses on Athabasca Glacier. The jumble of crevasses toward the icefield rim marks the location of three icefalls, where the glacier drops over steps in the bedrock.

Meltwater sculpts runnels into the surface of glacial ice, and sometimes enlarges crevasses, forming circular holes called millwells. The millwells connect to drainage systems within or beneath the glacier. The meltwater helps lubricate the base of the ice, enabling it to flow more easily. The subsurface streams in Athabasca Glacier discharge near the toe. Some of the streams have eroded an ice cave.

Glacial Erosion

The tremendous pressure produced by the weight of glacial ice gives glaciers awesome erosive power. Bedrock is shorn away, mountainsides are undercut and collapse, and the fragments are ground into bits and pieces. The resulting rubble, known to geologists as till, is the immediate product of glacial erosion. Glaciers incorporate till into their erosive arsenal. Picked up and carried on the underside of the ice, rock fragments are dragged across the bedrock, catching in cracks, and prying the rock apart. The bedrock scratches are called striations. You will see striations as you approach the toe of Athabasca Glacier.

How much rubble does Athabasca Glacier produce? On a hot summer day, its meltwaters deposit 570 tonnes of rubble and silt onto deltas in nearby Sunwapta Lake. This marginal lake, uncovered in 1938 by the retreating ice, will be completely filled with debris in the not-too-distant future.

Moraines

Although till is a product of destruction, glaciers create landforms from it called moraines. Lateral moraines are crested ridges pushed up alongside a glacier. The toe of Athabasca Glacier is flanked by wonderful examples. A terminal moraine is a horseshoe-shaped ridge created at the greatest advance of a glacier. The most recent terminal moraine of Athabasca Glacier abuts the slope of Mt. Wilcox, behind Columbia Icefield Information Centre. Recessional moraines mark annual halting places during a period of glacial retreat. The Forefield Trail cuts across a series of recessional moraines.

Global Warming

There have been 20 to 30 periods of glacial advance, or ice ages, during the last two million years. The most recent, the Little Ice Age was relatively minor. It lasted from approximately 1200 AD to the late 1800s. Many glaciers have disappeared since that time. Others, like Athabasca Glacier, have shrunk considerably. What has caused this retreat?

In a nutshell: global warming. The earth's climate has warmed rapidly during the last century, and glaciers have paid the price. The size of Athabasca Glacier is governed by two things: the amount of snow that falls annually on Columbia Icefield, and the amount of snow or ice that annually melts from the glacier's surface. The glacier will advance when the winter snow accumulation exceeds the amount of the previous summer's melt. It will retreat if the summer melt exceeds the amount of the previous winter's snowfall. Glacial advance and retreat are natural processes. But there is concern that humankind's effect on the environment—particularly the emission of "greenhouse gases" and the depletion of the atmospheric ozone layer—is contributing to unnatural global warming, and accelerated glacial retreat.

Glacial Retreat

How much does Athabasca Glacier shrink each year? In recent years, the annual retreat has averaged 1 to 3 m, measured lengthwise. Since 1870, the total retreat has been 1.6 km, or an average of 13 km per year. As impressive as this may seem, vertical shrinkage is also taking place. The total loss is hard to gauge visually on a year-to-year basis, but over the longterm it is staggering. It is estimated that Athabasca Glacier decreased 57 percent in area and 32 percent in volume between 1870 and 1971.

Why is this significant? Glaciers cover 11 percent of the world's surface and contain 75 percent of its freshwater in frozen form. As glaciers melt, this frozen reservoir is depleted. Some of the ice melting at the toe of Athabasca Glacier may have formed 800 years ago, before industrial pollution. Thus, melting glaciers represent the disappearance of nature's purest freshwater resources. At a time when demand for freshwater is increasing globally, the retreat of the world's glaciers becomes a vital concern.

Warning!

Travel on glacial ice is for equipped and knowledgeable mountaineers only! The toe of Athabasca Glacier is very dangerous to the casual walker. The chief danger is crevasses—slots in the ice that can be 30 m deep. Glacial ice is slippery. It is easy to lose your footing, especially during descent. If you fall into a crevasse you will be unable to climb out.

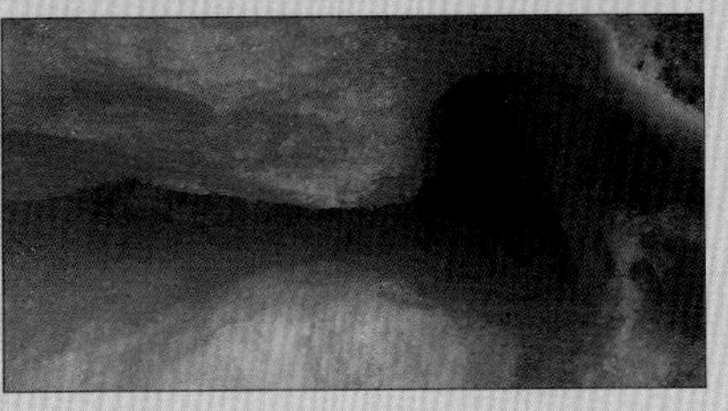

Ice on a glacier's surface is abrasive due to the high concentration of sediment. When you fall, your skin will not simply be cut. It will be torn away. Such injuries often become infected.

As many people find out to their horror, even gentle ice slopes are much harder to descend than they are to ascend.

What can you expect if you fall into a crevasse? Quick rescue is not likely. Death awaits most people who fall into crevasses unroped. Hypothermia, injuries sustained in the fall, and drowning are the major causes of death. Someone dies or is injured at the toe of Athabasca Glacier almost every year, despite the warnings. Stay off the ice!

Explorer Walter Wilcox first crossed Wilcox Pass in 1896. His party used the pass as a detour around the Athabasca Glacier and the Mt. Kitchener rockslide, which blocked travel in the Sunwapta Valley.

48. Wilcox Pass

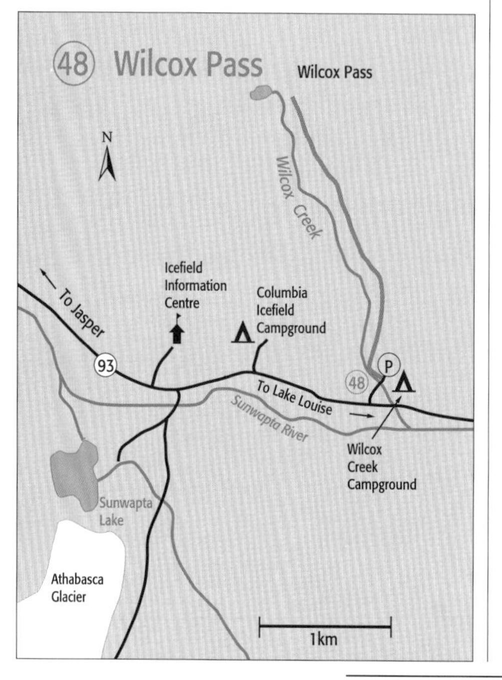

The Wilcox Pass trail provides an overview of the high mountains and spectacular glaciers on the northeast fringe of Columbia Icefield. This historic trail climbs steadily to alpine tundra, the haunt of bighorn sheep and grizzly bear. Dress warmly!

When the first travellers ventured north from Lake Louise in the 1890s, Athabasca Glacier

Route Information

Trailhead: Wilcox Creek campground on the east side of the Icefields Parkway, 106 km south of Jasper townsite, 2.8 km south of Columbia Icefield Information Centre, 124 km north of Lake Louise. The trailhead is on the north side of the access road, just off the Icefields Parkway.

Rating: harder, 4.5 km

Lighting: morning

blocked the valley that now contains the Icefields Parkway. Just beyond, lay the jumble of the Mt. Kitchener rockslide. Rather than attempting to cross the glacier with horses and tackle the narrow canyon beyond, the outfitters climbed over this alpine pass, and regained the Sunwapta Valley at Tangle Creek. The first explorer to make this detour was Walter Wilcox.

At the trailhead, you are in an old-growth forest dominated by Engelmann spruce. The larger trees are more than 400 years old, nearly 1 m in diameter, and 20 m tall. These are remarkable specimens given the severity of the local climate. The stumps in the first few hundred metres are remains of trees that were cut in the 1930s for use as bridge timbers during construction of the original Icefields Parkway.

After a steep climb, the trail gains a cliff edge that overlooks the Icefields Parkway and Athabasca Glacier. The mountain nearest you to the south is Mt. Athabasca. Behind it is Mt. Andromeda. Look for climbers—tiny, black specks on the expansive glaciers and icy faces of these mountains. West of Athabasca Glacier, spectacular Dome Glacier cascades from the rim of Columbia Icefield, between Snow Dome and Mt. Kitchener.

Veering away from the cliff edge, you turn your back on this icy scene and resume the moderate climb towards Wilcox Pass. You may encounter members of the resident band of bighorn sheep. The mountain to the east is Nigel Peak, named for Nigel Vavasour, cook on the mountaineering expedition that discovered Columbia Icefield in 1898.

Two more km of delightful hiking across alpine tundra leads to the expansive summit of Wilcox Pass (2375 m). The precise height of land is difficult to determine, but a large rock cairn serves as the turnaround point. Vegetation in the pass includes willows, sedges, rock lichens, mountain avens, mountain heather, and a variety of wildflowers.

The pass is frequented by grizzly bears, and occasionally by moose. Look for golden eagles overhead. The limestone bedrock beneath the pass contains a significant underground drainage system.

Grizzly Bear

The grizzly bear is the dominant mammal in the Rockies. Although a formidable animal, the grizzly in the Rockies is not a great hunter—90 percent of its diet is vegetarian. Berries and roots are the principal foods.

Grizzlies range from valley bottom to mountain top, feeding at low elevations in spring and autumn, and higher in the summer. They spend the months of November to April in a state of dormancy, in dens dug into steep mountainsides.

The adult male grizzly is 1.3 m tall at the shoulder, and can weigh in excess of 300 kg. The smaller female breeds on average every third year, and gives birth to a single cub (sometimes twins) while in the den. The female begins breeding on average at age seven.

Colour and size are not certain means of distinguishing between grizzly bears and black bears. Look for the grizzly's prominent shoulder hump and dished face. "Grizzly" refers not to the bear's disposition, but to its coat of grayish-tipped guard hairs.

Grizzly bears are not numerous. There are probably fewer than 200 in the Rocky Mountain parks. Recent studies indicate that because of its low reproductive rate, and the pressures of habitat disruption, hunting and poaching, the grizzly bear may become locally extinct in the central and southern Rockies.

Kinney Lake, known as the "mirror of the mount," lies at the foot of Mt. Robson, the highest peak in the Canadian Rockies. The lake was named for Reverend George Kinney, who took part in the first attempts to climb the mountain, in 1908 and 1909.

49. Kinney Lake

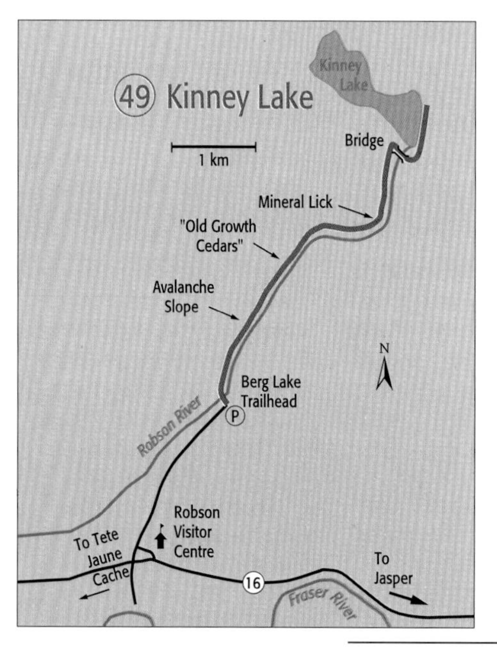

The hike to Kinney Lake is one of the best nature walks in the Rockies. It follows the first 5.2 km of the Berg Lake Trail. From the parking lot, the trail crosses the Robson River and follows its west bank, climbing gradually to the outlet of Kinney Lake. The wide trail is well-suited to families. Please use caution: the trail is

Route Information

Trailhead: Follow Highway 16 to Mt. Robson, 84 km west of Jasper townsite, 18 km east of Tete Jaune Cache. Turn north, and follow the sideroad 2 km to the parking lot at the Berg Lake trailhead.

Rating: harder, 5.2 km. A brochure may be available at Mt. Robson Visitor Centre.

Lighting: anytime

also popular with mountain bikers.

The annual precipitation at Mt. Robson is one and a half times that of Jasper townsite. The extra precipitation results when air is forced to rise over Mt. Robson's 3954 m summit. The precipitation, in conjunction with the longer growing season at this low elevation (862 m), creates a lush forest, with species more typical of interior and coastal rainforests than of forests in the Rockies. The indicator species are western red cedar, western hemlock, green alder, devil's club and thimbleberry.

After about a kilometre, the trail crosses an avalanche slope. Here, in late June, you will find one of the best wildflower displays on any trail in this book. Look for western (red) columbine, Indian paintbrush, harebell, spotted saxifrage, false solomon's seal, wild rose, wild strawberry, white geranium, calypso orchid, and cow parsnip.

The rainforest atmosphere of the Kinney Lake hike culminates a kilometre farther, where the trail enters an "old-growth" grove of western red cedar trees. These widely-spaced giants are probably 200 to 300 years old. Devils club, horsetail, queen's cup and ferns are common on the forest floor.

After leaving the cedar grove, the trail reveals a view of Mt. Resplendent, the second highest mountain in the park. It then crosses another avalanche slope, created by a snow slide in 1968. Although the park brochure characterizes avalanches as "the worst scourges of mountain regions," they are natural processes that help create new growth by opening sections of forest.

Calypso orchid

Three kilometres from the trailhead, you cross a boardwalk over a mineral lick. The damp soils here contain a concentration of salts and minerals. Look for the tracks of elk, deer, moose and mountain goats. They come to this lick for a nutritional boost. The tall shrub, red elderberry, grows nearby.

The outlet of Kinney Lake is a kilometre farther.

The lake was named for Reverend George B. Kinney, who took part in the first, unsuccessful mountaineering attempts on Mt. Robson in 1908 and 1909. To reach the viewpoint that overlooks the lake, cross the bridge and continue up the switchbacks to the top of a bluff. A boardwalk leads west (left) to the viewpoint. Across the blue-green waters are the avalanche-scarred slopes of Cinnamon Peak. To the north is Whitehorn Mountain, third highest peak in Mt. Robson Provincial Park.

Western Red Cedar

The western red cedar is the provincial tree emblem of BC. When mature, it is among the tallest-growing of the 17 native tree species in the Rockies. Its straight, 40 m trunk has shreddy, gray bark in vertical strips. The leaves of this evergreen conifer are frond-like, scaly and flat. In coastal rainforests, western red cedars can be gigantic trees. One of the largest recorded is 59 m tall, and 19 m in circumference near its base.

Western red cedar's soft, fragrant wood is resistant to rot, which has made it a popular choice with builders. Natives used it for totem poles, dugout canoes, boxes and clothing. Contemporary carpenters desire cedar for shingles, fence posts, siding, craftwork and boat timbers. Unfortunately, this tree has been subject to overcutting. Soon, the only old-growth pockets will be those that exist in protected areas such as Mt. Robson Provincial Park.

Overlander Falls cascade over a 10 m-high ledge on the Fraser River. The falls were named for a group of gold seekers, The Overlanders, who crossed western Canada by wagon, raft and foot in 1862.

50. Overlander Falls

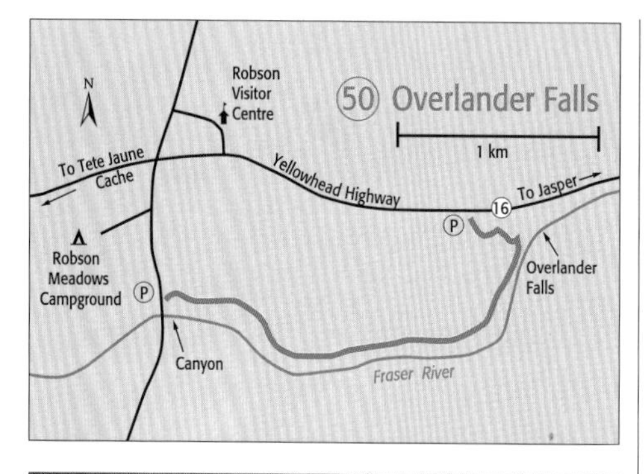

Route Information

Trailheads: South side of Highway 16, 19.6 km east of Tete Jaune Cache, 1.6 km east of Robson Visitor Centre, 80.4 km west of Jasper townsite. Or at the Fraser River bridge, 500 m south of Robson Meadows Campground at Mt. Robson

Ratings: From Highway 16, easy, 500 m.
From the Fraser River bridge, moderate, 1.9 km

Lighting: afternoon

Overlander Falls commemorates the epic journey of a group of gold seekers who crossed Canada in 1862. You can reach this 10 m-high waterfall on the Fraser River by two trails. For those with ample time, take the trail that begins on the north side of the Fraser River bridge, south of Robson Meadows campground. It winds along the steep banks of the Fraser River, and visits the ruins of a camp used during construction of the Grand Trunk Pacific Railway. For those who desire a shorter outing, follow the trail downhill from Highway 16.

The Fraser River is one of the longest rivers in western North America. From its sources on the continental divide southeast of Yellowhead Pass, it flows 1368 km to the Pacific Ocean at Vancouver. It drains 145,000 km^2 of British Columbia. The river was named for Simon Fraser, an explorer and trader with the North West Company, who followed the river from Prince George to the Pacific Ocean in 1808. The river is noted for its tumultuous rapids. "Hell's Gate," south of Lytton, is one of the most treacherous stretches of whitewater in North America.

In 1858, word reached the outside world of gold discovered along the Fraser River, and in the Cariboo Mountains west of the Rockies. Various agencies in eastern Canada enticed would-be gold miners from Europe with transportation arrangements, and promised to deliver them to the motherlode.

In 1862, a group of 125 from Liverpool England, departed Toronto for the gold country. They became known as the Overlanders, because most travel to western North America at that time had been completed by sailing "around the horn" of South America. The travel arrangements broke down at Fort Garry (now Winnipeg), and The Overlanders were left to fend for themselves. Together with some locals, they set out for Edmonton in a wagon train. From there, they tackled the crossing of the Rockies on foot, via the Athabasca, Miette and Fraser valleys.

Frequently short of supplies, The Overlanders resorted to butchering their cattle and horses, and shooting skunk, porcupine and chipmunks to provide rations. When they gained the upper reaches of the Fraser River, the going in the trackless forest became so difficult, that many took to the river on log rafts.

The Overlanders split into two groups. The ardent gold seekers rafted the Fraser River to Quesnel (kwuh-NELL). At least six of their number drowned—one had a premonition of his death and wrote of his drowning in his diary, just before attempting to run the rapid that claimed him. Those in the other group walked south to Kamloops. Among them was a pregnant woman, who gave birth to the first Euro-Canadian child born in the interior of BC.

After the tribulations of their 5600-km, five-month journey, most of The Overlanders could not face the further privations of the Cariboo goldfields, so they continued to the Pacific coast. Some of those who did prospect for gold helped establish the communities of Barkerville, Quesnel and Horsefly.

The Overlanders had set out equipped for a life of prospecting in western Canada. At the conclusion of the journey one of them commented: "Our mining tools were the only articles that we found to be unnecessary."

Overlander Falls is an insurmountable barrier to migrating chinook salmon from the Pacific Ocean. Were it not for the falls, the salmon might be able to reach the headwaters of the Fraser River.

Dwarf Dogwood

Dwarf dogwood is one of the most common and attractive wildflowers in both the Rockies and in Canada. It grows in damp, mossy areas of shaded forests. The prominent white "petals" are not part of the flower, but are modified leaves called bracts. The minuscule flowers are pale green, and yield a brilliant cluster of red berries in late summer—hence this plant's other folk name: bunchberry. Look for dwarf dogwood near Overlander Falls, along with three other common flowers of the coniferous forest: wild strawberry, queen's cup and twinflower.

Other Walks and Easy Hikes in Jasper National Park

51. Stanley Falls

Trailhead: East side of the Icefields Parkway, 15 km north of Columbia Icefield Information Centre, 88 km south of Jasper townsite. Park at a small parking area posted with a hiker symbol.
Rating: moderate, 2.5 km
Lighting: afternoon

After crossing a drainage dyke adjacent to the Icefields Parkway, the Stanley Falls trail passes through a narrow section of forest. When you emerge from this, turn south (right) onto the old road bed, abandoned when the Icefields Parkway was upgraded in the late 1950s. At the mouth of Beauty Creek, a rough track veers east (left) and follows the rim of a picturesque canyon than contains eight waterfalls. Use caution, there are no fences and the trail is rough. Stanley Falls is the last and highest waterfall. Always in the shade, it is difficult to photograph. However, some of the other cascades in the lower canyon are photogenic. This trail is sometimes used by woodland (mountain) caribou.

52. Sunwapta Falls and Canyon

Trailhead: West side of the Icefields Parkway, 48 km north of Columbia Icefield Information Centre, 55 km south of Jasper townsite. Follow the Sunwapta Falls Road 1 km to the parking lot.
Rating: viewpoint. Wheelchair accessible
Lighting: afternoon

At Sunwapta Falls, the Sunwapta River has been diverted from its former course by a glacial moraine. In following its newer path, the river has eroded a crack system in the Cathedral limestone to create the falls, and four other cascades in a canyon downstream. This lower canyon is reached by a 2 km walk along the north bank of the river, through open lodgepole pine forest. On the way, you can see remote mountains near the headwaters of the Athabasca River.

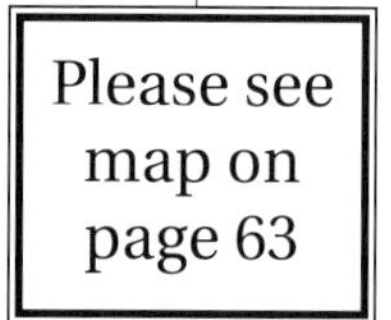
Please see map on page 63

53. Buck, Honeymoon and Osprey Lakes

Trailhead: East side of the Icefields Parkway, 50 km north of Columbia Icefield Information Centre, 53 km south of Jasper townsite.
Rating: easy, 1.5 km
Lighting: anytime

When glacial ice last receded from the floor of the Athabasca Valley, large blocks of ice detached and melted into the rubble. The lakes that resulted are known as kettle ponds. These three lakes are good examples. Buck Lake is 250 m straight ahead from the parking area. The trail to Honeymoon Lake and Osprey Lake branches north (left), about halfway to Buck Lake. This trail visits the south shore of Honeymoon Lake, before heading east through a black spruce bog to Osprey Lake. Wear rubber boots! Orchids grow at trailside, and moose and osprey are among the wildlife you may see in the area.

54. Goats and Glaciers Viewpoint

Trailhead: West side of the Icefields Parkway, 38 km south of Jasper townsite, 65 km north of Columbia Icefield Information Centre
Rating: viewpoint, 100 m
Lighting: morning and evening

The Goats and Glaciers Viewpoint is located on an outcrop of glacial till adjacent to the Athabasca River. Mountain goats that range on Mt. Kerkeslin to the east will congregate here to lick the sulphur-bearing minerals in the till. They use the lick most often in late spring. You can see classic examples of hanging valleys, across the river on the southwest side of the Athabasca Valley.

55. Horseshoe Lake

Trailhead: East side of the Icefields Parkway, 29 km south of

Cottonwood Slough

Jasper townsite, 74 km north of Columbia Icefield Information Centre
Rating: moderate, 600 m loop
Lighting: afternoon

This rough circuit visits the shores of a deep lake that has formed in the quartzite rubble of a rockslide. From the parking lot you descend to the lake's outlet—the waters drain underground through rocks beneath the trail. Keep straight ahead at the first two trail junctions. After 150 m, follow any of several paths to the cliffs on the lakeshore. Turn north (left), and follow rough paths along the shore, tracing the interior of the horseshoe back to a junction with the trail from the parking lot. Turn west (right). The lake is a favourite diving and swimming place for locals who can brave its chill waters.

56. Wabasso Lake

Trailhead: East side of the Icefields Parkway, 87 km north of Columbia Icefield Information Centre, 16 km south of Jasper townsite
Rating: moderate, 2.7 km
Lighting: anytime

Wabasso is a seldom-visited lake in the rolling, gritstone ridge country of the Athabasca Valley. Wabasso is a Cree word that means "rabbit." The trail undulates over a series of ridges, and at km 1.5, skirts a slough created by beavers. Keep left at all trail junctions. After climbing over another ridge, the trail drops to a picturesque cascade that drains the marshes below Wabasso Lake. The lake is 700 m farther. Although views are limited, you can see the Maligne Range on the east side of the valley, from Mt. Tekarra to Mt. Hardisty. Osprey nest at the lake. Keep right at all junctions on your return.

57. Cavell Lake

Trailhead: Follow the Icefields Parkway, 7 km south from Jasper townsite to Highway 93A. Turn west (right). Follow this road 5.2 km to the Mt. Edith Cavell Road. Turn west (right), and follow this road 12.5 km to the parking lot for the Tonquin Valley trailhead. Trailers and large RVs cannot negotiate the sharp turns of the Mt. Edith Cavell Road. Use the trailer drop-off on Highway 93A.
Rating: easy, 150 m
Lighting: early morning and evening

This road-width trail descends to a bridge at the outlet of Cavell Lake, revealing the postcard view of Mt. Edith Cavell.

58. Lac Beauvert

Trailheads: The boathouse at Jasper Park Lodge. Or take Highway 93A south from the corner of Hazel Avenue and Connaught Drive in Jasper townsite. Cross Highway 16. Turn east (left) onto the Lac Beauvert Road. Cross the bridge over the Athabasca River and follow the road to the Lac Beauvert parking lot.
Rating: moderate, 3.2 km loop

Lighting: anytime

Lac Beauvert is French for "beautiful green lake." The circuit of this horse-shoe-shaped lake adjacent to Jasper Park Lodge is an ideal family outing. The lodge originated in 1922. Earlier accommodation at the site was a camp called "Tent City," and possibly Henry House, a fur trade outpost built in 1811. The trail skirts the north and west shores of the lake and passes through open forest and grasslands that are important year-round range for elk. You may see Common loon and Canada geese on the lake. Complete the loop along walkways on the lodge's golf course.

Bald eagle

59. Cottonwood Slough

Trailhead: Park at Pyramid stables on the east side of the Pyramid Lake Road, 4 km north of Jasper townsite. The trailhead is on the west side of the road.
Rating: easy, 1.5 km
Lighting: afternoon and evening

There is a maze of hiking trails on the Pyramid Bench north of Jasper townsite. Unfortunately, due to excessive use by horses, most of these trails are in poor condition, and cannot be recommended. Because it has better drained soils underfoot, the trail to Cottonwood Slough (SLEW) is the best the area offers.

From the stables, take trail #6 which begins across the Pyramid Lake Road. After 150 m, take the left fork in the trail. In another 300 m, branch right. As it gains the banks above the first pond in the slough, the trail breaks out of lodgepole pine and aspen forest onto a dry, grassy, south facing slope, topped by Douglas firs. This vegetation association is one of the most rare in the Rockies. When the second pond comes into view, a spur trail branches downhill to allow a closer look. There is a large beaver lodge in this pond. The area is excellent for bird-watching.

60. Beaver Lake

Trailhead: Follow Highway 16, 3.7 km east of Jasper to the Maligne Lake Road. Turn east (right). Follow the Maligne Lake Road 28 km to the Beaver Creek picnic area at the south end of Medicine Lake.
Rating: easy, 1.6 km
Lighting: afternoon

The short walk to Beaver Lake is along the Jacques Lake trail, a wide, well-graded gravel path, ideal for families. The glacially-fed waters of the lake reflect the steeply tilted saw-tooth mountains of the Queen Elizabeth Ranges.

61. Mona, Lorraine and Moose Lakes

Trailheads: Follow Highway 16, 3.7 km east from Jasper to the Maligne Lake Road. Turn east (right). Follow this road 45 km to its end at the parking lot on the west side of Maligne Lake. There are two trailheads adjacent to this parking lot. The trail to Mona Lake and Lorraine Lake is the Skyline Trail. The trail to Moose Lake begins at the Bald Hills trailhead.
Ratings: Mona Lake, moderate, 2.4 km; Lorraine Lake, moderate, 2.1 km; Moose Lake, easy, 2.4 km loop
Lighting: anytime

The rockslide that dammed Maligne Lake was so colossal, it spread across the valley floor. Depressions in the rockslide debris have become natural hollows in which many small lakes have formed. To reach Mona Lake and Lorraine Lake, hike the Skyline Trail through open pine forest to the posted spur trails that lead southwest (left) to Lorraine Lake, and north (right) to Mona Lake, respectively. Mona Lake was named for one of Jasper's first female trail guides.

To reach Moose Lake, follow the Bald Hills trail and branch south (left) at the first junction in 300 m. In another kilometre, turn east (left) to the shore of Moose Lake. From the lake's north shore, a trail descends to Maligne Lake. The parking lot is then easily reached by walking north.

62. Miette Hot Springs Boardwalk

Trailhead: Follow Highway 16 east of Jasper, 42.9 km to the Miette Hot Springs Road. Turn south (right), and follow this road 19 km to its end at the Mi-

Lac Beauvert

ette Hot Springs parking lot. Trailers and large RVs are not permitted on this road. Park them at the trailer drop-off, 150 m from Highway 16.
Rating: easy, 800 m
Lighting: anytime

From the hot springs parking lot, walk south on the road across Sulphur Creek to the old hot springs building. Constructed in 1937, this building was used until deemed unsafe in 1984. The boardwalk beyond the old building leads to the outlets of the springs, the hottest (53.9°C) and most pungent in odour in the Rockies. You may see bighorn sheep near the parking lot.

63. Portal Lake

Trailhead: North side of Highway 16 at the picnic area in Yellowhead Pass, 23 km west of Jasper, 61 km east of Mt. Robson Visitor Centre, 79 km east of Tete Jaune Cache.
Rating: easy, 500 m
Lighting: anytime

A short stroll at Portal Lake is an ideal way to stretch your legs while driving the Yellowhead Highway. The trail follows the lake's east shore, and climbs onto a rocky knoll covered in a doghair forest of lodgepole pine. Although it is possible to loop back to the highway along the provincial boundary cut-line, this is a poorly defined, frustrating route. Return to the parking lot along the lakeshore. Yellow pond lilies grow in the lake. The cliffs along the west shore are Miette shale and slate.

64. Labrador Tea Trail

Trailhead: North side of Highway 16, opposite site 2 in Lucerne Campground, 34 km west of Jasper, 50 km east of Mt. Robson Visitor Centre, 68 km east of Tete Jaune Cache
Rating: easy, 2.5 km loop
Lighting: anytime

The Labrador Tea Trail (also called the Yellowhead Lake Trail) loops through a shaded lodgepole pine forest to the shore of Yellowhead Lake. Interpretive signs describe vegetation on the forest floor. Labrador tea is an evergreen shrub with showy white flowers. Natives and explorers made a strong tea from its leaves.

65. Fraser River Nature Trail

Trailhead: Site 39 in Robson Meadows Campground. Follow Highway 16 to Mt. Robson, 84 km west of Jasper, 18 km east of Tete Jaune Cache. Turn south and follow the road 1 km to the campground.
Rating: easy, 2 km loop
Lighting: anytime

This nature walk along the banks of the Fraser River is an ideal outing for those staying in the campground. Interpretive signs describe the common vegetation.

66. Rearguard Falls

Trailhead: South side of Highway 16, 90 km west of Jasper, 6 km west of Mt. Robson Visitor Centre, 12 km east of Tete Jaune Cache
Rating: easy, 300 m
Lighting: afternoon

Rearguard Falls is a spectacular, river-wide rapid on the Fraser River. These falls are the last barrier on the river that can be surmounted by chinook salmon as they return from the Pacific Ocean to spawn. The journey takes 10 weeks. Only one in 2500 eggs survives as an adult salmon that returns to the headwaters, four years after its birth. Look for the salmon here from mid-August to mid-September.

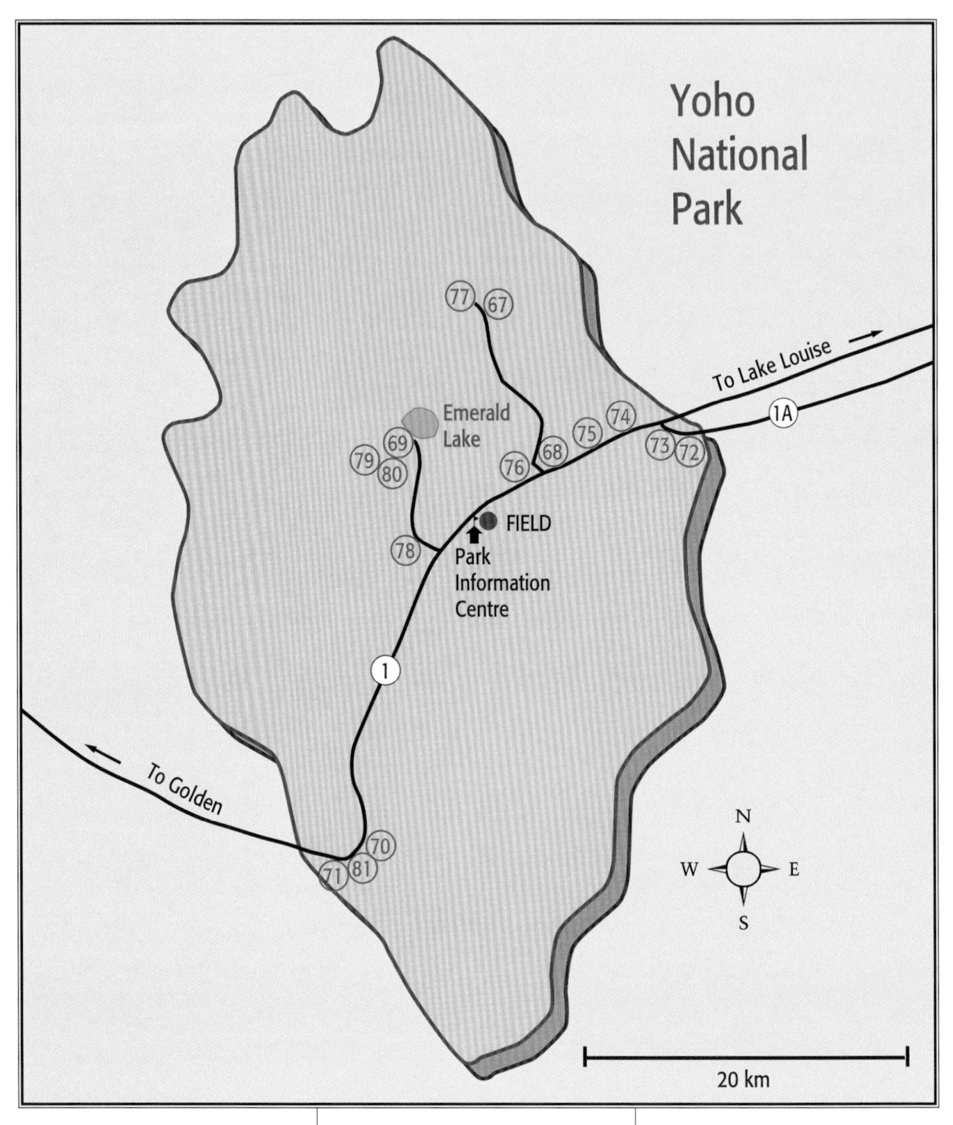

Yoho is a Cree expression of awe and wonder. Yoho National Park was established in 1886 as Canada's second national park. Though one of the smallest Rocky Mountain parks, Yoho's landscape has tremendous variety. The park's theme is "rockwalls and waterfalls."

The eastern part of the park features glaciers, icefields, lakes, deep valleys and the high peaks of the continental divide. The drier, warmer, southwestern area of the park features the broad valley of the Kicking Horse River, and abundant wildlife. Among the park's other attractions are a rich human history, and the soft-bodied fossils of the Burgess Shale.

Yoho National Park's theme is "rockwalls and waterfalls." Takakkaw Falls is the park's emblem. The falls are fed by meltwater from Daly Glacier on the Waputik Icefield. This view is from the Yoho Pass trail.

67. Takakkaw Falls

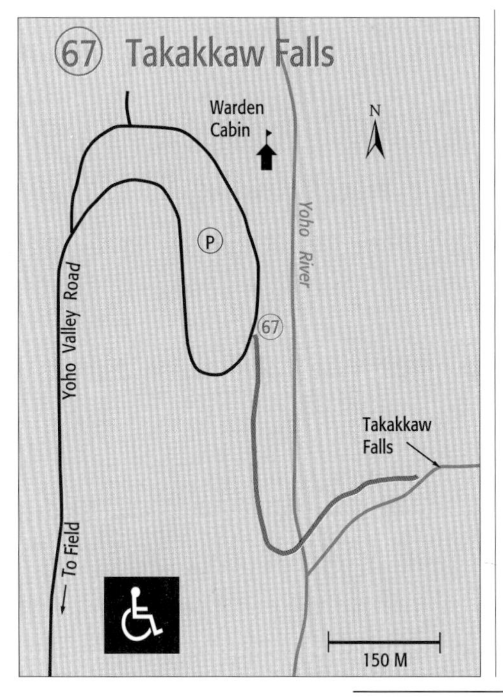

With a surveyed height of 254 m, Takakkaw (TAH-kuh-kah) Falls is one of the most impressive sites at roadside in the Rockies. More than any other walk or hike in Yoho, the paved trail to the base of the falls best displays the park's theme: "rock walls and water-falls."

The Yoho Valley Road is not plowed between

Route Information

Trailhead: Follow Highway 1 to the Yoho Valley Road, 3.7 km east of Field, 22.3 km west of Lake Louise. Leave trailers and large RVs at the trailer drop-off. Follow the Yoho Valley Road 14 km to its end at the Takakkaw Falls parking lot. Walk south to the trail.

Rating: easy, 600 m. Wheelchair accessible

Lighting: afternoon

October and June. Snow and avalanche debris frequently remain at roadside throughout the summer. At one point the road switchbacks sharply to by-pass a canyon. Vehicles more than 7 m long cannot turn in the tight radius, and must reverse along the middle switchback. Look for mountain goats, moose, bears, porcupines and hoary marmots during the drive.

Glacial ice of the Wisconsin Glaciation eroded the U-shaped trough of the Yoho Valley more deeply than its tributary valleys. So the mouths of these side valleys have been left hanging above the main valley floor. As a result, the Yoho is a valley of waterfalls. No less than eight cascades mark the locations where side valley streams plunge into the main valley. Today, the Yoho Glacier, architect of this valley, is but a remnant of its former self. It has receded north to the edge of the 40 km^2 Wapta Icefield. If you would like a good view of the glacier, walk north from Takakkaw Falls, 1 km to the Yoho Valley trailhead.

Takakkaw is a Cree expression that means "it is magnificent" or "it is wonderful." The name was given by William Cornelius Van Horne, President of the CPR. The first recorded visit to the falls was in 1897, by German explorer Jean Habel (AHH-bull). Habel's account of the wonders he saw in the Yoho Valley prompted Van Horne's visit to Takakkaw Falls, and was instrumental in the valley being added to the original 16 km^2 Mt. Stephen Reserve in 1901.

The amount of water in Takakkaw Falls varies with the season and with the time of day. It will be at maximum on hot afternoons in July and August. Boulders carried in the stream's flow can often be heard tumbling down the cliff. There have been occasions when boulders plugged the falls, temporarily stopping the flow. If you arrive in late afternoon or early evening, you may see a rainbow in the falls on sunny days.

In winter, the volume of the falls is reduced to a trickle. A broad shield of ice forms lower down, with a series of narrow pillars higher up. The frozen falls were first climbed in 1974, heralding the arrival of waterfall ice climbing as a significant winter activity in the Rockies.

For many years Takakkaw was touted as "the highest waterfall in Canada." However, measuring the height of waterfalls is an imprecise art. Surveyors argue as to whether the total drop, or only the highest cascade should be included. If you consider only the highest cascade, it is now generally agreed that Takakkaw Falls is third highest in Canada. First is Della Falls on Vancouver Island, followed by Hunlen Falls in Tweedsmuir Park, BC. Helmet Falls in Kootenay National Park is fourth highest.

The mountains immediately above Takakkaw Falls are part of the Waputik (WAH-poo-tick) Range. Waputik is a Stoney word that means "white goat." Mountain goats are frequently seen at the base of the cliffs near the falls.

What is Above Takakkaw Falls?

The landscape above Takakkaw Falls is one of the most spectacular in the Rockies. The water that feeds the falls empties from a marginal lake at the toe of Daly Glacier, one of five outlet valley glaciers of the 32 km^2 Waputik Icefield. This photograph shows a mountaineer's view of the lake, Daly Glacier and Mt. Balfour—the highest mountain in the area. You may obtain a distant view of this scene from the Yoho Pass and Iceline trails, on the opposite side of the Yoho Valley.

Locomotives such as Engine 314 were the workhorses on Yoho's "Big Hill" in the late 1800s. This particular locomotive demonstrated the dangers of operating on the mountain section of the CPR. In 1884, it ranaway and derailed coming down the Big Hill, killing one worker. Subsequently repaired, it exploded while going up the hill, killing two.

68. A Walk in the Past

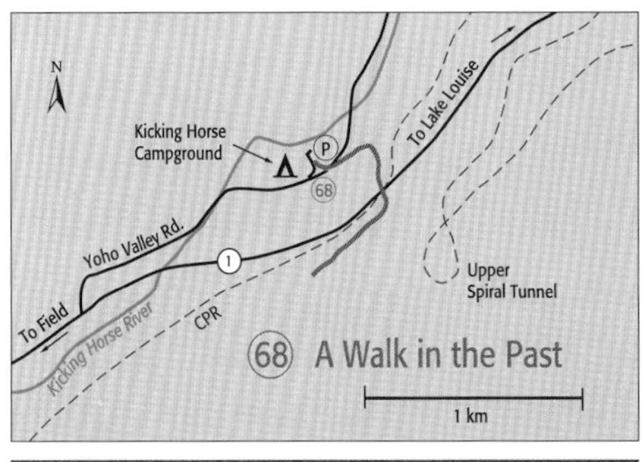

Route Information

Trailhead: Follow Highway 1 to the Yoho Valley Road, 3.7 km east of Field, 22.3 km west of Lake Louise. Follow this road 1 km to Kicking Horse Campground. Enter the campground and drive or walk to the interpretive theatre parking area. The trail begins at the display nearby.

Rating: moderate, 1.2 km. A brochure may be available at the trailhead.

Lighting: anytime

The six interpretive stops along A Walk in the Past explore the history of the Canadian Pacific Railway at the bottom of Yoho's notorious "Big Hill." You can also visit a stone bake oven in the campground 100 m west of the trailhead. The oven served a railway construction camp located here in 1884.

After crossing the Yoho Valley Road, the trail ascends toward the CPR main line through a damp, shaded forest that features western red cedar. Queen's cup, cow parsnip, horsetail, white geranium and a few devil's club grow in the undergrowth. The trail is following the route of a tote road, cleared in 1884 to pack supplies for railway construction.

The trail emerges at Cathedral Siding, one of three sidings on the Big Hill. There are deposits of coal soot and cinders beside the double set of railway tracks. These deposits accumulated during the 72 years of coal-fired railway operations that preceded the arrival of the diesel age in 1956. Please use caution crossing the tracks. Watch for oil and grease underfoot.

Across the tracks, the trail climbs to the original 1884 railway grade, abandoned when the Spiral Tunnels were completed. Part of this grade was subsequently used in The Kicking Horse Trail, the road completed from Lake Louise to Golden in 1927. A short climb leads to a gravel road and stop #5. You can see the upper portal of the Upper Spiral Tunnel directly upslope. The bark of some aspen trees here shows black claw marks left by bears. Turn west (right) and follow the road 200 m. Then veer southwest (left) on a trail to the last stop on this walk.

The CPR's contract with the government required that in no place could the grade of the line exceed 2.2 percent. The original grade surveyed above the steep ravine on the west side of Kicking Horse Pass was within this specification, but would have required tunnels and great expense to complete. The CPR was in trouble financially, and could not afford the time or the expense of constructing the line to specifications. Hence, General Manager, William Cornelius Van Horne, adopted a "temporary solution." He ran the rails straight down the hill in 1884. With a grade of 4.5 percent, this section of line soon became a railroader's horror.

Four, 150-tonne locomotives were required to haul a 14-car, 700-tonne freight train up the steep grade. The 14 km-trip took an hour. The wear and tear on equipment created tremendous, unforeseen expense. Scheduling, an imprecise art for a transcontinental railway in the late 1800s, was mayhem. Trains frequently stalled going uphill, and ran away coming down, sometimes derailing with loss of life. In addition, avalanches and washouts inundated the steep section of line.

A work crew clears the grade for the tote road on the Big Hill. The Walk in the Past Trail follows a section of the tote road.

Van Horne's temporary solution was finally rectified after 25 years, when the Spiral Tunnels were completed in 1909. These ingenious tunnels combine to add nearly 7 km to the length of the line, reducing the grade to 2.2 percent. Two locomotives could now do the work formerly done by four.

Construction of the tunnels cost 1.5 million dollars, required the efforts of 1000 workers and consumed 700,000 kg of dynamite. The crews completed the tunnels with remarkable accuracy. Each tunnel had two headings, that were excavated toward each other. Where the headings met, the error in alignment in each of the kilometre-long tunnels was less than 5 cm!

The End of the Line

During construction of the Spiral Tunnels, two narrow-gauge locomotives were used to haul away rubble. When the tunnels were completed, one of the locomotives was sold. The other was scavenged for parts and abandoned. Today, the last stop on this trail allows you to view the well-preserved remains of this locomotive, built by the Baldwin Works in Philadelphia, in 1885. The locomotive rests at the end of one of the three original spur lines on the Big Hill. Trains that lost control while descending the hill were diverted onto these spur lines, where, as one worker stated: "wrecks could take place without hindering traffic on the main line."

Emerald Lake is the largest lake in Yoho National Park. Pioneer guide and outfitter Tom Wilson discovered it in 1882. The massive limestone cliffs of The President and The Vice President are featured in this view from the lake's south shore.

69. Emerald Lake

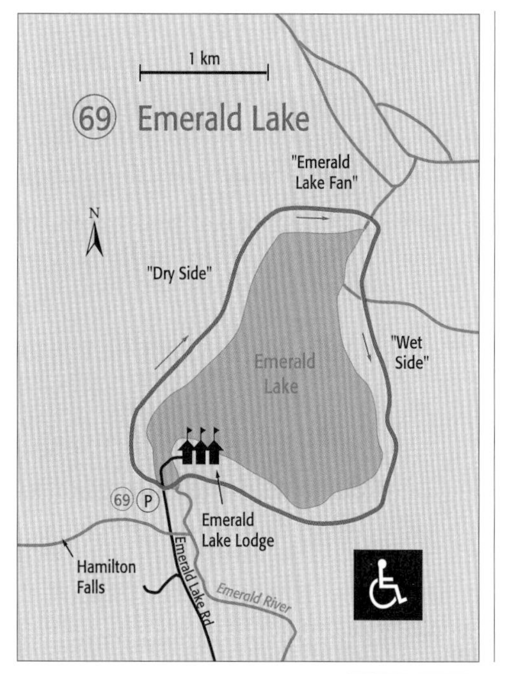

The Emerald Lake circuit is one of the most enjoyable nature walks in the Rockies. The first 500 m of trail is paved, and wheelchair access is possible for an additional 1.5 km. Walk the circuit in a clockwise direction, and keep right at all trail junctions.

With an area of 1.16 km^2, Emerald Lake is the

Route Information

Trailhead: Follow Highway 1 to the Emerald Lake Road, 2 km west of Field. Turn north and follow the road 8 km to its end at the Emerald Lake parking lot. The trailhead is adjacent to the bridge at the north end of the parking lot.

Rating: moderate, 4.8 km loop. Wheelchair accessible for 2 km

Lighting: anytime

largest lake in Yoho. It occupies a glacially-scoured hollow and has a maximum depth of 28 m. The outlet was dammed by an ice-age glacial moraine. The lake's surface is frozen from late November to early May. Rainbow trout, cutthroat trout, eastern brook trout, and slimy sculpin are the recorded fish species in Emerald Lake. Several pairs of common loon and a pair of osprey usually reside at the lake during summer. In spring and autumn, the waters are sometimes used as a stopover by Canada geese.

In your walk around Emerald Lake, you will notice marked transitions in the vegetation at trailside. The lake is frequently described as having a "dry side" and a "wet side." The "wet side" includes the east and south shores that lie at the base of shaded mountain slopes. The upper parts of these slopes hold snow most of the summer, and also receive a lot of rain. This cool, damp environment allows growth of a lush forest, more typical of wet coastal and interior forests in BC. The "dry side" of the lake (west shore) features a normal variety of vegetation for its location and elevation. It is only "dry" relative to the "wet side."

The Dry Side

The forest on the "dry side" contains subalpine fir, lodgepole pine and white spruce. This habitat suits Clark's nutcrackers, gray jays, red squirrels and American martens. In the undergrowth, Labrador tea and buffaloberry are the common shrubs. Pink wintergreen, arnica, dwarf dogwood and yellow columbine are attractive wildflowers. Five hundred metres from the trailhead, the trail crosses a large avalanche path, where snow avalanches from the upper slopes of Emerald Peak sweep the mountainside each winter and spring. The supple willows and alders that grow here are favourite foods of moose.

In the view southeast from the avalanche slope, the peak directly behind Emerald Lake Lodge is Mt. Burgess. A similar view was featured on the Canadian ten dollar bill from 1954 to 1971. To the east (left) of Mt. Burgess is Mt. Field. Farther east (left) is Wapta Mountain. It was on the ridge that connects Mt. Field and Wapta Mountain that Charles Walcott of the Smithsonian Institution discovered the 530 million-year-old soft bodied fossils of the Burgess Shale in 1909.

Beyond the avalanche path, the character of the forest changes frequently. There are drier areas of lodgepole pine and Douglas fir, and damper places that feature a few western yew trees and western red cedar.

The Emerald Fan

After passing some springs in the lake bottom and a horse-hiker barrier, the trail swings east (right) onto an alluvial fan, a landform created from rubble carried by glacial melt streams. Because of rocky soils, cold air drainage, the ever-changing courses of the streams, and the high water table under the gravels, it is difficult for vegetation to grow on the alluvial fan. Trees include lodgepole pine, white birch and gnarled white spruce. Juniper and willows grow beneath them. The trees are exposed to the full brunt of winds from across the lake. Some of the trees near the

Yellow Lady's Slipper

Easily recognized, the orchid, yellow lady's slipper, is one of the most beautiful wildflowers in the Rockies. The pouch-like slipper hangs slightly from a stem that is 20 cm to 30 cm in height. The interior of the pouch features purple highlights. This flower grows in damp areas of shaded woods, and occasionally on open gravels close to water, as on the Emerald Lake alluvial fan. It blooms mid-June to mid-July.

Although yellow lady's slipper can be locally common, picking the flower frequently kills the plant. Please leave this beautiful flower for others to enjoy.

lakeshore "flag" the prevailing southwest wind, by growing branches only on their northeast sides.

In summer, the alluvial fan can be transformed from ice box to furnace. Intense light and heat result when sunlight reflects off the rocks. Many of the mat-like plants are pale on the undersides of their leaves, in order to reflect the light and heat.

As harsh as the environment on the alluvial fan sounds, nature decorates it with many wildflowers and flowering shrubs. Mats of yellow mountain avens, bearberry and twinflower are found in the drier areas. The wetter areas support cotton grass sedge meadows, blue-eyed grass, and a variety of orchids, including: yellow lady's slipper, tall white bog orchid and hooded lady's tresses. White camas and Indian paintbrush are common at trailside.

Looking west across the lake from the alluvial fan, the horn mountain shapes of the Van Horne Range are prominent. These mountains were named for William Cornelius Van Horne, vice-president and general manager of the CPR during its construction. The highest peak visible is Mt. King, with a small niche glacier on its north flank. Farther south (left), the other glaciated peak is Mt. Vaux (VOX) in the Ottertail Range.

The bridge on the east side of the fan crosses one of the main inlets to the lake. This stream deposits fine sediments, building a delta. Emerald Lake is one of a few places in the Rockies where a delta and an alluvial fan are found together. Pondweed, horsetail and sedges grow here, providing cover for waterfowl and food for moose. Wheelchairs cannot proceed beyond this point.

The Wet Side

Across the bridge, the forest immediately becomes more dense. Welcome to the wet side of the lake. Here you find forest more typical of interior rainforests than the Rockies. Shrub-like western red cedar are interspersed among ancient white spruce, subalpine fir, and a few western hemlock and Douglas fir. Intense forest fires have not occurred on this side of the lake for three hundred years, allowing this "old-growth" forest to develop. In the undergrowth, green alder, ferns, thimbleberry, devil's club, horsetails, queen's cup and foam flower are common. After you pass the Burgess Pass junction, scan the lakeshore ahead for moose. Please use caution on the boardwalks. The wood is often slippery.

Emerald Lake Lodge

The Emerald Lake circuit finishes with a short climb to the crest of the moraine that dams the lake. This pile of glacial rubble was deposited at the end of the Wisconsin Glaciation, 11,000 years ago. Emerald Lake Lodge has been constructed on top of this moraine. The main lodge building includes part of the original chalet constructed by the CPR in 1902. The lodge was completely redeveloped in 1985–86.

To reach the parking lot, walk through the lodge grounds to the bridge at the lake's outlet. To the north, are the massive, glacier-capped cliffs of The Vice President (named for the vice-president of the CPR). To the south, Mt. Burgess is reflected in the lagoon that has formed behind the moraine. Cliff swallows provide constant aerial entertainment, and fish rise occasionally below. In the evening, the bridge is a good place to watch the rapid comings and goings of little brown bats. These winged mammals swoop over the lake, feeding on insects. During daytime, they congregate under the eaves of the lodge.

Devil's Club

Ask any mountaineer to name the plant with the worst reputation in British Columbia. "Devil's club" will invariably be the answer. Growing in the damp undergrowth of cedar rainforests, this tall (up to 3 m) shrub has a natural armour capable of inflicting great pain: the succulent stem is covered in sharp spines that cause inflammation of the skin. The huge, maple-like leaves are also fringed underneath with spines. Devil's club adds insult to injury. Brush against it after a rain, and it will give you a good soaking, too. Mountaineers in the Rockies are fortunate this plant grows only in isolated, low elevation wet belts, principally on the western slopes.

Despite its poor reputation, devil's club in fruit is beautiful to behold. Its white flowers yield shiny red berries, that sit upright atop the stem. Look, but don't touch!

Most of the Leanchoil Hoodoos still contain capstones. Some geologists consider these to be the finest examples of till hoodoos in the world.

70. Leanchoil Hoodoos

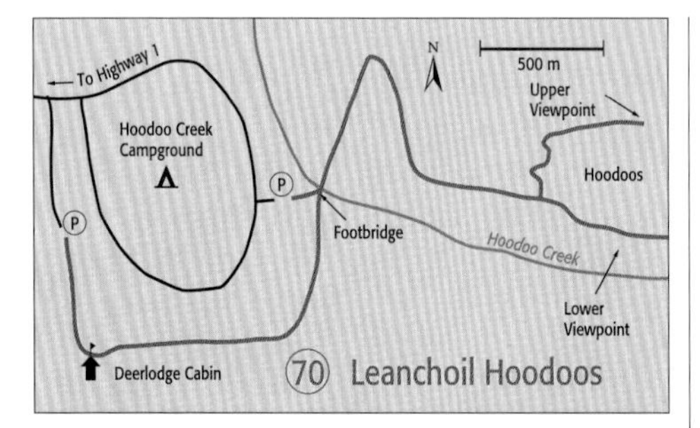

Route Information

Trailhead: Follow Highway 1 to Hoodoo Creek Campground, 22.6 km west of Field. Turn east (left) and follow the campground road 600 m to a junction. Turn west (right) on a gravel road, and follow this 400 m to the Deerlodge-Hoodoos trailhead. When the campground is closed (September to June), you may have to park at the gate adjacent to Highway 1, and walk to the trailhead.

Rating: harder, 3.1 km

Lighting: anytime

There are two starting points for the hike to the Leanchoil (lee-ANN-coil) Hoodoos. The route from Deerlodge trailhead offers an opportunity for a quick side trip to Deerlodge cabin, the first warden patrol cabin built in Yoho. Beyond the cabin, the trail circles to the rear of the campground through a damp forest of lodgepole pine and white spruce. The trail emerges after 1.5 km at a footbridge across Hoodoo Creek. If you are staying in the campground, you may choose to begin the hike here.

It is only 1.6 km from the Hoodoo Creek bridge to the upper viewpoint at the hoodoos. However, the trail gains 450 m of elevation in that distance. With an average grade of roughly 30 percent, this is by far the steepest hike in this book. Please keep to the trail and avoid shortcutting the corners.

There is no drinking water on the trail.

From the footbridge the initial climb is on a dry, south-facing sideslope at the mouth of the creek. This is perfect soil and exposure for Douglas fir. Large, fire-scarred specimens of this tree are prominent at trailside. Soon the trail swings into the Hoodoo Creek valley. In places it is exposed to a steep drop. Use caution.

The cool, moist air channelled along the creek produces a marked transition in the forest about a kilometre from the footbridge. The Douglas firs give way to subalpine fir, white spruce and lodgepole pine. Feathermosses cover the forest floor, along with the wildflowers dwarf dogwood and queen's cup. Calypso orchids bloom here in June.

At the viewpoint trail junction, those who are tired may want to take the right fork to the lower viewpoint. For the best view, take the left fork to the upper viewpoint. This section of trail is the steepest, but the view down onto the hoodoos is worth the effort.

Chancellor Peak looms to the south of Hoodoo Creek. Its summit towers 2150 m above the highway.

The Leanchoil Hoodoos have been eroded by wind and water from a blanket of glacial rubble called a kame terrace. The terrace was deposited along the flank of the Kicking Horse Valley during the Wisconsin Glaciation. Most of these hoodoos are topped by capstones that have protected the columns from erosion, while the surrounding till has weathered away. A small bench above the hoodoos marks the end of trail. The lofty mountain to the east is Chancellor Peak.

Leanchoil is a Scottish name connected with the construction of the Canadian Pacific Railway. The mother of Donald Smith, a CPR stockholder and financier, lived in a Scottish manor named Leth-na-Coyle. The name was applied to a nearby railway siding in 1884.

Tree Lichens

The branches of many trees in the damp forest along Hoodoo Creek are covered in hair-like growths, commonly called "Spanish moss" or "old man's beard." These growths are not moss, they are tree lichens. Lichens are a sophisticated vegetation, in which a fungus and an algae coexist. The fungus provides shelter for the algae, and the algae produces food for both.

Some of the more common tree lichens are the greenish *Alectoria* and *Usnea* species (photo), the black *Bryoria* species, and the brilliant green wolf lichen. Elsewhere in the Rockies, these plants are a staple food for woodland (mountain) caribou.

At Wapta Falls, the Kicking Horse River plunges over a 30 m ledge that spans the width of the river. At high water, the roar of the falls is audible from the trailhead, more than 2 km distant.

71. Wapta Falls

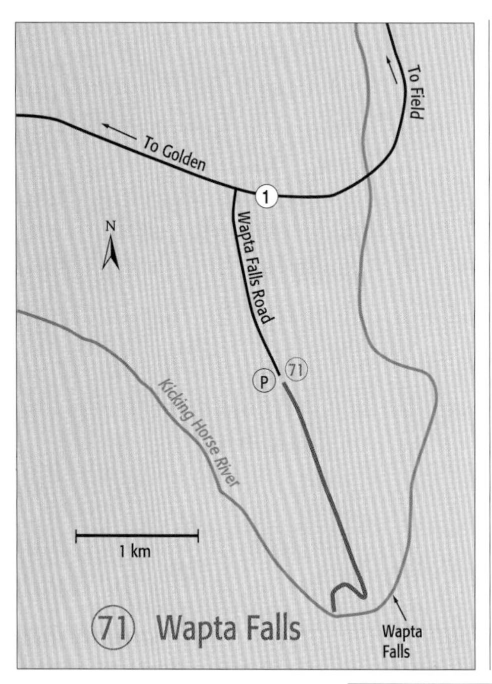

The Wapta Falls trail is an ideal family outing. It travels through forest to the waterfall, a 30 m–high ledge that spans the Kicking Horse River.

The initial kilometre of trail is along the edge of a clearing originally intended for a road to the falls. The open montane forest here is typical of

Route Information

Trailhead: Follow Highway 1, 24.7 km west of Field. Turn south (left) onto the Wapta Falls Road. Follow this road 1.6 km to the trailhead. There are plans to close the Wapta Falls Road, in which case you will have to walk or bike the 1.6 km to the trailhead.

Rating: harder, 2.4 km

Lighting: anytime

the drier, low elevations in southwestern Yoho National Park. White spruce, lodgepole pine, Douglas fir, cottonwood poplar, trembling aspen and white birch are the trees. Wood lilies, pink wintergreen, bearberry and juniper are common in the undergrowth. Black bear, wolf, ruffed grouse and white-tailed deer are seen by fortunate visitors.

As the trail narrows, it enters a forest that is more dense. A short climb leads to the upper viewpoint, above the falls. Please keep within the fence. Just upstream is the confluence of the Beaverfoot River and the Kicking Horse River. For a closer view of the falls, continue downhill. A short spur trail branches left to the mid-level viewpoint which offers the most pleasing prospect of the falls. Return to the main trail and continue downhill another 350 m to a gravel beach on the riverbank. At low water, you can walk towards the falls. Outcrops in the river indicate former locations of the falls.

In August 1858, James Hector's party from the Palliser Expedition explored the central Rockies. Led by two Iroquois guides, Nimrod and Erasmus, the party reached the confluence of the Beaverfoot River and Kicking Horse Rivers, above Wapta Falls. While struggling with his horse, Hector was kicked in the chest by the horse and rendered unconscious. His men assumed him dead, and were preparing to bury him, when to their mutual surprise, Hector revived. Although injured and in great pain, Hector was on his horse again the next day, as the party headed east toward the continental divide. In his journal Hector remarked that his men now called the river along which they travelled "The Kicking Horse." It had previously been known by the Stoney name Wapta, which means "river."

The Kicking Horse is the largest river in Yoho National Park, and drains virtually the entire park area of 1313 sq km. At Wapta Falls, the peak volume has been measured at 255 cubic metres per second. The Kicking Horse was designated a Canadian Heritage River in 1989.

Wapta Falls are being cut through an outcrop of the 500-million-year-old shale of the McKay (muck-EYE) formation. Some glaciologists speculate that before the Wisconsin Glaciation, the Kicking Horse River flowed south into what is now Kootenay National Park. When the ice age ended, a moraine blocked the southerly course of the river, diverting it west where it found a weakness in the shale and created the falls. Captured by a lower valley, the Kicking Horse River then eroded a canyon northwest to the Columbia River near Golden.

Bearberry

Bearberry is an evergreen shrub at montane elevations, and is one of the most common plants in the ground cover. It grows as a trailing vine, and forms mats on dry slopes. The delicate, urn-shaped flowers bloom in early summer. They are white with pink edging, and hang downward from the stem. Glossy red berries replace the flowers by August. As the plant's name suggests, these berries are a favourite food of black bears. However, the bears prefer to eat the berries in spring, after they have spent a winter on the vine.

Bearberry is also known as kinnikinnik (KINNY-kin-ick), Algonquin for "a mixture that is smoked." Natives fashioned a primitive tobacco from its dried leaves, fruits and bark. Bearberry is a member of the heath family of plants, that includes blueberries and mountain heather. There are three bearberry species in the Rockies, two of which occur at higher elevations. One of the higher-growing species is not evergreen. Its leaves turn bright red in late August, and then fall off the plant.

Other Walks and Easy Hikes in Yoho National Park

72. The Great Divide

Trailhead: Highway 1A, 3 km east of its junction with Highway 1 in Yoho, 10.7 km west of Lake Louise Village
Rating: viewpoint. Wheelchair accessible
Lighting: anytime

The Great Divide in Kicking Horse Pass marks the point where Divide Creek branches. One fork flows east into Alberta, and the other flows west into BC. This tiny creek sends waters to both the Atlantic Ocean and Pacific Ocean, and forms the boundary between two provinces and two national parks. The dividing creek is an artificial feature. Its bed has been reinforced with concrete and boulders.

Interpretive displays highlight the differences between the eastern slopes and western slopes of the Rockies, and describe the activities of the Interprovincial Boundary Survey from 1913 to1925. The Great Divide is a good place for train buffs. The CPR main line is a few metres away. A cairn adjacent to the railway tracks commemorates explorer James Hector, who discovered Kicking Horse Pass in 1858.

73. Ross Lake

Trailhead: Highway 1A, 2 km east of its junction with Highway 1, 1 km west of The Great Divide, 11.7 km west of Lake Louise Village. Park on the north side of the road.
Rating: moderate, 1.2 km
Lighting: afternoon

Ross Lake is a glacial tarn, scoured from the bedrock by a glacier that once flowed from the hanging valley above. The lake is reached by a walk through subalpine forest, following the route of an old logging road. The picturesque lake is backed by 400 m-high limestone cliffs that are home to a band of mountain goats. Ross Lake was named for James Ross, a CPR construction boss.

Please see map on page 98

74. Sherbrooke Lake

Trailhead: Wapta Lake picnic area on the north side of Highway 1, 11 km east of Field, 15 km west of Lake Louise Village
Rating: harder, 2.8 km
Lighting: morning

The Sherbrooke Lake trail gains 190 m of elevation through subalpine forest to the shores of a glacial lake nestled between Mt. Ogden and Paget Peak. You may see many wildflowers along the trail, including violets and several species of orchids. Near the lake, there are many downed trees that toppled during a severe thunderstorm in 1984. Mt. Niles is the prominent peak beyond the head of the lake. Scan the cliffs for mountain goats, and look for moose, elk and bears on the avalanche slopes across the lake.

75. Lower Spiral Tunnel Viewpoint

Trailhead: North side of Highway 1, 7.4 km east of Field, 18.6 km west of Lake Louise Village
Rating: viewpoint. Wheelchair accessible
Lighting: morning and afternoon

The original line of the CPR descended the Big Hill from Wapta Lake to Field directly—a grade of 4.5 percent. Wrecks occurred when trains ran away. In 1909, the two Spiral Tunnels were completed, adding 7 km to the length of the line, and reducing the grade to 2.2 percent. One thousand workers and 700,000 tonnes of dynamite were required in their construction. The Lower Spiral Tunnel in Mt. Ogden is visible from this viewpoint. Approximately 30 trains a day pass through the tunnel, so have patience if you want to see a train loop over itself while negotiating this portion of the Big Hill. The Yoho Valley is visible to the north.

76. Centennial Trail

Trailhead: Follow Highway 1 to the Yoho Valley Road, 3.7 km east of Field, 22.3 km west of Lake Louise. Follow this road to the first bridge over the Kicking Horse River (100 m west of Kick-

ing Horse Campground). The trail begins on the north side of the road, west of the bridge, and follows the river upstream.
Rating: easy, 2.5 km loop
Lighting: anytime

The Centennial Trail was constructed to commemorate the national parks centennial in 1985. It follows the Kicking Horse River, and provides excellent views across the valley to Cathedral Crags and the north glacier on Mt. Stephen, particularly at sunset. The riverbank features diverse vegetation, including many wildflowers.

A few hundred metres from the trailhead, the trail crosses a prominent avalanche slope on Mt. Field. In the spring of 1989, an avalanche from this slope swept across the river, damaging some facilities in the campground. Look for mountain goats on the cliffs above.

The cliffs of Mt. Field to the north, and Mt. Stephen across the valley, feature mine portals, used during the heyday of the Monarch Mine and Kicking Horse Mine. Lead, silver and zinc were the principal minerals sought. Mining ended in 1952.

Where the trail rejoins the Yoho Valley Road, turn south (right), cross the bridge, leave the road and follow the gravel path into the campground.

77. Laughing Falls

Trailhead: Follow Highway 1 to the Yoho Valley Road, 3.7 km east of Field, 22.3 km west of Lake Louise. Leave trailers and large recreational vehicles at the trailer drop-off. Follow this road 14 km to its end at the Takakkaw Falls parking lot. Walk north through the Takakkaw Falls campground to the Yoho Valley trailhead.
Rating: harder, 4.7 km
Lighting: morning

The original carriage road in the Yoho Valley was completed in 1910, and led beyond Takakkaw Falls. Hence the first section of this trail, across alluvial fan and through subalpine forest, is road width. There is a good, distant view of Yoho Glacier from the trailhead. Short sidetrips at km 2.6 lead east (right) to views of Angel's Staircase Falls, and southwest (left) to Point Lace Falls. The trail then narrows and climbs steeply. At km 4, a short side trail leads west (left) to Duchesnay Lake. You may see moose here. The trail crosses the Little Yoho River on a bridge just downstream from Laughing Falls. The falls are reached by walking a short distance west along the north bank of the Little Yoho River. On sunny days, you may see a rainbow in the spray in early morning.

Natural Bridge

78. Natural Bridge

Trailhead: Follow Highway 1 to the Emerald Lake Road, 2 km west of Field. Turn north (right), and follow the road 1.5 km. Turn west (left) into the paved parking area.
Rating: viewpoint. Wheelchair accessible
Lighting: afternoon

Natural Bridge marks the point where the Kicking Horse River encounters a relatively resistant rock outcrop in an area of otherwise weak shales. The rock has been tipped vertically, offering more resistance to the river. Formerly, the river cascaded over the lip of rock as a waterfall. But over time it has eroded downward into a crack behind the lip, creating the dogleg bridge. At high water, the Kicking Horse River flows completely over the bridge.

79. Hamilton Falls

Trailhead: Follow Highway 1 to the Emerald Lake Road, 2 km west of Field. Turn north (right), and follow the road 8 km to its end at the Emerald Lake parking lot. The trailhead is at the southwest corner of the parking lot. (See map, page 103)
Rating: easy, 800 m
Lighting: morning

Hamilton Falls cascade over a limestone cliff at the shaded base of Mt. Carnarvon. The trail features vegetation normally found in interior rainforests, including western red cedar. Bunchberry, thimbleberry, foam plant, queen's cup and ferns dominate the undergrowth. Part of the old water collection system for Emerald Lake Lodge is visible at the base of the falls.

Laughing Falls

80. Emerald Basin

Trailhead: Follow Highway 1 to the Emerald Lake Road, 2 km west of Field. Turn north (right), and follow the road 8 km to its end at the Emerald Lake parking lot. The trailhead is adjacent the bridge, at the north end of the parking lot.
Rating: harder, 4.3 km
Lighting: morning and afternoon

Emerald Basin is a glacial valley north of Emerald Lake, hemmed by the summits of the President Range. The first 1.4 km of this trail follows the Emerald Lake trail. The trail then veers north (left) for 600 m across the alluvial fan, and then northwest (left) into the trees. After a steep climb, the trail levels in a pocket of old-growth forest, that features western red cedar, western hemlock and Douglas fir. Beyond this, the trail emerges into the lush growth of an avalanche slope on the flanks of Emerald Peak. As the vegetation thins, the trail becomes indistinct. Ahead is a hanging glacier, notched in the sheer limestone cliffs of The President and The Vice President. To the south, you can see Mt. Burgess and the summit of Mt. Stephen.

81. Deerlodge

Trailhead: Follow Highway 1 to Hoodoo Creek Campground, 22.6 km west of Field. Turn east (left) and follow the campground road 600 m to a junction. Turn west (right) on a gravel road, and follow this 400 m to the Deerlodge-Hoodoos trailhead. When the campground is closed (September to June), you may have to park at the gate adjacent to Highway 1, and walk to the trailhead.
Rating: easy, 500 m
Lighting: anytime

Constructed in 1904, Deerlodge was the first warden patrol cabin in Yoho. Warden John Tocher and his wife May lived in the cabin from 1920 to 1926, when the railway was the only connection to the outside world. Tocher brought the cookstove to the cabin by slinging it between two packhorses, and fording the Kicking Horse River. The cabin was restored in 1961, and there are plans to restore it again. You may see beaver, moose, black bear and great blue heron in the area.

Kootenay National Park

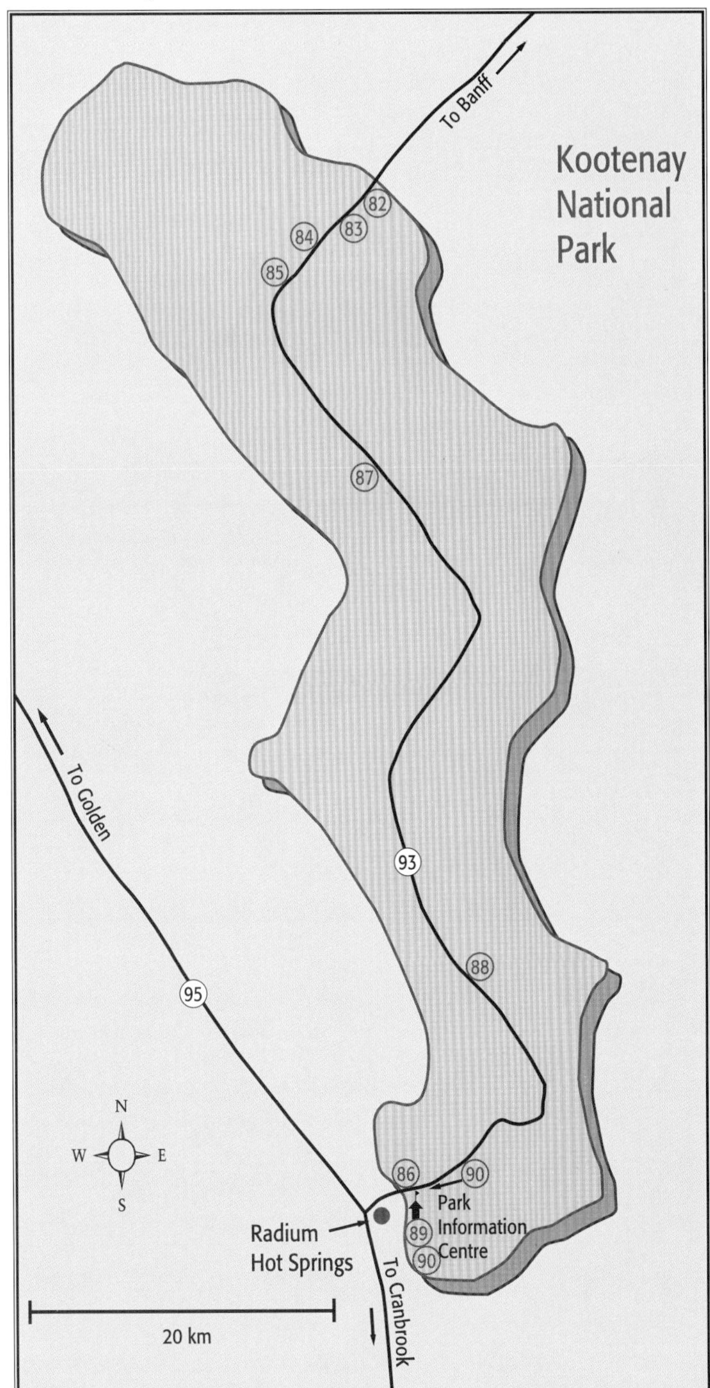

Kootenay National Park was established in 1920. British Columbia provided the necessary land, and in return the Canadian government constructed the Kootenay Parkway to connect Banff and the Columbia Valley. It was the first highway completed across the Rockies. Kootenay is a native word that means "people from beyond the hills." The name has various spellings. Anthropologists now prefer Kutenai.

The Walks and Easy Hikes in Kootenay National Park visit a burnt forest, a dolomite canyon, an alpine valley glacier, and the outlets of three mineral springs. The Juniper Trail, in the southwestern corner of the park, introduces you to the drier, warmer climate of the Columbia Valley. There are excellent opportunities to see wildlife on these trails: elk, deer, moose, bears, mountain goats and bighorn sheep.

The blackened stumps and silver spars in Vermilion Pass are the remains of a subalpine forest that burned in 1968. The Fireweed Trail makes a short loop through the burn, where a new forest is growing from the remains of the old.

82. Fireweed Trail

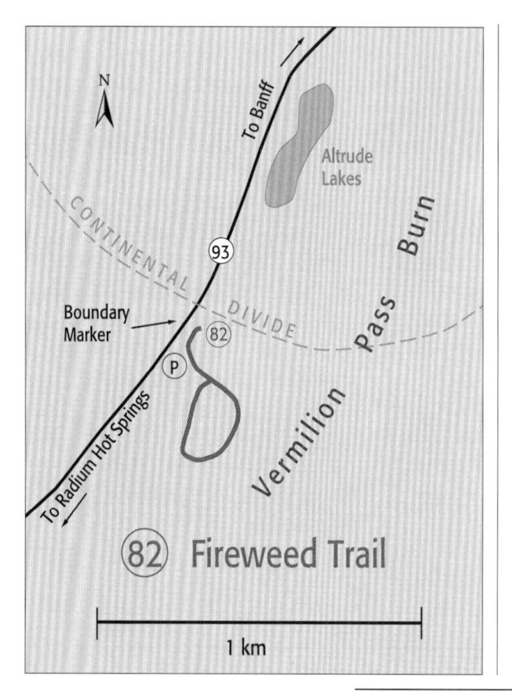

The Fireweed Trail loops through the Vermilion Pass Burn, providing a close-up view of the rebirth of a forest.

The summer of 1968 was hot and dry across most of western Canada. On the afternoon of July 8, the temperatures in Banff and Kootenay climbed to 30°C, and winds were strong. At 4:30 pm, a bolt of lightning struck the slopes of Mt. Whymper, just west of Vermilion Pass. Fanned by

Route Information

Trailhead: South side of the Kootenay Parkway (Highway 93 South) at the continental divide, 10.2 km west of Castle Junction, 94.5 km east of the junction with Highway 95

Rating: easy, 1 km loop

Lighting: anytime

the winds, the lightning spark kindled quickly. In three minutes, the mountainside was in flame. The Vermilion Pass Burn had begun.

Sixty-five firefighters were on the fireline within six hours, but the forest fire burned out of control for three days. On July 12 the weather began to cool. The following day, rain came to the firefighters' aid, and by July 18 the fire was out. The Vermilion Pass Burn consumed 26.3 km^2 of subalpine forest, forced closure of the Kootenay Parkway, and cost $160,000 to fight. It sounds like a disaster, but this fire was part of a natural and essential process of succession—the regeneration of the forest.

Forest fires kill diseased tree stands, reduce competition for moisture and sunlight, create stable seed beds by burning off loose soil layers, trigger the mass release of seeds, return minerals to the soil, and create habitat for wildlife. They enhance the mosaic of habitats in an ecosystem, and promote biodiversity.

However, not all forested areas burn with regularity. Old-growth forests develop in areas that escape fire for centuries. These forests become refuges for species that do not depend on fire to propagate their seeds, or create habitat.

The Vermilion Pass Burn consumed a mature forest of Engelmann spruce and subalpine fir, with scattered lodgepole pine. The resin-sealed cones of the lodgepoles were cracked open by the blaze, resulting in a mass seeding of this species. The lodgepole saplings quickly outgrew the less densely seeded spruce and fir, to become the most common tree in the first stage of the fire succession forest.

By the year 2030, most of these lodgepole pines will be past their prime. Windfall and disease will take their toll. The longer-lived Engelmann spruce and subalpine fir will then succeed the lodgepoles to again become the dominant trees. If the spruce and fir seed a second generation of trees before another fire, the area will be described as a climax forest.

Studies of the Vermilion Pass Burn have yielded some interesting facts that illustrate the beneficial effects of forest fires. Within four years of the burn, there were nearly twice as many species of vegetation within the burned area, as in the adjacent unburned area. The number of bird and wildlife species using the burned area also increased, relative to before the fire.

Avalanche terrain in Vermilion Pass has doubled in area since the burn, due to the removal of large tree stands that formerly prevented the snow from sliding. Three new slidepaths now cross the Kootenay Parkway.

Common Fireweed

Among the silvery skeletons of the burned forest, common fireweed is sure to catch your eye. At home on disturbed ground, this plant often grows in thickets. Each plant features a multitude of pink flowers, atop a stem that may reach 2 m in height. The lowest flowers open first, and it is usual for flowers, buds and purple seed pods to be present on the same plant in late summer. The flowers shed a thick, yellow pollen in late July. Common fireweed is the territorial emblem of the Yukon.

Mountain fireweed (river beauty) is a smaller plant that grows at higher elevations and along glacial melt streams.

The Stanley Glacier trail leads through the Vermilion Pass Burn into a glacial hanging valley. Highlights of the trail include an array of wildflowers, an 800 m-high limestone cliff, and views of Stanley Glacier.

83. Stanley Glacier

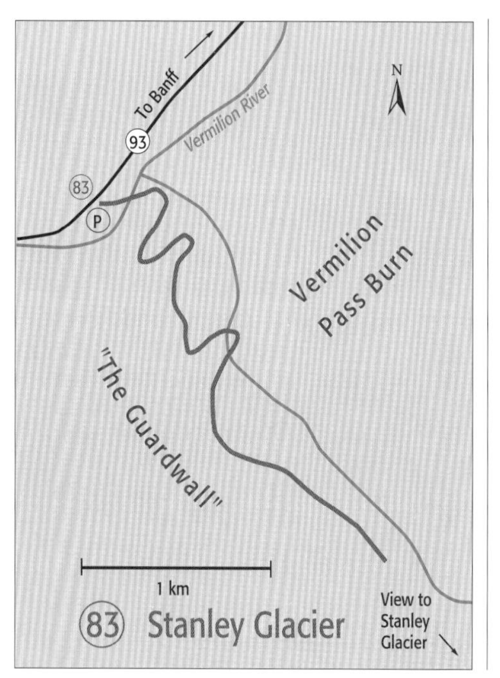

The Stanley Glacier trail leads into a spectacular glacial valley, and offers close-up views of three major processes that have shaped the environment: fire, avalanches, and glaciation. The trail is initially steep, gaining 220 m of elevation in the first 2.4 km.

Leaving the parking lot, the trail crosses the Vermilion River and climbs into the Vermilion Pass Burn. Most of the living trees at trailside are lodgepole pines that began growth after this 1968

Route Information

Trailhead: South side of the Kootenay Parkway (Highway 93 South), 13.4 km west of Castle Junction, 91.5 km east of the junction with Highway 95
Rating: harder, 4.2 km
Lighting: anytime

fire. After completing the climb, the trail descends slightly to a footbridge across Stanley Creek. The descent is from the crest of a terminal moraine, pushed up by Stanley Glacier when it extended this far down the valley.

The next 1.8 km of trail is a delight in mid-summer. In the aftermath of the forest fire, with the shading canopy of trees removed, a variety of sun-loving wildflowers has invaded the area. Camas, fireweed, fleabane, pink wintergreen, arnica, yellow columbine, ragwort and vibrantly coloured Indian paintbrush are the most common species. Damp areas feature bog orchids and gentians.

At one point, the trail separates burned from unburned forest. On your right are mature Engelmann spruce, on the left are blackened timbers and stumps. You will not see as many young pines here as you saw near the trailhead. Regeneration of trees in this part of the burn is progressing slowly, because cold air that drains from Stanley Glacier collects here, shortening the growing season.

The colossal, 800 m-high limestone cliff on the southwest side of the valley is known as the Guardwall. The dark streaks on the cliff are water seeps and lichen. In winter, the seeps freeze into sheets of ice and become a destination for waterfall ice climbers. The northeast side of the valley features steep avalanche paths, swept annually by snow slides. At trailside are the sun-bleached remains of trees uprooted by the sliding snow and by the winds it generates.

A sign on a rocky knoll marks the end of maintained trail. This is a good place to view Stanley Glacier. Several lobes of the glacier terminate at the cliff edge. You may hear the creaking and groaning of the ice as it creeps forward, and if fortunate, witness an ice avalanche. Meltwater that cascades over the cliffs is sometimes caught in updrafts, creating waterfalls that seem to disappear in mid-air.

The upper valley toward the glacier is a barren world of boulders and scree. It is home to mountain goat, hoary marmot, pika and white-tailed ptarmigan. Stanley Peak was first climbed in 1901, by a party that included Edward Whymper, of Matterhorn fame. Lord Frederick Stanley was the 6th Governor General of Canada. His name also adorns North American ice hockey's ultimate prize, the Stanley Cup.

White-tailed ptarmigan

U-Shaped Valley

The original valleys in the Rockies were V-shaped, and were the products of erosion by water. When glacial ice advanced into these valleys, it undercut the adjoining mountainsides, causing them to collapse. This created widened, U-shaped valleys known as troughs. You can see the U-shape of the Stanley Glacier valley in the view north from the end of the trail.

The interpretive trail at Marble Canyon follows the canyon created by a retreating waterfall, and crosses Tokumm Creek seven times on sturdy bridges. The 600 m-long canyon has a maximum depth of 39 m.

84. Marble Canyon

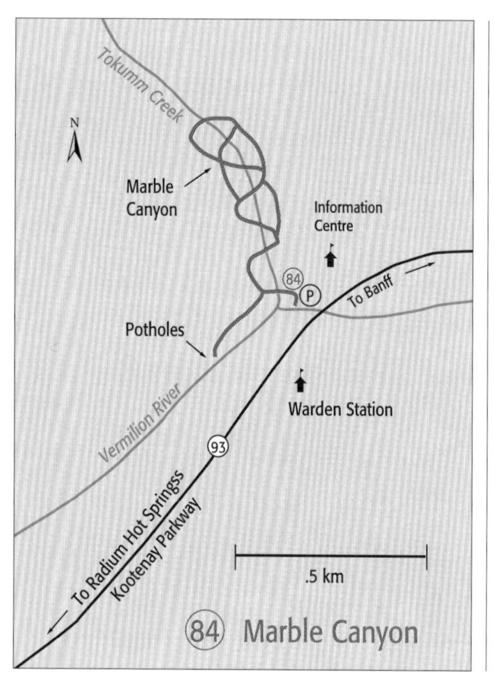

It has been said that in the Rockies, "the sound of rushing water is the sound of a canyon growing." When you walk the Marble Canyon interpretive trail, you witness the truth in this statement. The trail follows the route of a "migrating" waterfall, the principal agent in the canyon's creation.

As with most canyons in the Rockies, Marble Canyon is at the mouth of a hanging valley—in this case, where Tokumm Creek joins the Vermil-

Route Information

Trailhead: Northwest side of the Kootenay Parkway (Highway 93 South), 17.2 km west of Castle Junction, 88 km east of the junction with Highway 95
Rating: easy, 800 m
Lighting: late morning and early afternoon

ion River. (Tokumm is a native word that means "red fox.") At the first bridge across Tokumm Creek, you will be greeted by a blast of cold air—a potent illustration of the canyon's effect on local climate. The temperature on the bridge can be 10°C colder than on the trail 20 m away. Glaciers 20 km up the valley create a cold air flow, that is further cooled in the shaded depths of the canyon.

Twinflower

The trail crosses the canyon seven times on sturdy bridges. At the second bridge, you can see a natural arch—a lip of rock that resisted erosion. This arch marks the waterfall's location, 9000 years ago. Please don't attempt to cross it. People have died from falls at this spot. The large sedimentary boulder near the fifth bridge is a glacial erratic, deposited here when the glacier that carved Tokumm Creek valley receded. Cracks in its surface have filled with soil, and a tree has taken root. Spray from the canyon saturates the thin soils on the canyon rim. This causes the soils to creep toward the abyss. Only mosses, lichens and plants with mat-like characteristics can anchor these soils and grow here.

Marble Canyon's gradual, northwestward curve resulted from the water enlarging a crack system in the bedrock. The canyon's deepest point is the 39 m-drop beneath the seventh bridge, the present location of the waterfall. The principal rock types in the canyon are limestone, and the more resistant dolomite. Dolomite will naturally become the lip of the waterfall in this canyon, resisting the water's flow while the surrounding limestone is more easily eroded. The constant pounding at the base of the waterfall creates a plunge pool, which enlarges over time and begins to undercut the lip of the waterfall above. Eventually, gravity, the shattering effects of frost, and the sheer hydraulic force of the water prevail. The hanging, dolomite lip of the waterfall collapses into the plunge pool, and the brink moves a few metres upstream. In this manner Marble Canyon's waterfall has "migrated" more than 600 m upstream in 11,000 years.

Is It Marble?

Some people consider the name "Marble Canyon" a misnomer, claiming that there is no marble in the canyon. By strict geological definition, this is correct. True marble is limestone in which the carbonates have been recrystalized by heat or by pressure. However, in common use, "marble" means any sedimentary rock that can be polished. The 540 million-year-old Cathedral dolomite in Marble Canyon is polished constantly by glacial silt in the water, and yields a fine finish. So in layman's terms, it is marble. The best example is the whitish-coloured rock at the brink of the waterfall.

Slightly downstream from Marble Canyon, there are potholes eroded into another exposure of highly polished dolomite. You can view them on your return by taking the branch trail to the southwest (right), just before you recross the first bridge.

The Ochre Beds are clay that has been stained red and yellow by iron oxide carried in spring water. The ochre was a valuable ritual material and trading item for Kutenai natives from the interior of BC.

85. Ochre Beds and Paint Pots

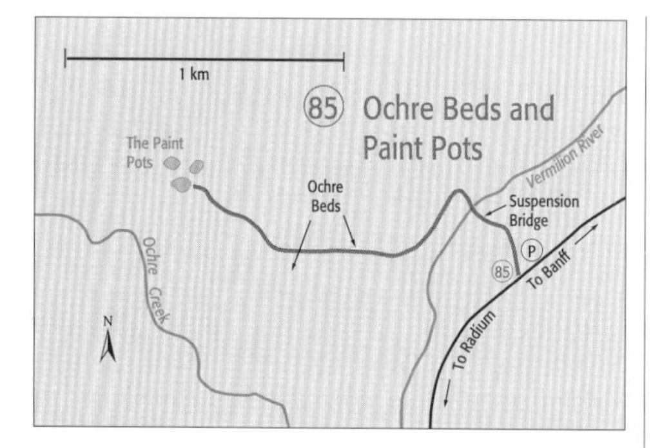

Route Information

Trailhead: North side of the Kootenay Parkway (Highway 93 South), 19.7 km west of Castle Junction, 85 km east of the junction with Highway 95
Rating: easy, 1 km
Lighting: anytime

The walk to the Ochre Beds and Paint Pots leads to colourful deposits of clay and the outlets of three mineral springs. On the way, you are treated to a crossing of the Vermilion River by suspension bridge. Wildlife is common here. Look for wolf, coyote, deer, elk, moose, American marten, grizzly bear and black bear. You may see their tracks in the clay.

The clay at the Ochre Beds was created from sediments deposited on the bottom of an ancient glacial lake. The remarkable colours result from saturation of the clay with iron rich water. This water percolates to the surface nearby at the outlets of three mineral springs—The Paint Pots. The iron compounds in the water have also stained rocks and vegetation in the Vermilion River, providing its name.

The Ochre Beds were known to Kutenai natives from southeastern BC as "the place where the red earth spirit is taken." The Kutenai gathered the colourful clay, formed it into cakes and baked it in fire. The resulting compound was ground into powder and mixed with animal fat or fish grease to create a body paint, used in rituals.

The Kutenai discovered that the "red earth" was a valuable trading commodity. Once or twice a year, they would cross the Rockies to hunt bison and trade with the Stoneys at Kootenay Plains on the North Saskatchewan River. One of their trade and travel routes, the Kutenai Trail, went north from the Ochre Beds. Ochre and bison bones have been found at many archaeological sites along the Kutenai Trail in Yoho and Banff national parks.

A pack of gray wolves (timber wolves) frequents the Ochre Beds. Look for their tracks in the clay.

In the early 1900s, the Ochre Beds were developed as a source of pigment for paint. The clay was excavated and hauled overland to Castle Junction, then shipped to Calgary by train. The enterprise soon failed. Equipment remains at the Ochre Beds, rusting beside mounds of clay collected for a harvest that was never completed.

Please do not to walk in the ochre deposits, or remove any of the material. The clay will stain clothing and shoes, and disturbances of this soil take many years to disappear.

The Paint Pots

The Paint Pots are cone-shaped, mineral spring outlets, where water emerges at 10.7°C. So they are mineral springs, not hot springs. Either the water does not filter far enough underground to become super-heated, or it becomes mixed with cold water on its return to the surface. The combined volume of flow is 330 litres per minute.

The cones around the Paint Pots are accumulations of iron oxide, precipitated from the spring water as it emerges. As the iron rim grows in height, the pool of the spring becomes deeper. Eventually the depth of water creates a back pressure greater than the pressure of the flowing spring water. The spring is then forced to seek another outlet where the resistance is less, leaving behind an abandoned or "choked" cone. There are several choked cones near the Paint Pots.

The two largest Paint Pots contain a mixture of spring and surface water, and are greenish in colour. The water of the smallest Paint Pot is clear. Cotton grass and tall white bog orchids grow in the moist area nearby.

The Juniper Trail descends from the Kootenay Parkway to Sinclair Creek, and then climbs to viewpoints on the rim of Sinclair Canyon. Bighorn sheep are often seen on this hike.

86. Juniper Trail

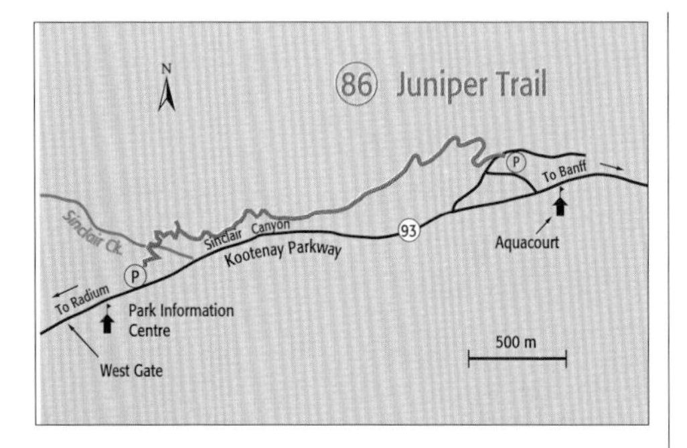

Route Information

Trailhead: North side of the Kootenay Parkway (Highway 93 South), 103.5 km west of Castle Junction, 1.2 km east of the junction with Highway 95, 200 m east of the Kootenay Park gate
Rating: harder, 4.6 km loop
Lighting: anytime

The Juniper Trail is the most "up and down" outing in this book. The trail initially descends abruptly to Sinclair Creek, and then makes a steady climb to the rim of the canyon above. The rewards for hiking this steep trail are spectacular views over the Columbia Valley, and an appreciation of the diverse vegetation in the area of Radium Hot Springs.

As the trail switchbacks steeply down to Sinclair Creek, notice the changes in the vegetation produced by the damp, cool canyon air. Mosses appear on the trunks of Douglas fir trees, and feathermosses carpet the forest floor in the shade of western red cedars. Before you cross the creek on the bridge, walk upstream a short distance on a rough trail for a view of the waterfall at the mouth of Sinclair Canyon.

Across the bridge, the trail begins its climb to the rim of Sinclair Canyon. If you pay attention to the surrounding vegetation, you will notice another pronounced change at the first switchback. The cedars and feathermosses promptly disappear, replaced by widely-spaced Douglas firs, with an understory of grasses, bearberry and juniper. This vegetation is typical of the adjacent Columbia Valley, which features a milder climate than the Rockies. Because of their steepness and sunny aspect, slopes like this one remain virtually snow-free all winter, and provide important habitat for bighorn sheep.

From the second and highest viewpoint, you can look west to Mt. Farnham in the Purcell Range of the Columbia Mountains. Wetlands to the north in the Columbia Valley are important stopovers and nesting areas for migratory birds. More than 200 species have been recorded.

The short descent north delivers you to a parking area near the hot springs aquacourt. If a dip in the hot springs is not in your itinerary, follow the sidewalk west (right), 1.4 km to the trailhead. This takes you through the depths of Sinclair Canyon, but you won't see Sinclair Creek. When the Kootenay Parkway was constructed, the creek was buried in a culvert.

The Columbia River, into which Sinclair Creek empties, occupies a tremendous rift in the earth's surface. Known as the Rocky Mountain Trench, this rift parallels the western boundary of the Rockies from Montana to the Yukon. Here, it separates the Rockies from the older Columbia Mountains.

Before construction of hydroelectric dams on the Columbia River, chinook salmon could migrate from the Pacific Ocean along the river, to spawn at its headwaters. The dams have proved insurmountable barriers, and attempts to re-establish the salmon run have failed. The annual migration is now curtailed 600 km downriver from here. Salmon are an important source of food for animals and native peoples. The salmon's disappearance has greatly altered the upper Columbia River.

Juniper

Juniper is an evergreen cypress-family shrub. There are three species in the Rockies. Prickly juniper grows in circular patches. Creeping juniper grows from a trailing vine. The shrub-like Rocky Mountain juniper may reach 5 m in height. Creeping juniper and Rocky Mountain juniper have shreddy bark and scaly leaves, like their enormous cypress cousin, western red cedar.

Prickly juniper is the most common juniper in the Rockies, and is aptly named. Contact with the spiky needles produces a rash in some people. All junipers grow berries, which vary in colour from green to gray to purple, depending on age. The berries may stay on the plant for two summers, and provide food for birds and squirrels. In days past, they were used to flavour gin. The photo shows a branch of Rocky Mountain juniper.

Other Walks and Easy Hikes in Kootenay National Park

87. Vermilion River

Trailhead: Numa Creek picnic area on the west side of the Kootenay Parkway (Highway 93 South), 24.5 km west of Castle Junction, 80.5 km east of the junction with Highway 95
Rating: easy, 100 m
Lighting: anytime

This is the backpacker's trailhead for access along Numa Creek to the Rockwall. However, the short walk to the bridge across the Vermilion River is a good way to stretch your legs while driving the Kootenay Parkway. Here, the river is carving a canyon through shales and slates of the Chancellor group of formations. The Vermilion River separates the eastern main ranges to the east, from the western main ranges to the west.

88. Dog Lake

Trailhead: East side of the Kootenay Parkway (Highway 93 South), 78 km west of Castle Junction, 27 km east of the junction with Highway 95, 500 m south of McLeod Meadows campground.
Rating: moderate, 2.6 km
Lighting: anytime

The trail to Dog Lake is an ideal excursion for campers staying at McLeod Meadows Campground. From the picnic area, the trail skirts the rear of the campground and crosses the Kootenay River on two bridges. It then climbs away from the river through a Douglas fir forest. Western wood lilies bloom here in early summer. After you cross a low ridge, the sounds of the highway disappear, and the trail drops toward peaceful Dog Lake. The lake's outlet shows evidence of a beaver dam. By crossing a footbridge, you can follow a rough and wet anglers' track to the lake's east shore. Many of the lodgepole pine trees in this part of the Kootenay Valley have been afflicted by pine bark beetle—hence the discoloured foliage.

Please see map on page 113

89. Valleyview

Trailhead: Follow the Redstreak Campground road, which begins 500 m south of the junction of the Kootenay Pa way with Highway 95. T trailhead is 200 m west of the entrance to Redstreak Campground, on the north (left).
Rating: moderate, 1.2 km
Lighting: anytime

The Valleyview Trail traverses steep, grassy slopes that support an open Douglas fir forest. You reach a viewpoint that overlooks the Columbia Valley. Red squirrel, pileated woodpecker and ruffed grouse inhabit the surrounding forest. In late spring and early summer, a variety of wildflowers blooms on the sunny slopes. The last 300 m of trail is a staircase that descends to Radium Hot Springs townsite.

90. Redstreak

Trailheads: To hike downhill: follow the Redstreak Campground road, which begins 500 m south of the Kootenay Parkway and Highway 95. The trailhead is at Loop H in the campground. To hike uphill: begin at the rear of the Hot Springs Aquacourt on the Kootenay Parkway.
Rating: moderate, 2.3 km
Lighting: anytime

The Redstreak Trail is recommended to campers who would like to visit the hot springs, and obtain a spectacular view into Sinclair Canyon en route. The sidetrail to the canyon viewpoint is 300 m north of the campground. Look for bighorn sheep on the steep, grassy slopes on the opposite of the canyon. Back on the main trail, you drop steadily to the hot springs, and the forest becomes increasingly damp and dense. The young trees immediately above the Aquacourt seeded after a 1967 forest fire. "Redstreak" refers to the red limestones and dolomites of the Beaverfoot Formation, exposed nearby along the Redwall Fault.

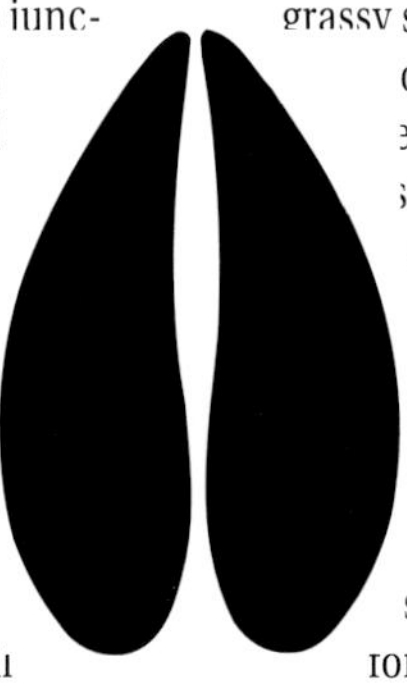

Moose track

Waterton Lakes National Park

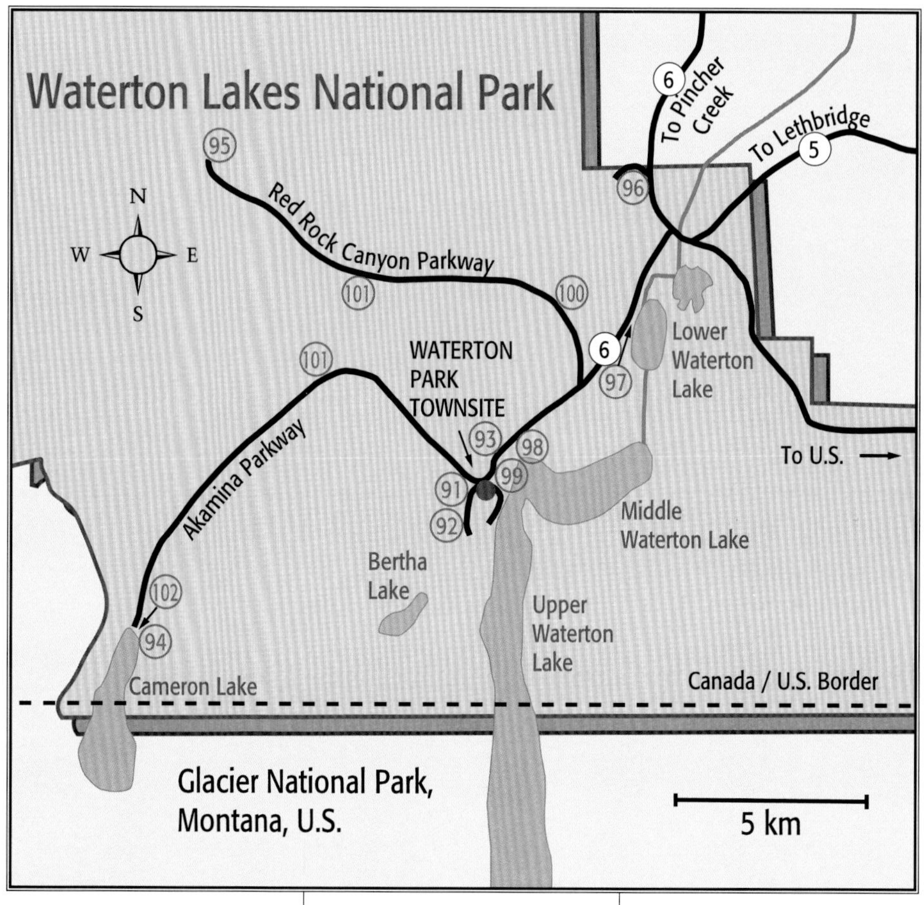

Waterton Lakes National Park is located in the extreme southwestern corner of Alberta. It is the smallest Rocky Mountain national park, including 525 km^2 of prairie and front ranges. Waterton's theme is "where the mountains meet the prairie."

The Walks and Easy Hikes in Waterton feature the mountain–prairie contact, the park's vibrant human history, interesting geology, and diverse plant and animal life. More than one half of Alberta's plant species are found in Waterton. The wildflower displays of late spring and early summer are among the best in the Canadian Rockies.

Cameron Falls is one of the highlights of the walk around Waterton townsite. The rock beneath the falls is 1.5-billion-year-old limestone—the oldest rock visible in the Rockies.

91. Cameron Falls and Waterton Townsite

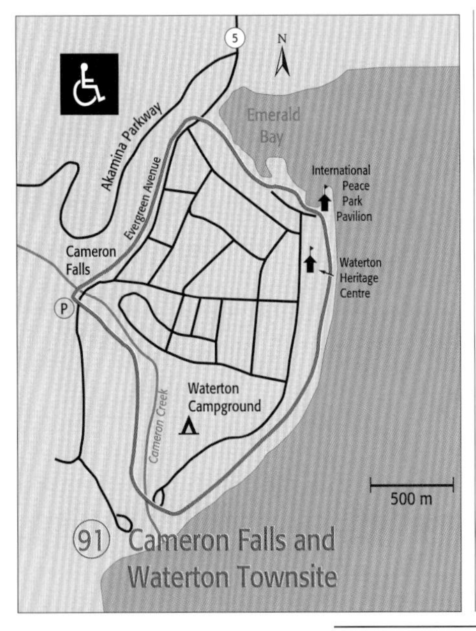

This circuit of Waterton Park townsite is an ideal introduction to Waterton Lakes National Park. Cameron Falls makes a logical starting point for this walk, which follows a brick sidewalk for most of its length.

Cameron Falls cascades over a 10 m-high limestone step. This limestone is the 1.5 billion-year-old Waterton Formation—the oldest rock vis-

Route Information

Trailhead: West side of Waterton Park townsite at Cameron Falls. Follow Cameron Falls Drive west to the parking lot at the bridge over Cameron Creek.
Rating: easy, 3.2 km loop. Wheelchair accessible
Lighting: Cameron Falls are lit best in the morning.

ible in the Canadian Rockies. A short trail on the north (right) of the waterfall offers access to the rim of the canyon that has been cut by Cameron Creek.

From Cameron Falls, cross the road and follow the path southeast along Cameron Creek toward Upper Waterton Lake. The creek bed shows evidence of shoring and man-made diversions, designed to mitigate flash-floods. In some years, the creek has undergone a thousand-fold increase in volume between the lowest flow of winter, and the peak flow of summer. Waterton Park townsite is also susceptible to flooding from high waters on the lake. The most recent serious flooding was in 1975.

If the day is typical, it will be windy. The park's average daily wind speed is 32.5 km per hour. Chinook winds, which can raise the temperature 40°C in a few hours, contribute to the warmest winters in the province of Alberta. However, the winds also bear wetter fruit. The park has the greatest annual precipitation in the province.

With a maximum depth of 157 m, Upper Waterton Lake is the deepest lake in the Canadian Rockies. It is 11.1 km long, has an area of 941 ha, and is by far the largest of Waterton's 80 lakes and ponds. It holds approximately 645 million cubic metres of water. The southern reach of the lake extends 4.5 km into Glacier National Park, Montana.

The MV "International" has plied the waters of Upper Waterton Lake since 1927.

There are 17 native species of fish in Waterton Lakes National Park, and 8 introduced species. The largest fish on record in the park was a 23.2 kg lake trout caught in Upper Waterton Lake in July 1920. The Blackfoot (Siksika) know the Waterton Lakes by several names, one of which means "big water."

Turn north (left) at the lakeshore, and follow the sidewalk towards town. You can make a sidetrip to the Waterton Heritage Centre. Exhibits in this building describe the human and natural history of the park. The International Peace Park Pavilion is a few hundred metres north. It was constructed in 1982, the 50th anniversary of Waterton-Glacier International Peace Park. The peace park, an expression of goodwill between Canada and the United States, was the first established in the world.

The *International* departs from the nearby marina on Emerald Bay, touring Upper Waterton Lake into US waters. The maiden voyage of the *International* was in 1927, the year that the Prince of Wales Hotel opened. At the bottom of Emerald Bay there is a paddle wheel steam ship, brought to Waterton in 1907 to tow log booms. Later it was moored at the dock, and used as a tea room. It was scuttled in 1918. Today, the novelty of a shipwreck inland attracts divers from throughout western Canada.

After passing the marina, turn south (left) on Evergreen Avenue to return to the Cameron Falls parking lot, or turn north (right) to access the Prince of Wales and Linnet Lake trails.

The Oldest Rock in the Rockies

How did 1.5-billion-year-old limestone from the sedimentary basement of the Rockies come to rest on the surface? The particles of mud, sand and pebbles that became the rocks in the Rockies, were deposited on the floors of ancient seas in horizontal layers. During mountain building, which lasted from approximately 120 million to 60 million years ago, compressive forces pushed these sedimentary formations northeastward. Within the earth's crust, higher temperatures rendered the rock pliable. Under the pressure, the rock bowed into folds. Some of these folds broke, and massive sheets of rock were freed to slide as thrust sheets, riding upward and over adjacent rock to the northeast. Since then, the younger rocks atop the sedimentary stack of the thrust sheets have been eroded, exposing the ancient underlying rocks.

The Bertha Falls trail explores the montane forest south of Waterton Park townsite. It leads to a viewpoint that overlooks Upper Waterton Lake, and then follows Bertha Creek to a picturesque waterfall.

92. Lower Bertha Falls

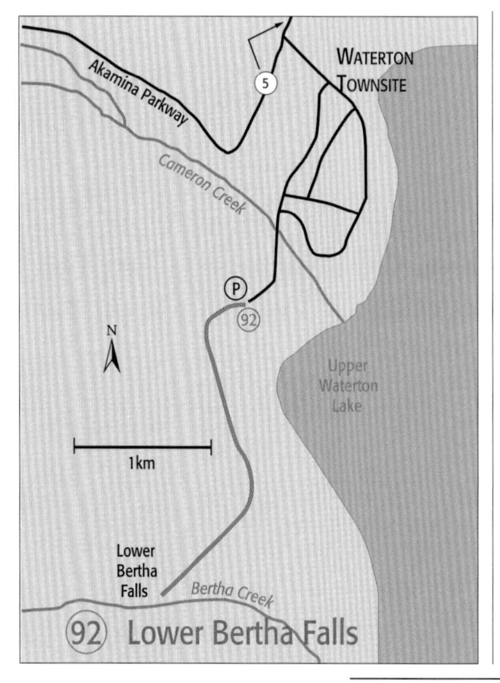

The hike to Lower Bertha Falls explores the montane forest along the west shore of Upper Waterton Lake, and delivers you to a picturesque waterfall—a cool, shady destination on a hot day. The interpretive stops along the trail are explained in a brochure that may be available at the park information centre. Keep right at all trail junctions.

The forest along this trail has been affected by avalanches, blowdowns, beetle infestations and

Route Information

Trailhead: Bertha Lake trail in Waterton Park townsite, on Evergreen Avenue, 500 m south of Cameron Falls

Rating: moderate, 2.9 km

Lighting: morning

forest fires. It sounds like a roll-call of destruction. Although many of the transformations that take place in this forest are subtle, nature often employs less subtle means to bring about beneficial changes. The blowdown on the Bertha Falls trail took place June 7, 1964, when wind speeds reached more than 160 km per hour. In all, 201 hectares of the park were affected by blowdowns that day. Blowdowns remove weakened trees and expand habitat by creating openings in the forest.

At km 1.7 the trail emerges from the trees to reveal a wonderful panorama of Upper Waterton Lake and the mountains along its east shore. You can see Mt. Cleveland, the highest mountain in Glacier National Park, Montana. Limber pine, an uncommon tree in the Rockies, grows near this viewpoint.

From the viewpoint en route to Lower Bertha Falls, you obtain this panoramic view of Upper Waterton Lake.

Leaving the viewpoint, the trail swings to the southwest, and climbs gradually along Bertha Creek. (Do not follow the lakeshore trail south from the viewpoint.) It is 1.2 km to Lower Bertha Falls. The water cascades in a veil across a tilted, resistant outcrop of the 1.5 billion-year-old Altyn Formation. At the base of the falls, the stream has been captured by the edge of another resistant rock formation, producing a right-angle turn in the flow.

This area is in the path of a prominent storm track. The storm winds bring plant seeds from the interior of BC. The high annual precipitation and shade along lower Bertha Creek favours their growth. So you may see some plant species here that are normally found in interior or coastal rainforests of BC. The avalanche paths across the creek on Mt. Richards are some of the most extensive in the park. The trail beyond the falls climbs steeply for 2.8 km to Bertha Lake. "Bertha" was Bertha Ekelund, an early Waterton resident who was jailed for passing counterfeit money.

Mountain Pine Beetle

The mountain pine beetle infests over-mature lodgepole pine trees. The female beetle bores into tree bark and deposits her eggs in the soft, cambium layer. The worm-like burrowings which the female and her off-spring chew beneath the bark, girdle the tree and kill it by drying up the sap flow. You can see these burrowings on dead pines beside the trail to lower Bertha Falls.

The most recent mountain pine beetle infestation in Waterton ran its course between 1976 and 1983. More than half the pines in the park were killed. Some individual stands were totally wiped out. The severity of this infestation was amplified because many of Waterton's forest stands are over-mature. For the past 50 years, all forest fires have been suppressed in the park. Without the rejuvenating process of fire, nature has resorted to other means, such as infestations of pine beetle, to regenerate the forest.

The death of the pines has exposed a greater area of the forest floor to sunlight, resulting in new growth needed by some wildlife. Removal of the pines has also made way for succession to a forest dominated by white spruce and Douglas fir, the climax species for this area.

One objective of national park policy is to ensure the continuation of natural processes. Although this forest looks devastated, it is not. A natural transformation is taking place that will ultimately benefit all the species that live here.

From the Bear's Hump, you can look over Waterton Park townsite and Upper Waterton Lake. But you work hard for this view: the trail gains more than 200 vertical metres in only 1.2 km.

93. Bear's Hump

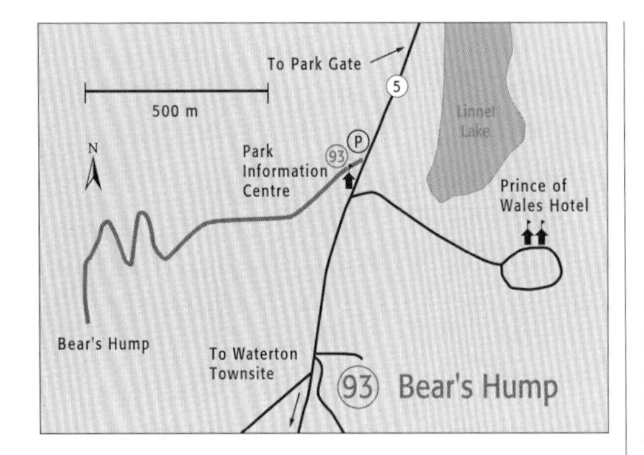

The Bear's Hump is a limestone bluff on a ridge that extends from Mt. Crandell, north of Waterton Park townsite. The trail to the Bear's Hump is the second steepest in this book. Your reward for completing this unrelenting climb is a panorama that includes the Waterton Lakes, Waterton Park townsite, and the contact between mountain and prairie for which the park is famous. Waterton is a windy park, and the Bear's Hump is one of its windiest places. Take a sweater and windbreaker with you. Avoid this hike when there are thunderstorms nearby.

From the Bear's Hump, Upper Waterton Lake is the centrepiece in the view. The lake has an area of 941 hectares, is 11.1 km long, 750 m wide, and extends 4.5 km into Montana. It holds an estimated 645,200,000 cubic metres of water. With a maximum depth of 157 m, it is the deepest lake in the Canadian Rockies.

The U-shaped valley that contains Upper Waterton Lake was created by an ice-age glacier that undercut the adjacent mountainsides. Middle Waterton Lake and Lower Waterton Lake were formed in a different manner. They are kettle ponds, created by the melting of detached blocks of glacial ice when the glacier receded.

Boulders, silt and rubble are carried away from mountains in streams and rivers, and deposited where the angle of the stream bed lessens, building an alluvial fan. Waterton Park townsite is built on the alluvial fan formed where Cameron Creek descends from its hanging valley into the Waterton Valley. Geologists speculate that much of the material in alluvial fans in the Rockies was deposited during a tremendous meltwater surge between 6000 years ago and 7000 years ago. Material is still being deposited on the Waterton fan today, although diversions of Cameron Creek (designed to prevent flooding) have interfered with the natural process.

Looking north from the Bear's Hump, you can see where the front ranges of the Rockies end abruptly on the prairie. During mountain building approximately 85 million years ago, the rock formations that make up Waterton's mountains were thrust northeastward as a cohesive, 6.5 kilometre-thick mass of rock, known as the Lewis Thrust Sheet. This huge slab of rock slid 60 km to 70 km, and came to rest atop undisturbed, relatively flat shales. The mountains were literally pushed onto the prairie. The effect is still visible today.

A Natural Dam/A Man-made Dam

The streamlined contours of the Bear's Hump indicate that it was completely covered by glacial ice during the Wisconsin Glaciation. Before that ice age, the Bear's Hump extended southeast toward Vimy Peak on the opposite side of the lakes. The Bosporus, the narrow strait that links Upper Waterton Lake and Middle Waterton Lake, was eroded through this ridge by the ancestral Waterton Glacier. Evidence of the connecting ridge can be seen in the knoll beneath the Prince of Wales Hotel, and in the rocky spur known as "The Couch," that extends to waterline on the east side of the Bosporus.

Glaciers removed this natural rock dam. But in 1919, a proposal was made to build a concrete dam at the Bosporus, to impound Upper Waterton Lake for irrigation. A dam would have greatly altered the ecology and the appeal of the national park. The proposal was dismissed by James B. Harkin, Commissioner of Dominion Parks. Unfortunately, dams have since been constructed downstream on the Waterton River, and on other tributaries of the South Saskatchewan River.

Cameron Lake is located in a glacially-carved valley in the extreme southwest corner of Alberta. Mt. Custer, at the south end of the lake, is in Glacier National Park, Montana.

94. Cameron Lake

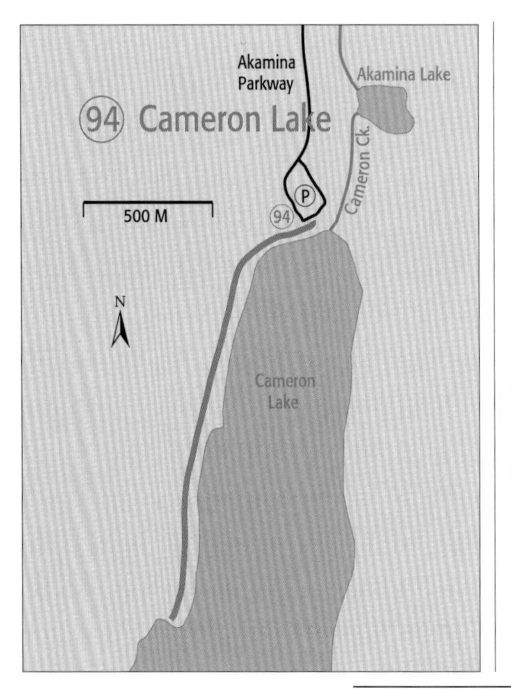

The Cameron Lake trail takes you into the extreme southwest corner of Alberta—a place where two parks, two provinces and two countries meet. The trail follows the west shore of the lake through subalpine forest. The trail is flat, making it an ideal excursion for families.

Although glaciers have long been absent from Waterton's mountains, their legacy is evident at Cameron Lake. The lake is situated in a bowl-

Route Information

Trailhead: Follow the Akamina Parkway, 16 km southwest from Waterton Park townsite to the end of the road at the Cameron Lake parking lot.
Rating: easy, 1.6 km
Lighting: morning and late afternoon

shaped valley known as a cirque. A glacier that once occupied the flanks of Mt. Custer at the far end of the lake, eroded this cirque. The glacier flowed north. When it receded, it deposited a moraine that now impounds the waters.

The most common tree species in the subalpine forest around Cameron Lake are Engelmann spruce and subalpine fir, both coniferous. There are many ways to differentiate between these tree species, but to the casual visitor with an interest in botany, needles provide the easiest clue. Fir needles are flat. Spruce needles are spiky and square, and will roll between your fingers. Lodgepole pines have needles in pairs. If the needles are in bundles of five, the tree is the less common whitebark pine, or limber pine.

Tree bark also provides a clue for identification. Engelmann spruce bark is reddish-brown and scaly. The bark of the subalpine fir is silvery-gray and smooth, with resin blisters. (Please be gentle with tree branches and needles, and do not trample surrounding vegetation.)

Rufous hummingbird

The subalpine forest is often called the "snow forest." The area around Cameron Lake has some of the heaviest snowfall in Alberta. The spire-like form of the subalpine fir helps shed the heavy snow load.

The undergrowth at trailside around Cameron Lake features the wildflowers: arnica, queen's cup, cow parsnip, foam flower, dwarf dogwood, purple geranium, false hellebore and pearly everlasting. Red monkey flowers are common. This attractive plant is a favourite with hummingbirds and amateur botanists. It occurs in the Rockies only in Waterton and Jasper national parks.

The ridgecrest above the west shore of Cameron Lake separates Waterton Lakes National Park in the province of Alberta, from the Akamina-Kishinena Recreation Area in BC. The boundary between Canada and the US follows a more arbitrary line. The 49th parallel cuts across the extreme south end of Cameron Lake. Hence, Mt. Custer is entirely within Glacier National Park, in the US. The mountain was not named for the famous general, but for Henry Custer, a topographer with the US Boundary Survey of the 1860s.

Avalanche Paths

Snow avalanches are one of the most important and common natural processes in the Rockies. Accumulations of snow can slide as a mass down a mountainside, when triggered by certain snow and weather conditions. The force of the avalanche and the wind blast it generates, create a swath in the forest. Supple willows and alders survive by bending. Perennial grasses and wildflowers survive by being flattened beneath the snow.

Avalanches create openings in the forest that allow sunlight to reach the ground. These openings promote the growth of vegetation eaten by elk, deer, moose, and bears. The avalanche paths at the end of the Cameron Lake trail are frequented by grizzly bears. They feed on the lush growth of plants like cow parsnip.

The red, white and green rocks in Red Rock Canyon are 1.5-billion-year-old mudstone of the Grinnell Formation, one of the oldest rock formations visible in the Rockies. The canyon features fossils, intriguing geology, and the opportunity to see bighorn sheep.

95. Red Rock Canyon

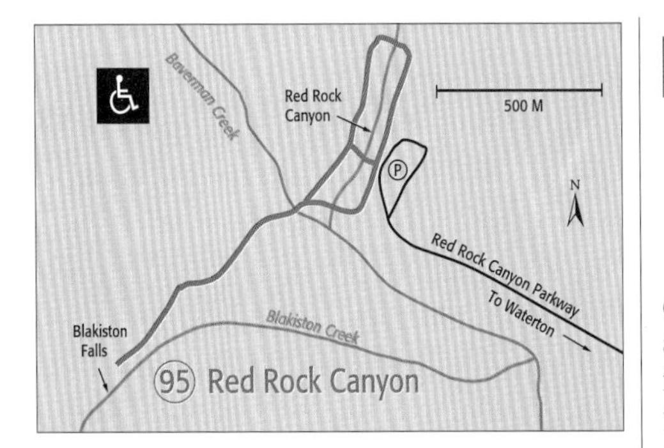

Route Information

Trailhead: Follow the Red Rock Canyon Parkway, 15 km from its junction with Highway 5, to where it ends at the parking lot at Red Rock Canyon.
Rating: easy, 700 m loop. Wheelchair accessible
Lighting: anytime

The paved trail at Red Rock Canyon makes a circuit of one of the most colourful attractions in the Rockies. The red rock in the canyon is 1.5-billion-year-old mudstone, known as argillite (ARE-jill-ite). This rock was created from iron-rich sediments deposited on ancient tidal mud flats. Where the mud flats were exposed to air, the iron oxidized and turned red. The green and white rocks in the canyon are also argillite, but contain iron that did not oxidize.

Red Rock Canyon is 23 m deep, and began forming 10,000 years ago. Its steep walls indicate rapid erosion. The potholes were created by swirling rocks trapped in eddies. Red Rock Canyon has some interesting features. These include ripple rock, which records wave action along a prehistoric shoreline. On the east side of the canyon, the trail crosses a honeycomb of mud cracks. These cracks opened where mud dried on the ancient tidal flat. The cracks were later filled with a different type of sediment. The formation was subsequently turned to rock by the pressure of other sediments that accumulated rapidly above.

At trailside you can see examples of a fossil formation known as a stromatolite. These reef-like accumulations were created 1.5 billion years ago, from calcium carbonate produced by algae. Similar algae grow today, creating reefs in warm, shallow seas elsewhere in the world.

The last item of geological interest is an intrusion of igneous (once molten) rock near the mouth of the canyon. Nearly all the rock in the Rockies is sedimentary in origin. However, blobs of molten rock sometimes oozed into cracks within the hardened sedimentary layers.

Bighorn sheep

The gray igneous rock here is a lava known as basalt (BAY-salt). There are phenocrysts in this rock—star-shaped crystals of feldspar.

A native travel route called the Buffalo Trail crossed South Kootenay Pass and followed Blakiston Creek past the mouth of Red Rock Canyon. Seasonal native hunting camps have been found near the canyon, and date to 8000 years ago.

You may extend this outing by walking a kilometre southwest from the mouth of Red Rock Canyon, to the viewing platform at Blakiston Falls. The falls were named for Lt. Thomas Blakiston, meteorologist with the Palliser Expedition of 1857–60. Blakiston was probably the first European to record a visit to what is now Waterton Lakes National Park. He travelled along Blakiston Creek in 1858.

Too Many Feet

Since the Red Rock Canyon Parkway was completed, millions of people have visited the canyon. The effect of millions of pairs of feet on the mudstone around the canyon has been very damaging. Whereas erosion of the rock by water is a natural process, excessive erosion resulting from foot traffic here is not. By all means, appreciate the canyon. But please, keep to the paved walkway and bridges, and spare the 1.5-billion-year-old mudstone from further damage.

The band of bighorn sheep that frequents Red Rock Canyon has also suffered from interacting with visitors. These animals are so accustomed to handouts, they now expect to be fed by everyone. Please refrain. Feeding the sheep endangers both them and you.

Waterton's famous mountain-prairie contact is the highlight in this view from the Bison Paddock Viewpoint.

96. Bison Paddock Viewpoint

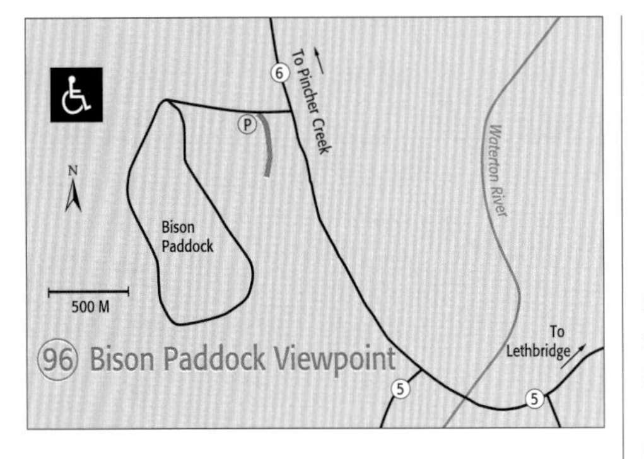

Route Information

Trailhead: Follow Highway 6, for 2 km north from its junction with Highway 5, to the Bison Paddock Road. Turn west (left) and park on the south (left).
Rating: easy, 300 m. Wheelchair accessible
Lighting: morning

There is no finer place to appreciate Waterton's mountain–prairie contact than the Bison Paddock Viewpoint. Here, the rolling shortgrass prairie, dotted with kettle lakes, ends abruptly at the base of Bellevue Hill and the front ranges of the Rockies.

The grasses and wildflowers of the bison paddock prairie represent the natural vegetation of the northern interior plains. There are very few pockets of this vegetation left, and that is part of the tale of the bison's demise. It is estimated that 60 million bison lived on the interior plains in 1790. When horses and rifles were introduced onto the bison's range, the animal was subjected to a senseless slaughter by both whites and Natives. The prairie was burned and put under the plough as settlers arrived. Diseases imported with domestic cattle took a heavy toll.

What was the net result of all this pressure? By 1890, the population of the plains bison was 1090. The decimation of this species was a double tragedy, unparalleled in history, for it also spelled the end of the traditional way of life for Plains Natives.

The return of the plains bison from the brink of extinction can be attributed to Walking Coyote, who captured bison in southern Alberta in 1874, an sold some of them to two ranchers in Montana. In 1907, the Canadian government purchased 716 bison from the captive Montana herd. Descendants of these animals now live at Elk Island National Park, and here. The Waterton Lakes bison paddock was established in 1952, with one bull and five cows. Today, it holds approximately two dozen bison.

The bison paddock area features many glacial landforms. The lakes are kettle ponds. The sinuous, moraine ridges are eskers, deposited in streams that flowed beneath glacial ice. Oval-shaped mounds are drumlins—created when a glacier advanced over existing moraines. Kames are conical-shaped piles of rubble, deposited at a glacier's edge by meltwater flowing from the glacier's surface. The viewpoint is on a kame.

There are also many archaeological sites in this vicinity. The Buffalo Trail from South Kootenay Pass crossed the area of the paddock. A nearby cliff was used as a bison jump.

Bison track

Bison

The bison (BYE-sun) is the largest land mammal in North America. The popular name "buffalo" is more correctly applied to certain wild cattle of Asia and Africa. Adult males are 1.7 m tall at the shoulder, and weigh 725 kg to 1000 kg. There are two species: plains and wood. The bison in the Waterton Lakes paddock are plains bison.

Bison make wallows and roll in the dirt. The dirt reduces irritation from insects and shedding skin. It is not uncommon for a bison to tolerate birds on its back. The birds bring relief by eating insects from the bison's coat.

Bison have a heavy and clumsy appearance that belies their agility and speed. They can sprint 60 km per hour. They are territorial and defensive, and may readily show aggression if you approach too closely. If you drive the loop road through the bison paddock, please remain in your vehicle. Bison can be long-lived. One of the original bison held in the Banff paddock was 38 when it died.

Other Walks and Easy Hikes in Waterton Lakes National Park

97. Kootenai Brown's Grave

Trailhead: Follow Highway 5, for 5.4 km north of Waterton Park townsite, or 3 km south of its junction with Highway 6. The trailhead access road is on the east.
Rating: easy, 500 m
Lighting: anytime

This trail visits the grave of John Kootenai Brown, who was in many ways the father of Waterton Lakes National Park. A character who epitomized the "wild west," Brown's pre-Waterton life read like an encyclopedia of adventure. He served with the British Army in India, made and lost a fortune in the Cariboo gold fields, served as a police constable at Cranbrook, ran whiskey, was a pony express rider, trapped furs, and was accused and acquitted of murdering a business partner. Brown first saw the Waterton Lakes in 1865. He returned three years later to settle near the mouth of Blakiston Creek.

Brown's idyllic life of guiding and trapping at Waterton was disrupted in the 1890s. He had witnessed the demise of the plains bison, and now increasing numbers of visitors were threatening other wildlife. Together with local ranchers, Brown pressured the federal government to set aside a reserve in the area. In 1895 the Kootenay Lakes Forest Reserve was established. (The Waterton Lakes had been originally known as the Kootenay Lakes.) Brown became the first guardian of the protected area.

Please see map on page 125

In 1911, the reserve was proclaimed a national park, and its name was changed to Waterton Lakes. At age 71, Brown became the park's first superintendent; a position he held for three years. The park area was then increased thirty-fold, requiring a younger man in the patrol saddle. Brown died in 1916. He is buried on the shore of Lower Waterton Lake, between the graves of his two wives.

98. Linnet Lake

Trailhead: East side of Highway 5, 400 m north of the park information centre
Rating: easy, 1 km paved loop
Wheelchair accessible
Lighting: anytime

The Linnet Lake trail was paved in 1985 as a park project to commemorate the national parks centennial. The lake is a kettle pond. The surrounding forest features Douglas fir, balsam poplar, white birch, lodgepole pine, and the shrub, saskatoon. The linnet is a type of finch.

99. Prince of Wales

Trailheads: East side of Highway 5, 400 m north of the park information centre. Or from the Emerald Bay picnic area, east side of Highway 5, 300 m south of the park information centre
Rating: moderate, 2 km loop
Lighting: anytime

The Prince of Wales Hotel was the brainchild of Louis Hill, president of the Great Northern Railway. With Glacier National Park established as a tourist draw in the US, Hill sought to expand his business with side trips into Canada.

Construction of the hotel began in 1926. Chinook winds that gusted to 144 km per hour, pushed the hotel 20 cm off its foundation. Nonetheless, the hotel opened the following summer, and soon became part of Waterton's trademark view.

The hotel sits atop a glacial deposit known as a kame—a conical pile of boulders and sediments, that was deposited at the edge of a retreating glacier by meltwater. This kame is especially high because it accumulated on a bedrock bench.

The trail loops around the base of the kame, crossing a pebbled beach to the Bosporus—the narrows that separate Upper Waterton Lake and Middle Waterton Lake. Archaeologists have inventoried an 8000-year-old native fishing camp here. The stunted and gnarled shapes of the trees are evidence of Waterton's windiness. After following the lakeshore north to the Linnet Lake trailhead, the Prince of Wales Trail climbs back over the kame, and descends to the picnic area at Emerald Bay.

100. Bellevue Prairie

Trailhead: Follow the Red Rock Canyon Parkway for 2.9 km from Highway 5, to where the road makes a prominent turn to the west (left). Park on the east (right). The trail is not indicated, but heads north from the road.
Rating: easy, 1–2 km
Lighting: morning

On the Bellevue Prairie you explore the place where mountains and prairie meet. Although Waterton's peaks are not high by Rockies' standards, the abrupt manner in which they rise from the rolling prairie makes this a unique setting among the Walks and Easy Hikes.

Waterton is extraordinarily rich in plant life. The park is home to 1270 plant species, including 870 vascular species—55 percent of the total in Alberta. Of these, 113 species are rare in Alberta, 43 species are rare in Canada, and 34 species are unknown in Alberta outside the park. The Bellevue Prairie is a remnant of the shortgrass prairie that originally covered much of central North America. Some of the plant associations found here do not occur elsewhere in the Rocky Mountain parks. The wildflowers are spectacular, and the walk is highly recommended to the amateur botanist, particularly in late spring and early summer.

The Bellevue Prairie is known to glaciologists as an eskerine complex. An esker is a sinuous ridge of gravelly material, deposited by meltwater flowing beneath a glacier. Many eskers snake their way across this prairie. Their windward sides are devoid of trees, but in the shade and shelter of these low ridges, stunted aspens and limber pines grow.

Osprey

The Buffalo Trail was an ancient native travel route between BC and the plains of Alberta. It crossed Bellevue Prairie. Many archaeological artifacts have been found in the area, including rock structures associated with ritual sites, buffalo jumps, campsites, and the ruts left by native sleds.

It is possible to traverse Bellevue Prairie to Indian Springs near the Bison Paddock, but most walkers venture a kilometre or two out onto the prairie, and then backtrack to the Red Rock Canyon Parkway.

101. Crandell Lake

Trailheads: North side of the Akamina Parkway, 6.6 km from Waterton Park townsite. Or, follow the Red Rock Canyon Parkway, 6 km from its junction with Highway 5. Turn south (left) onto the Canyon Camp Road (1.2 km past Crandell Campground), and follow this 400 m to the parking lot.
Ratings: From Akamina Parkway, easy, 1.6 km; From Red Rock Canyon Parkway, moderate, 2.4 km
Lighting: anytime

Crandell Lake is situated on a rocky bench that separates the Cameron Creek and Blakiston Creek valleys. During the Wisconsin Glaciation, glacial ice flowed from the south over this bench, and scooped out the hollow that now contains the lake. Both trails to the lake follow the route of an old wagon road, constructed in 1902 to allow access to the Discovery oil well on Cameron Creek. E.H. Crandell was a Calgary businessman who helped finance the well. The trails feature good displays of wildflowers, and there is a sandy beach at the lake's north end.

102. Akamina Lake

Trailhead: Follow the Akamina Parkway, 16 km from Waterton Park townsite to the Cameron Lake parking lot. The trailhead is on the east side of the parking lot.
Rating: easy, 500 m
Lighting: anytime

Akamina Lake is a peaceful body of water, a short walk from the hubbub of the Cameron Lake parking lot. The trail winds through wet subalpine forest to a platform on the lakeshore. You may see moose, waterfowl and fish. Horsetail, ferns, arnica and foam flower are some of the common plants in the undergrowth. Akamina (ah-kah-MEE-nuh) is a Kutenai word that means "high bench land."

General Information

Walks and Easy Hikes for the Elderly and Young Families

The following outings are recommended to the elderly and to families with young children:

Akamina Lake
Annette Lake
Athabasca Falls
Bankhead
Beaver Lake
Bison Paddock Viewpoint
Blakiston Falls (Red Rock Canyon)
Bow Falls
Bow Lake
Bow River
Bow Summit
Cameron Falls and Waterton Townsite
Cameron Lake
Cavell Lake
Deerlodge
Discovery Trail
Emerald Lake
Fenland Trail
Fraser River
Great Divide
Hamilton Falls
Howse Valley Viewpoint
Johnson Lake
Johnston Canyon (lower falls)
Kootenai Brown's Grave
Labrador Tea Trail
Lac Beauvert
Lake Louise
Linnet Lake
Lower Spiral Tunnel Viewpoint
Maligne Canyon (teahouse loop)
Marble Canyon
Marsh Trail
Miette Boardwalk
Mistaya Canyon
Montane Trail
Moraine Lakeshore
Moraine Lake Rockpile
Ochre Beds and Paint Pots
Overlander Falls (from Highway 16)
Path of the Glacier
Pocahontas (lower trail)
Portal Lake
Rearguard Falls
Red Rock Canyon
Schäffer Viewpoint (Maligne Lake) (use lakeshore trail for return)
Stewart Canyon
Sunwapta Falls
Takakkaw Falls
Tunnel Mountain Hoodoos
Upper Waterfowl Lake
Vermilion River

Wheelchair Accessible Walks and Easy Hikes

The following trails are wheelchair accessible, although in some instances, natural and artificial barriers preclude access to the full trail length. Inclines are usually present, and an assistant is recommended.

Annette Lake
Athabasca Falls
Beaver Lake
Bison Paddock Viewpoint
Bow Falls
Bow Lake
Bow River
Bow Summit (from the upper parking lot)
Cameron Falls
Deerlodge
Emerald Lake (north shore, first 2 km)
Fenland Trail
Great Divide
Howse Valley Viewpoint
Johnston Canyon (lower falls)
Kootenai Brown's Grave
Lac Beauvert (west shore)
Lake Louise Shoreline
Linnet Lake
Lower Spiral Tunnel Viewpoint
Maligne Canyon (teahouse loop)
Marsh Trail
Miette Boardwalk
Natural Bridge
Red Rock Canyon
Schäffer Viewpoint (Maligne Lake)
Stewart Canyon (first 700 m)
Sundance Canyon (first 3.8 km)
Sunwapta Falls (path at east edge of parking lot)

Takakkaw Falls
Tunnel Mountain Hoodoos
Whistlers (tramway to boardwalk)

Walks and Easy Hikes from Campgrounds

Many of these outings are ideal for after-dinner outings, or as rainy-day diversions.

Campground	Walk or Easy Hike
Bow Valley	Montane Trail
Castle Mountain	Silverton Falls
Chancellor Peak	Deerlodge Leanchoil Hoodoos Wapta Falls
Columbia Icefield	Wilcox Pass
Crandell	Crandell Lake
Hoodoo Creek	Deerlodge Leanchoil Hoodoos Wapta Falls
Johnston Canyon	Johnston Canyon
Kicking Horse	A Walk in the Past Centennial Trail
Lake Louise	Bow River
Lucerne	Labrador Tea Trail
McLeod Meadows	Dog Lake
Pocahontas	Pocahontas/ Punchbowl Falls
Redstreak	Redstreak Valleyview
Robson Meadows	Fraser River Overlander Falls
Takakkaw Falls	Laughing Falls Takakkaw Falls
Tunnel Mountain	Tunnel Mountain Hoodoos
Waterton Townsite	Cameron Falls Linnet Lake Prince of Wales Lower Bertha Falls
Wilcox Creek	Wilcox Pass

The Author's Favourite Walks and Easy Hikes

Athabasca Falls
Athabasca Glacier
Bear's Hump
Bison Paddock Viewpoint

Bighorn sheep lambs

Bow Summit
Emerald Lake
Fenland Trail
Howse Valley Viewpoint
Johnston Canyon
Lake Louise
Maligne Canyon
Marble Canyon
Moraine Lake Rockpile
Ochre Beds and Paint Pots
Parker Ridge
Path of the Glacier
Takakkaw Falls
Upper Waterfowl Lake
Whistlers

National Park Regulations and Etiquette

- Vehicles stopping in national parks must pay the appropriate use fee at a park entry point or visitor information centre.
- Firearms may not be transported through a national park unless securely locked, or dismantled.

- Hunting and trapping of wildlife is not permitted.
- Anglers must obtain a national park fishing permit, and be familiar with closures and catch quotas for the waterbodies they intend to fish.
- It is illegal to disturb, remove or deface any natural, cultural or historic object.
- It is illegal to approach, feed or harass wildlife.
- Do not enter a closed area.
- Camp in designated campgrounds only.
- Light fires only in metal fire boxes provided. Use firewood sparingly.
- Mountain biking is permitted only on specific trails.
- Keep to maintained trails when hiking. Do not shortcut switchbacks.
- Keep pets restrained at all times. There are restrictions on taking dogs into the backcountry overnight.
- Respect the rights of others to solitude. Hike and camp in small groups.
- Observe quiet hours at campgrounds between 10:00 pm and 7:00 am.

Safety

There are hazards in the Rockies that may be unfamiliar to you. As anywhere in the mountains, common sense is your best friend. The following will help ensure that your visit is a safe one.

- Do not approach, entice or feed wildlife.
- Do not park or walk in posted avalanche or closed areas.
- Keep off snow-covered slopes. The snow in summer snow banks is abrasive and cuts skin easily. It may also conceal treacherous ice slopes.
- Keep off glacial ice.
- Stay on your side of the guardrail at viewpoints, waterfalls and canyons. Approach unfenced viewpoints with extreme caution.
- Do not drink surface water from roadside or in heavily-visited areas.
- Do not drive on paved shoulders. Park only in designated pull-offs. Observe the posted speed limit. Slow down in areas frequented by wildlife, or if you see wildlife at roadside. Be on the lookout for cyclists.
- Altitude increases the effects of sun and wind. Dress appropriately for walks and hikes. Use sunscreen. Wear sunglasses and a sun hat. Carry extra clothing and some food and water.
- Frost may develop on road surfaces at any time of the year, especially in the mountain passes. Be prepared for winter driving conditions between September and June, and equip your vehicle accordingly.
- Keep to the trails when hiking. Avoid taking "shortcuts." If you begin to tire excessively, retrace your route to the trailhead.

Metric/Imperial Conversions

METRIC	IMPERIAL
1 millimetre (mm)	0.0394 in
1 centimetre (cm)	0.394 inches
1 metre (m)	3.28 feet
1 kilometre (km)	0.62 miles
1 hectare (ha)	2.47 acres
1 square kilometre (km^2)	0.386 square miles
1 kilogram (kg)	2.205 pounds
1 tonne (t)	0.9842 UK tons (1.102 US tons)
1 litre (L)	0.22 UK gallons (0.264 US gallons)
1° Celsius (C)	1.8° F

IMPERIAL	METRIC
1 inch	2.54 centimetres (cm)
1 foot	0.305 metres (m)
1 mile	1.61 kilometres (km)
1 acre	0.405 hectares (ha)
1 square mile	2.59 square kilometres (km^2)
1 pound	0.4536 kilograms (kg)
1 UK ton	1.016 tonnes (t)
1 UK gallon	4.55 litres (L)
1 US ton	0.9072 tonnes (t)
1 US gallon	3.78 litres (L)
1° Fahrenheit	0.55° C

90 km per hour equals 56 miles per hour.
50 km per hour equals 31 miles per hour.
The freezing point is 0°C.
One hectare is 100 m by 100 m.

- A rough formula for converting distances and heights from metric to imperial, is to multiply by 3 and add 10 percent of the product. Example: 30 m x 3 = 90, plus 9 = 99. Therefore, 30 m equals approximately 99 feet.

Tips for 35 mm Photography

Light is the substance of good landscape photographs. If you have a particular destination in mind, carefully consider the time of day and the resulting angle of light. Many of the best-known scenes in the Rockies are lit best before mid-morning.

Lakes are usually calm at dawn and dusk. These are the times to take reflection photographs. Direct sunlight disturbs the air and may cause the surface to ripple.

The large mammals are most active at dawn and dusk in summer.

The horizon is blocked at most locations in the Rockies. At sunrise and sunset, the best effects are not obtained by including the sun in the photograph, but by capturing the colourful lighting opposite the sun. Called alpenglow, this lighting precedes sunrise and follow sunset. You may want to underexpose slightly, 1/2 to 1 stop, to saturate colours at these times of day.

Snow will often be present in your compositions. You will frequently encounter difficult lighting situations that incorporate opposing values of sunlit snow and shade. Bracket exposures. Shaded snowscapes will appear dull unless you overexpose. Take a light meter reading off your barc hand and use this for the scene.

To obtain details of people or objects in the foreground of bright landscapes, take a close-up light meter reading from the foreground subject and use this exposure for the scene. In some cases, the extraordinary contrast between foreground lighting and background lighting goes beyond the limits of film. Expose for the background and infill the foreground with flash, or use a neutral density filter to darken the brightest part of the scene.

If you have two camera bodies, dedicate each to a different kind of film. Load one with 25 ISO, 50 ISO, 64 ISO, or 100 ISO film. Load the other with 200 ISO or 400 ISO film. This will give you flexibility with regard to lighting, depth-of-field, colour saturation and tripod work.

At higher altitudes, film registers a bluish cast because of the greater incidence of ultraviolet light. Equip your lenses with UV filters. You can use a polarizing filter to cut glare in photos that include water and ice.

Carry a selection of lenses from 24 mm to 300 mm, and a sturdy tripod. Carry lots of film. Fingerless gloves take the chill out of cold weather work.

Watch for condensation and frost on lens elements when you step from a warm vehicle into the cold outdoors. On really cold mornings, hold your breath when releasing the shutter so as not to get vapour in the foreground.

Keep your equipment lightweight, accessible and well-organized. You will be more inclined to carry it with you. Ensure that your camera is ready with the lens best suited to the kind of photo you seek—telephoto for wildlife, or wide-angle for landscape. This will minimize set-up time when a good scene presents itself.

Carry your camera equipment over the shoulder in a case or bag rather than in your hands. You will tire less easily.

Think ahead to anticipate lighting. Linger a while if things are not initially favourable. As with most endeavours, patience with photography usually pays.

Contacts

Parks Canada welcomes comments on your experience in the mountain national parks. You can fill out comment forms at park information centres. Superintendents of the individual parks may be contacted using the addresses below.

The author and the publisher of *Walks and Easy Hikes* would also like to hear about your experience in the Rockies. If you have suggestions, corrections or omissions concerning this book, please forward them to the author in care of:

Altitude Publishing
Box 1410
Canmore, AB
Canada T0L 0M0
403-678-6888

Banff National Park
P.O. Box 900
Banff, AB T0L 0C0
403-762-1500

Park information centre, Banff 762-4256
Park information centre, Lake Louise 522-3833

Banff warden office 762-1470
Lake Louise warden office 522-3866

Jasper National Park
P.O. Box 10
Jasper, AB T0E 1E0
403-852-6161

Park information centre, Jasper 852-6176
Park information centre, Columbia Icefield 761-7030
Park warden office 852-6155

Yoho National Park
P.O. Box 99
Field, BC V0A 1G0
604/250-343-6324*

Park information centre 343-6783
Park warden office 343-6784

Kootenay National Park
P.O. Box 220
Radium Hot Springs, BC
V0A 1M0
604/250-347-9615*

Park information centre, west gate 347-9505
Park warden office 347-9361

Waterton Lakes National Park
Waterton Park, AB T0K 2M0
403-859-2224

Park information centre 859-2224
Park warden office 859-2224

Bow Valley Provincial Park
403-673-3985

Mt. Robson Provincial Park
P.O. Box 579
Valemount, BC V0E 2Z0
604/250-566-4325*

* Area code 604 changes to area code 250 in October 1996.

Emergency Telephone Numbers

Banff National Park
Ambulance 762-2000
Fire 762-2000
Hospital 762-2222
Lake Louise Medical Clinic: 522-2184
RCMP 762-2226
Warden office 762-4506

Jasper National Park
Ambulance 852-3100
Fire 852-3100
Hospital 852-3344
Medical clinics 852-4885, 852-4456
RCMP 852-4848
Warden office 852-6156

Yoho National Park
Ambulance 344-6226
Fire 343-6028
Hospital 344-2411, 403-762-2222
RCMP 343-6316
Warden office 343-6324 ext. 253

Kootenay National Park
Ambulance 1-374-5937
Fire 347-9333
Hospital 342-9201
Medical Centre 342-9206
RCMP 347-9393
Warden office 347-9361

Waterton Lakes National Park
Ambulance 859-2636
Fire 859-2636
Hospital (Pincher Creek) 627-3333, (Cardston) 653-4411
Clinic (Pincher Creek) 627-3321
RCMP 859-2044
Warden office 859-2224

Bow Valley Provincial Park
Emergency Services 591-7767
RCMP: Ask operator for Zenith 50,000

Mt. Robson Provincial Park
Ambulance 1-800-461-9911
RCMP 566-4466

Recommended Reading

General Reference

Gadd, Ben. *Handbook of the Canadian Rockies.* Jasper: Corax Press, 1995. If it's not in this Handbook, it's not in the Rockies.

Pole, Graeme. *Rockies SuperGuide.* Canmore: Altitude Publishing, 1996. A full-colour frontcountry guide.

Pole, Graeme. *Classic Hikes in the Canadian Rockies.* Canmore: Altitude Publishing, 1994. Selected backcountry hiking trails, full colour, with maps.

Birding

Holroyd, G.L. and Howard Coneybare. *Birds of the Rockies.* Edmonton: Lone Pine, 1990.

Peterson, R.T. *A Field Guide to the Western Birds.* Boston: Houghton Mifflin, 3rd edition, 1989. The standard reference for western North America.

Scotter, G.W., Ulrich, T.J. and E.T. Jones. *Birds of the Canadian Rockies.* Saskatoon: Western Producer Prairie Books, 1990. Excellent photography.

Van Tighem, Kevin, and Andrew LeMessurier. *Birding Jasper National Park.* Jasper: Parks and People, 1989.

Geology

Ford, Derek, and Dalton Muir. *Castleguard.* Ottawa: Minister of the Environment, 1985. A clear and lavishly illustrated description of natural processes at Castleguard Cave and Meadows, but relevant to the alpine throughout the Rockies.

Kucera, Richard E. *Exploring the Columbia Icefield.* Canmore: High Country, 1987.

Sandford, R.W. *The Columbia Icefield.* Banff: Altitude Publishing, 1993.

Human History

Boles, G., R. Laurilla and W. Putnam. *Place Names of the Canadian Alps.* Revelstoke: Footprint, 1990.

Hart, E.J. *Diamond Hitch.* Banff: Summerthought, 1979. Stories of trail life and an illustrated history of the guides and outfitters who opened up the Rockies.

Hart, E.J. *Jimmy Simpson: Legend of the Rockies.* Canmore: Altitude Publishing, 1991.

Holterman, Jack. *Place Names of Glacier/Waterton National Parks.* Glacier Natural History Association, 1985.

Marty, Sid. *A Grand and Fabulous Notion.* Toronto: NC Press, 1984. The founding of Banff National Park and Canada's national park system.

Pole, Graeme. *The Canadian Rockies: A History in Photographs.* Banff: Altitude Publishing, 1991. Human history from 1884 to the 1950s, illustrated with 130 photographs.

Schäffer, Mary T.S. *A Hunter of Peace.* Banff: The Whyte Foundation, 1980. On the trail with Mary Schäffer, in quest of Maligne Lake.

Canadian Pacific Railway

Bain, Donald. *Canadian Pacific in the Rockies.* Calgary: The British Railway Modellers of North America. (In ten volumes)

Berton, Pierre. *The National Dream.* Toronto: McClelland and Stewart, 1970.

Berton, Pierre. *The Last Spike.* Toronto: McClelland and Stewart, 1971.

Berton, Pierre. *The Great Railway Illustrated.* Toronto: McClelland and Stewart, 1972.

Cruise, D. and Alison Griffiths. *Lords of the Line.* Markham: Penguin Books 1989.

Lavallée, Omer. *Van Horne's Road.* Montreal: Railfare Enterprises, 1974.

McKee, Bill, and Georgeen Klassen. *Trail of Iron.* Calgary: Glenbow-Alberta Institute, 1983.

Turner, Robert D. *West of the Great Divide: The Canadian Pacific in British Columbia 1880-1986.* Victoria: Sono Nis Press, 1987.

Yeats, Floyd. *Canadian Pacific's Big Hill.* Calgary: The British Railway Modellers of North America, 1985.

Caribou track

Vegetation

Anonymous. *Trees and Forests of Jasper National Park.* Jasper: Parks and People, 1986.

Bush, C. Dana. *Wildflowers of the Rockies.* Edmonton: Lone Pine, 1990. Colour illustrations.

Kujit, J. *A Flora of Waterton Lakes National Park.* Edmonton: University of Alberta Press, 1982. Most of the species that occur in the Rockies are found in Waterton. An excellent reference for both novice and expert. Illustrations. Unfortunately, now out of print.

Lauriault, J. *Identification Guide to the Trees of Canada.* Toronto: Fitzhenry and Whiteside, 1989.

MacKinnon, A.J. Pojar and R. Coupé. *Plants of Northern British Columbia.* Edmonton: Lone Pine, 1993. Flowers, grasses, trees, shrubs, mosses and lichens in the Central Rockies; particularly those of the subalpine and alpine.

Moss, E.H. and J.G Packer. *The Flora of Alberta.* Toronto: University of Toronto Press, 1983. The standard technical reference. No illustrations.

Porsild, A.E. and D.T. Lid. *Rocky Mountain Wild Flowers.* Ottawa: National Museum of Natural Sciences, 1979. Colour illustrations.

Scotter, G.W. and H. Flygare. *Wildflowers of the Canadian Rockies.* Toronto: McClelland and Stewart, 1992. Good colour photographs.

Stanton, C. and N. Lopoukine. *The Trees and Forests of Waterton Lakes National Park.* Forestry Service and Environment Canada, undated. Available at Waterton Lakes National Park information centre.

Zwinger, A. and B.E. Willard. *Land Above the Trees.* Tucson: University of Arizona Press, 1989. An excellent guide to ecology above timberline.

Caribou antlers

Elk antlers

Moose antlers

Mule deer antlers

Wildlife

Burt, W.H. and R.P. Grossenheider. *Mammals.* Boston: Houghton, Mifflin, 3rd edition, 1980. The standard Peterson reference for North America.

Holroyd, G.L. and Howard Coneybare. *Birds of the Rockies.* Edmonton: Lone Pine, 1990.

National Geographic Society. *Field Guide to the Birds of North America.* Washington, D.C.: National Geographic Society, 2nd edition, 1987.

Peterson, R.T. *A Field Guide to the Western Birds.* Boston: Houghton Mifflin, 3rd edtion, 1989.

Murie, O.J. *Animal Tracks.* Boston: Houghton and Mifflin, 1974. An excellent field guide with a wealth of information on animal behaviour.

Schmidt, D. and E. Schmidt. *Alberta Wildlife Viewing Guide.* Edmonton: Lone Pine, 1990.

Scotter, G.W. and T.J. Ulrich. *Mammals of the Canadian Rockies.* Saskatoon: Fifth House, 1995.

Scotter, G.W. and Ulrich, T.J. and E.T. Jones. *Birds of the Canadian Rockies.* Saskatoon: Western Prairie Producer Books, 1990.

Van Tighem, Kevin. *Wild Animals of Western Canada.* Banff: Altitude Publishing, 1992.

Van Tighem, Kevin and Andrew LeMessurier. *Birding Jasper National Park.* Jasper: Parks and People, 1989.

Glossary

Alluvial fan (ah-LOO-vee-ull) A fan-shaped landform created from rubble that drops from stream flow, where a steep mountain stream enters a broad valley.

Alpine ecoregion The vegetation zone above treeline, characterized by rocky soils, and by scattered, low-lying wildflowers, lichens and mosses.

Arête A narrow, rugged mountain ridge.

Avalanche An accumulation of snow that releases as a mass and sweeps the mountainside below.

Bedrock Rocky outcrops on the surface, or the rock that underlies surface boulders, soils and vegetation.

Chinook (shih-NOOK) A warm wind that blows eastward at the mountain front.

Cirque glacier An accumulation of ice that erodes rearwards and downwards into bedrock, creating a bowl-shaped pocket called a cirque (SURK).

Climax species The species of trees and vegetation that culminate the process of succession. In the montane forest, this is Douglas fir and white spruce. In the subalpine forest, it is Engelmann spruce and subalpine fir.

Continental Divide The height of land that separates rivers that flow east to the Atlantic Ocean or north to the Arctic Ocean, from rivers that flow west to the Pacific Ocean.

CPR The Canadian Pacific Railway was Canada's first transcontinental railway. It was constructed through the Rockies between 1882 and 1884. The railway, and the tourism industry it developed, were responsible for the establishment of Banff and Yoho national parks.

Delta A fan-shaped landform created from fine sediments that drop out of the flow where a stream enters a lake.

Doghair forest A dense, uniformly-aged stand of lodgepole pine, created by a natural mass seeding after a forest fire.

Dolomite Limestone rock in which water seeped into the lime sediments before they lithified. Calcium was replaced by magnesium.

Douglas fir

Engelmann spruce

Lodgepole pine

Douglas fir One of the indicator trees of the montane ecoregion. The Douglas fir usually grows on dry, south-facing slopes. Characteristics: coniferous; 30 m to 40 m tall; straight or gracefully curving trunk; furrowed, cork-like bark. Named for the botanist David Douglas.

Eastern Main Ranges The mountains along the continental divide between Banff and Yellowhead Pass.

Ecoregion A vegetation zone defined by altitude. There are three ecoregions in the central Rockies: montane, subalpine and alpine. The boundaries between them are not precise, varying with local climate and topography.

Engelmann spruce One of the two most common trees in the subalpine ecoregion. Characteristics: coniferous; 20 m to 30 m tall; shreddy, reddish-brown bark; spiky, squarish needles that roll between your fingers. Named for George Engelmann, a 19th century botanist.

Erratic A rock or boulder transported from its place of origin by glacial ice.

Fault A fracture in the bedrock. The rock on one side of the fracture has moved relative to the rock on the other side.

Feathermosses Leafless, rootless plants that prefer damp, shaded locations. Common on the floor of the subalpine forest.

Foothills Hills on the eastern slope of the Rockies.

Forefield The area immediately in front of a glacier. Covered by glacial ice less than 150 years ago, and characterized by rubble, meltwater streams and scant vegetation.

Formation A distinctive layer of rock that represents a particular past environment. Formations are often named for areas where they are prominent, or for where they were first studied.

Front Ranges The easternmost ranges of the Rockies.

Frost hollow A shallow depression where cold air collects, stunting the growth of vegetation. Common adjacent to glaciers, in high valleys, and at the mouths of mountainside streams.

Glacial landforms Surface features created by glaciers and their meltwater streams. Includes: moraines, drumlins, eskers, kames, and kettle ponds.

Glacier A mass of ice formed from consolidated snow and moving slowly downhill under its own weight.

Great Glaciation The most extensive ice age of the last 2 million years. It lasted from 240,000 years ago to 128,000 years ago. The ice sheets were 1 km thick.

Hanging valley A tributary valley that glacial ice did not erode as deeply as the adjacent major valley. Hence the mouth of the hanging valley "hangs" above the valley into which it empties.

Hoodoo A resistant pillar of glacial till.

Hot spring A natural outlet for groundwater that has been heated within the earth's crust.

Icefield An expansive area of glacial ice, found at elevations above 2430 m.

Interior plains The extensive, flat area of central North America.

Karst Underground drainage in limestone bedrock.

Kettle pond A lake that fills a hollow created where a detached block of glacial ice melted into the underlying glacial rubble.

Kruppelholz German for "crippled wood." Gnarled and stunted forms of Engelmann spruce, subalpine fir, whitebark pine, lodgepole pine, and Lyall's larch. Found at treeline, on cliff edges, or near glaciers.

Lateral moraine A crested ridge of glacial rubble pushed up alongside a glacier.

Limestone Sedimentary rock created from deposits of lime, or from the skeletal remains of primitive marine life.

Little Ice Age A minor, global glacial advance that lasted from 1200 AD until the late 1800s.

Lodgepole pine One of the indicator trees of the montane ecoregion. Characteristics: coniferous; 5 m to 20 m tall; a straight trunk that is often devoid of branches in the lower half; needles in pairs; scaly gray bark, often with a reddish-orange hue. Cones are sealed with resin and must be cracked open by fire for effective seeding.

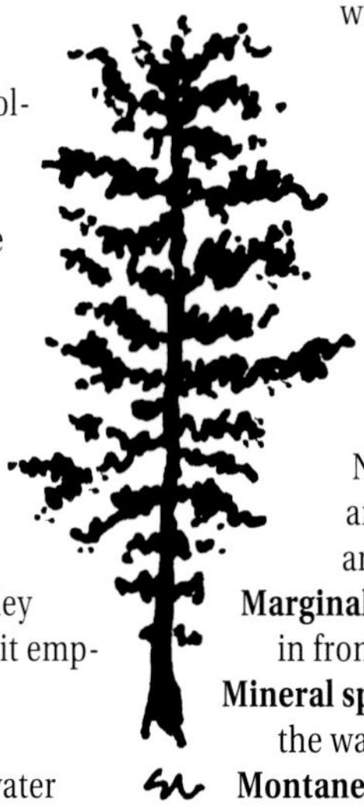

Lyall's larch (LIE-ull's) A tree of the upper subalpine ecoregion. Characteristics: coniferous; 5 m to10 m tall; ragged-looking; pale green needles that turn gold in autumn and are shed. Named for David Lyall, a naturalist and surgeon with the British Boundary Commission.

Lyall's larch

Marginal lake A lake that forms immediately in front of a glacier.

Mineral spring A natural water spring where the water does not emerge hot.

Montane ecoregion The vegetation zone in the major valley bottoms and on lower mountainsides.

Moraine (more-RAIN) A deposit of glacial till.

Niche glacier (NEESH) A type of catchment glacier that forms in an indentation on a mountainside. Sustained by windblown snow. Often peculiar in shape.

Outlet valley glacier A glacier that flows from an icefield into an adjacent valley.

Old-growth forest A forest which in which the climax species have seeded more than one generation.

Palliser Expedition An expedition sent by the British Government in 1857, to explore central and western Canada.

Plunge pool A rounded depression in the bedrock beneath a waterfall, resulting from the incessant pounding of water.

Potholes Circular depressions drilled into the bedrock near falls and rapids by boulders trapped in eddies and backwaters.

Western red cedar

Quartzite A quartz-rich sandstone in which the quartz particles have liquefied and then reconsolidated, binding the rock together. A metamorphic rock.

Rock flour Minute particles of glacial sediment that are suspended in lake water. These particles reflect the blue and green wavelengths of light, giving the lakes their colours.

Rock lichens Rootless, leafless plants that grow on rocks and cliffs.

Sandstone A rock made from sand grains, and usually containing quartz.

Sediment Mineral soil or chemical material transported from elsewhere by wind, water or glaciers.

Sedimentary rock Rock formed from the accumulation of sediments. The sediments come from other rocks (creating sandstone, shale, conglomerate, gritstone, siltstone and tillite); from chemical action (creating limestone and dolomite); or from the skeletal remains of marine life (creating limestone).

Strike valley A valley eroded into the interface between two thrust sheets.

Subalpine ecoregion The vegetation zone between the montane and alpine ecoregions. Found on mountainsides, and in valley bottoms at higher elevations.

Subalpine fir One of the two common trees in the subalpine ecoregion. Characteristics: coniferous; 20 m to 30 m tall; conical shape with a spire-like crown; silvery bark with resin blisters; branches that curl upwards.

Succession A natural process of change from youth to maturity in a vegetation community.

Syncline A U-shaped fold in layered rock, produced by compressive forces during mountain building.

Tarn A small mountain lake or pond, often in a hollow that was scoured from the bedrock by glacial ice. Tarns are frequently fed by glacial meltwater, and dammed by moraines.

Terminal moraine A horseshoe-shaped ridge of till pushed up by a glacier and marking the maximum extent of a glacial advance.

Terminus The lower end of a glacier. Also called the toe or snout.

Thrust fault A fracture in the earth's crust, along which an assemblage of rock has slid upwards and over adjacent rock.

Thrust sheet An assemblage of rock that slid along a thrust fault.

Till Rock rubble deposited by glaciers and their meltwater streams.

Tillite Till that has become rock.

Tree lichens Rootless, leafless plants that grow on tree trunks and branches.

Treeline The upper limit of tree growth, usually 2200 m on south-facing slopes. Treeline may be considerably lower on north-facing slopes or near glaciers. Treeline separates the subalpine ecoregion from the alpine ecoregion.

Tufa Crumbly limestone rock created by chemical action at the outlet of a mineral spring.

Tundra A treeless area at high elevation or near a glacier. Vegetation comprises wildflowers, low-growing shrubs, sedges, mosses and rock lichens.

Subalpine fir

U-shaped valley A valley that has been eroded or enlarged by glacial ice. Also called a trough.

Western red cedar An uncommon tree in the Rockies, found only in areas of excessive precipitation. Characteristics: coniferous; up to 40 m tall; scaly, frond-like leaves; gray bark that is shredded in vertical strips; aromatic wood. The provincial tree of BC.

White spruce A characteristic tree of the montane ecoregion, especially along riverbanks and on flood plains. Similar to Engelmann spruce, with which it hybridizes.

Whitebark pine Found on cliff edges and windy locations, usually in the subalpine ecoregion, sometimes in kruppelholz form. Characteristics: coniferous; grayish-brown bark; needles in bunches of 5; branches frequently flag the prevailing wind.

Wisconsin Glaciation An ice age that lasted from 75,000 to 11,000 years ago. Ice sheets were a kilometre thick. There were three distinct advances of glacial ice during this period. Two of these extended from the Rockies, eastward to the plains.

White spruce

Index

The Author

Graeme Pole lives in Field, BC. He is a licensed interpretive guide, and a keen hiker and mountaineer. He brings to this work many years of experience, observation and research in the Canadian Rockies. Graeme is author of *Canadian Rockies SuperGuide, The Canadian Rockies: A History in Photographs, Classic Hikes in the Canadian Rockies, and The Spiral Tunnels and The Big Hill.* When not hiking, taking photographs and writing, Graeme serves with the British Columbia Ambulance Service, as a paramedic and Unit Chief in Field.

With royalties from the sales of this and other books, Graeme supports the reforestation work of *Trees for the Future.*

Colour photography: Graeme Pole and Marnie Pole: Mountain Vision

Additional photography:

Carole Harmon: 2, 68, 99, 111

Don Harmon: 36

Stephen Hutchings: 32, 49, 61, 65, 83, 97, 112

Dennis Schmidt: 46 bottom, 82 top, 91 top, 96, 133 top, 135 top, 139, front cover (inset right)

Esther Schmidt: 17 top, 44 top, 80 top, 117 bottom, 121 top, 141, front cover (inset left)

Archival photographs:

Whyte Museum of the Canadian Rockies: 22, 23, 50 top (hand coloured by Carole Harmon), 54 (hand coloured by Carole Harmon), 101

Glenbow Archives: 73, 102